For Bill Ellis and Diane E. Goldstein

Slender Man Is Coming

Slender Man Is Coming

Creepypasta and Contemporary
Legends on the Internet

Edited by
Trevor J. Blank
Lynne S. McNeill

Utah State University Press
Logan

© 2018 by University Press of Colorado

Published by Utah State University Press
An imprint of University Press of Colorado
245 Century Circle, Suite 202
Louisville, Colorado 80027

 The University Press of Colorado is a proud member of
the Association of University Presses.

The University Press of Colorado is a cooperative publishing enterprise supported, in part, by Adams State University, Colorado State University, Fort Lewis College, Metropolitan State University of Denver, Regis University, University of Colorado, University of Northern Colorado, Utah State University, and Western State Colorado University.

∞ This paper meets the requirements of the ANSI/NISO Z39.48-1992 (Permanence of Paper).

ISBN: 978-1-60732-780-6 (pbk.)
ISBN: 978-1-60732-781-3 (ebook)
DOI: https://doi.org/10.7330/9781607327813

Library of Congress Cataloging-in-Publication Data

Names: Blank, Trevor J., editor. | McNeill, Lynne S., editor.
Title: Slender Man is coming : creepypasta and contemporary legends on the Internet / edited by Trevor J. Blank, Lynne S. McNeill
Description: Logan : Utah State University Press, [2018] | Includes bibliographical references and index.
Identifiers: LCCN 2018000471| ISBN 9781607327806 (pbk.) | ISBN 9781607327813 (ebook)
Subjects: LCSH: Folklore and the Internet. | Slender Man (Legendary character) | Contagion (Social psychology) | Memes. | Urban folklore. | Horror tales.
Classification: LCC GR44.E43 S54 2018 | DDC 398.2—dc23
LC record available at https://lccn.loc.gov/2018000471

Contents

Acknowledgments

The creation of this volume has been a true labor of love, and we owe a debt of gratitude to a number of people for their time and support. First, we would like to thank our spouses, Angelina Blank and Stephen VanGeem, for their kindness and patience as we worked through the publication process. We are grateful to John Bodner for organizing the panel that helped kick-start this project and to Ian Brodie and the editorial staff at *Contemporary Legend* for their assistance in developing the special issue from which this book was born. Our thanks also go to Michael Spooner, Kylie Haggen, Rachael Levay, and the incredible staff at Utah State University Press and the University Press of Colorado for the meticulous attention to detail and assistance in crafting this book into its present form. Finally, Bill Ellis and Diane E. Goldstein, to whom this book is dedicated, have inspired and mentored both of us over the years and we are grateful for their support and tutelage.

Slender Man Is Coming

Figure 0.1. Original caption: "One of two recovered photographs from the Stirling City Library blaze. Notable for being taken the day which fourteen children vanished and for what is referred to as 'The Slender Man'. Deformities cited as film defects by officials. Fire at library occurred one week later. Actual photograph confiscated as evidence.—1986, photographer: Mary Thomas, missing since June 13th, 1986." (http://knowyourmeme.com/memes /slender-man.)

Introduction

Fear Has No Face
Creepypasta as Digital Legendry

Trevor J. Blank and Lynne S. McNeill

ON JUNE 10, 2009, THE PHOTO SHOWN HERE (on page 2), captioned as shown, hit the Internet. The user who posted the image, Victor Surge, uploaded a second photo as well. The images aren't scary or shocking as much as they are uncanny; it can take a moment to realize that there's something strange being depicted. The captions, referencing events and explanations that sound both alarming and plausible (the fire, the disappearance of the children, the missing photographer), add to the unsettling nature of the photos. Both images depict children in the foreground and a tall, slim figure in the background. The blurry creature appears to be male given its height and apparel, a plain black suit, although its features are largely indiscernible. In one photo (figure 0.1), there is a suggestion of tentacles emerging from its body—what the caption, in a perfect mimicry of official statements on disturbing events, attributes to film distortion. In the other photo (figure 0.2), the children are clearly upset and frightened, while the accompanying caption implies that they have fallen prey to the mysterious, faceless character lurking behind them. These two images were posted to the Something Awful web forum in response to a thread asking users to create a creepy paranormal image, inviting participants to craft something that could pass as believable and authentic. This was the birth of Slender Man.

Slender Man is, perhaps, the best example of an intentionally created legend that has hit all the right notes required to be believable, and while the character initially resided mostly in the corners of the Internet, he's been stepping into the limelight lately, with a growing notoriety that has intrigued folklorists and folk alike. The original photos posted under the alias Victor

DOI: 10.7330/9781607327813.c000

3

Figure 0.2. Original caption: "We didn't want to go, we didn't want to kill them, but its persistent silence and outstretched arms horrified and comforted us at the same time . . .—1983, photographer unknown, presumed dead." (http://knowyourmeme.com /memes/slender-man.)

Surge (real name Eric Knudsen) make excellent use of the legend genre's predominant qualities of realism and plausibility—they are presented as largely unexplained, with missing details and fragmented origins. Had they been tidier, or more coherent, Slender Man may have been relegated to a small segment of Internet lore; as it is, Surge's post captivated the imaginations of other users who embraced and ran with the new character, adding details and features through fan art, short stories, and multimedia.

Narrative and visual art of Slender Man were supplemented almost immediately by video-based additions to the burgeoning canon (or Slender Man Mythos, as it became known), with the YouTube found-footage series Marble Hornets appearing in 2009.[1] The series features a young man named Jay watching his missing friend Alex's film school project and slowly realizing that Slender Man played a role in his friend's disappearance. Jay posts clips of Alex's films and begins making recordings himself to solve the mystery. Video games quickly became another major source of Slender Man exposure, with the popular game *Minecraft* incorporating a Slender-like figure known as Enderman, and several independent games emerging with a focus on Slender Man himself. The first game, a free, independently

Figure 0.3. Pages from the *Slender* game show the style that has often been associated with Slender Man—scribbled writing and panicked tone.

developed first-person survival game called *Slender: The Eight Pages*, came out in 2012 and builds on some of the early established tropes of the character, such as his forest origins and disturbance of electrical devices (figure 0.3).[2] This game and its sequel, *Slender: The Arrival,* were and continue to be popular subjects for reaction and Let's Play videos, highlighting that the appeal goes beyond the experience of first-person play and extends into a shared sense of mutual tension and release.[3] More recently, indie game designer DVloper's *Slendrina* (2015) and *Granny* (2017) games have provided players with new elements to grow the Mythos; Granny is presented as Slender Man's mother-in-law, and Slendrina as his daughter.

The emic genre that is commonly referenced on the Internet for the Slender Man phenomenon and its many visual, narrative, and video-based manifestations is "creepypasta," a word that emerged on the Internet around 2007. Creepypasta is derived from the Internet slang *copypasta*, which in turn derives from the phrase *copy/paste*, serving as shorthand for any block of text that is repeatedly copied and pasted to various online forums. In the process, the narrative texts often undergo modification, annotation, and/or reinterpretation by new posters in a folkloric process of repetition and variation. Creepypasta is, in short, creepy copypasta. More specifically, it is an emergent genre of Internet folklore that involves the creation and dissemination of a particular style of creative horror stories and images. Targeted and circulated primarily to and by younger audiences, creepypasta draws on the disturbing, monstrous, strange, grotesque, and/or unknown while invoking the thematic and structural qualities of legendary narratives, including the use of personal narratives; ritual; ostension; familiar "real" settings, contexts, and ancillary characters;[4] and an accompanying air of plausibility in an effort to elicit feelings of playful uneasiness, paranoia, and genuine fright among audiences. Emanating from the bowels of Internet forums, wikis, social media, and websites like 4chan and Reddit, the creepypasta genre has been sustained in large part by the repeated sharing or reposting/rewriting/reimagining of these stories, and further buoyed by subsequent discursive commentaries about the nuanced qualities of their contents or composition that have arisen in response to their circulation online. Slender Man is arguably the most well-known example of creepypasta in circulation, and the character's infamy was solidified by a tragedy that drew the digital bogeyman into the real world and into the national media spotlight.

Indeed, it wasn't until May 31, 2014, that the Slender Man stepped fully—and unfortunately—into a wider spotlight. On that day, in Waukesha, Wisconsin, twelve-year-olds Morgan Geyser and Anissa Weier lured their friend Payton Leutner into the woods, stabbed her nineteen times, and left her to die. Leutner managed to make her way out of the forest, where she was rescued by a passerby and taken to the hospital. When the two girls were asked why they had stabbed their friend, they claimed to have committed the crime for Slender Man, drawing inspiration from creepypasta.[5] Overnight, Slender Man became the new leading man on the stage of contemporary legend characters, and "creepypasta" became a household term.

CLASSIFYING SLENDER MAN: LEGEND, MYTHOS, CREEPYPASTA

Many folklorists recognize that the online narratives about Slender Man fall into the broad category of legends: narratives told as true or possibly true, set in the real world and in historical time. The genre of legend is the form through which we rhetorically negotiate and examine questions of possibility and belief, and the digital setting of Slender Man's origins make the specific classification of contemporary legend especially apt. Classic definitions of contemporary legends often focus on the narrative form in addition to thematic content and methods of transmission that highlight the contemporary nature of the form: "A short traditional narrative, or digest of a narrative, that has no definitive text, formulaic openings and closings, or artistically developed form; alternatively described as modern, urban, or belief legends, folktales or myths . . . Frequently, they also are disseminated through the mass media, novels, and short stories or by email, fax, and photocopier and therefore have a wide international circulation" (Smith 1997, 493).

There has long been an understanding, however, that legends also exist in many nonnarrative forms. Legends may appear as visual images with limited or no text: photoshopped or recontextualized images that often circulate in the wake of current events, providing additional vernacular commentary on the situations at hand.

Legends are also often embodied through the process of ostension, the acting out of a legend (the term is derived from the Latin *ostendere*, to show, rather than to tell). Ostension is key to almost all contemporary legend complexes, but especially so in today's multimedia contexts of use and creation.[6] Of the many narrative forms of folklore, supernatural and contemporary legends lend themselves best to ostension through their connection to present-day society and questions of possibility. Local legends can be investigated through "legend tripping," the process of visiting a legend site to explore and test the narratives. Contemporary legends can lead to action, such as boycotting or promoting a brand after hearing a story about the corporation's business practices. Other kinds of ostensive behaviors are examined in this volume—cosplay, pranking, and play—as well as "reverse, ostension" on the Internet, in which collective action leads to a narrative, rather than the other way around (Tolbert 2013).

While folklorists may call Slender Man legendary, there are other important emic terms in use by the people who create and share the content online. "Mythos" is a concept that is used widely to describe the entirety of a world (often fictional) that exists around a given figure or source. Fans, scholars, and content creators work within the shared mythos of a given show, film, book or book series, game, or character to consume and develop that world further. A common example of this is the mythos of Cthulhu, a creature invented by American horror writer H. P. Lovecraft and expanded upon by numerous other writers, artists, game designers, and fans. The Cthulhu Mythos is larger than the creation of any one person, even Lovecraft himself as the originator of the idea. Fans and other writers have worked hard to develop the story and the worldview, and to bring aspects of Cthulhu to life, similar to the many versions of the Necronomicon, Lovecraft's fictional magical book, that have been written. The sense that a mythos has or takes on a life of its own helps to blur the line between official information and folkloric information about things like origins and precursors. The Slender Man Mythos incorporates all the creations that focus on him as a subject—the entire fictional, ever-growing world that he inhabits as well as the actual creative processes that have generated information about him. As Tim Evans points out later in this volume, the creation and acknowledgment of a mythos provides Slender Man a depth and significance that he might not otherwise achieve.

One popular addition to the Mythos has been the creation of historical precedents for Slender Man. Shortly after the original images appeared, stories of a German legendary figure known as Der Großmann (Der Großmann 2014) began to appear online, often appearing in the form of tidbits of information uncovered through research. An account supposedly translated from a 1702 source describes an alleged incident involving Der Großmann:

> My child, my Lars . . . he is gone. Taken, from his bed. The only thing that we found was a scrap of black clothing. It feels like cotton, but it is softer . . . thicker.
> Lars came into my bedroom yesterday, screaming at the top of his lungs that "The angel is outside!" I asked him what he was talking about, and he told me some nonsense fairy story about Der Großmann. He said he went into the groves by our village and found one of my cows dead, hanging from a tree. I thought nothing of it at first . . . But now, he is gone. We must find Lars, and my family must leave before we are killed. I am sorry, my son . . . I should have listened. May God forgive me. (Der Großmann 2014)[7]

Images purporting to be woodcuts from the sixteenth to eighteenth centuries combine with these reports to greatly confuse readers and researchers alike (figure 0.4).

Figure 0.4. A doctored version of a mid-1500s original that featured a normal skeleton. (http://www.slendermanfiles.org/home/16th-century-german-woodcuts.)

Of course, not all examples of the Slender Man Mythos tie into historical posturing. In some cases, Slender Man is said to have been a victim of bullying (Kitta 2019) or a member of a family. One surprising element of the Slender Man Mythos is that he sometimes has a daughter, Skinny Sally—a young girl whom he is typically depicted as treating quite gently and paternally, although she is at times shown with multiple shallow wounds.

Images and stories about Slender and Sally are often taken as decidedly fictional, in contrast to other creations, like historically grounded narratives and photoshopped images, that aim for a confusing depiction of reality.

The focus on fiction here highlights one of the most intriguing aspects of Slender Man's existence as a legendary figure—legends, by definition, deal largely with belief and possibility, but the idea of a crowdsourced mythos speaks to a distinct awareness of fabrication. Slender Man is a new kind of creation: one intentionally created as a fiction, but one that has emulated the look and feel of legend so well that its emic categorization is understandably multivalent.[8] This folk appropriation of Slender Man in creepypasta embodies what Michael Dylan Foster calls the folkloresque: "popular culture's own (emic) perception and performance of folklore," asserting that it "refers to creative, often commercial products or texts . . . that give the impression to the consumer . . . that they derive directly from existing folkloric traditions" (Foster 2016, 5; see also Tolbert, chapter 4). Expounding further, Foster notes:

> A common aspect of a folkloresque item of popular culture is that it is imbued with a sense of "authenticity" . . . derived from association with "real" folklore. This capacity to connect an item to an established body of tradition has the effect of validating the work in which it appears, increasing its appeal to popular audiences. Because the folkloresque is often part of mass-mediated popular culture, in many cases it leads to greater exposure to a wider audience for local and culture-specific traditions; in some cases this inspires a feedback loop in which the folkloresque version of the item is (re)incorporated into the folk cultural milieu that it references. (Foster 2016, 5)

This feedback loop is often at the heart of vernacular discourse surrounding Slender Man and creepypasta in general. The nature of the information created about Slender Man is such that it denies its own creation—it is often as easy to find evidence for Slender Man's historical presence in antiquity as it is to find proof that he was created from whole cloth in 2009. Concepts such as "truth" and "proof" have become surprisingly permeable these days, and it is perhaps no surprise that concepts like fiction and reality can be reconciled fairly easily.[9] The mediated environment of the Internet allows even fictional worlds to serve as shared spaces of creation and interaction (see McNeill 2015). Add to that the notion of the "Tulpa Effect," the idea that collective thought can create reality, and it starts to seem inconsequential that Slender Man's fictional origins are so firmly verifiable.[10] It is also important to note that there are many legitimate precedents in folk and popular culture for Slender-like characters: the Pied Piper, Men in Black, the Silence (Dr. Who), the Observers (Fringe), the Gentlemen (Buffy the Vampire Slayer), the Blair Witch, and Jack Skellington (*The Nightmare Before Christmas*), to name a few.[11] Clearly, this is salient imagery for fear and horror.

Slender Man isn't the only character that represents a blend of online genres, though he is currently the most prominent. There are a number of types of creepypasta in circulation, some visual and some narrative, and some that take on unique forms, like the epistolary presentation of Kris Straub's Candle Cove, which first appeared online in 2009. Candle Cove is a short, fictional forum discussion, appearing to take place over an expanse of time (indicated by such realistic phrases as "Sorry to resurrect this old thread . . . "), apparently conducted among a group of several different people (none of whom know each other). They talk about a television show they all recall watching and being frightened by during the early 1970s:

SKYSHALE033
SUBJECT: RE: CANDLE COVE LOCAL KID'S SHOW?

> Thank you Jaren!!! Memories flooded back when you mentioned the Laughingstock and channel 58. I remember the bow of the ship was a wooden smiling face, with the lower jaw submerged. It looked like it was swallowing the sea and it had that awful Ed Wynn voice and laugh. I especially remember how jarring it was when they switched from the wooden/plastic model, to the foam puppet version of the head that talked.

MIKE_PAINTER65
SUBJECT: RE: CANDLE COVE LOCAL KID'S SHOW?

> ha ha i remember now too. ;) do you remember this part skyshale: "You have . . . to go . . . INSIDE."

SKYSHALE033
SUBJECT: RE: CANDLE COVE LOCAL KID'S SHOW?

> Ugh mike, I got a chill reading that. Yes I remember. That's what the ship always told Percy when there was a spooky place he had to go in, like a cave or a dark room where the treasure was. And the camera would push in on Laughingstock's face with each pause. YOU HAVE . . . TO GO . . . INSIDE. With his two eyes askew and that flopping foam jaw and the fishing line that opened and closed it. Ugh. It just looked so cheap and awful.
> You guys remember the villain? He had a face that was just a handlebar mustache above really tall, narrow teeth.

KEVIN-HART

SUBJECT: RE: CANDLE COVE LOCAL KID'S SHOW?

i honestly, honestly thought the villain was pirate percy. i was about 5 when this show was on. nightmare fuel.

The last post in the discussion thread reveals that the show was never real, that the kids were watching static the whole time. The implications are wonderfully chilling: a show that only children can see, with content that seems to push the nonsensical nature of children's programming to a terrifying level. Candle Cove succeeds for many of the same reasons that Slender Man does; a compelling yet incomplete picture has been created, one that *feels* plausible to readers and viewers. While there have been some evolutions of the original Candle Cove story on both the folk and popular levels (a few sample episodes created for YouTube, and a 2015 show on the SyFy channel), Candle Cove has not had the cultural impact that Slender Man has.

It is clear that not all creepypastas are equal. Much like any familiar offline legend, creepypasta is subject to the communal (re)shaping that all folk forms undergo. Just as some legends rise to the top and spread like wildfire, so too do some creepypastas. There's a clear sense of traditional competence that has developed in the creepypasta creator and fan communities over time; the emic term *crappypasta* highlights that not all pastas are going to be equally appealing or successful. As YouTuber HoodoHoodlumsRevenge describes them, crappypastas are creepypastas that are so horrible that they've become "adorable."[12] One (in)famously bad example, known colloquially as "Man Door Hand Hook Car Door," is based on the classic contemporary legend "The Hook." While this text sees a decent amount of circulation, it's entirely because it fails as a creepypasta:

> Anonymous 06/19/12 (Tue) 00:38 No. 10311088
> man & girl go out to drive under moonlight. they stop at on at a side of road.
> he turn to his girl and say:
> "baby, I love you very much"
> "what is it honey?"
> "our car is broken down. I think the engine is broken. ill walk and get some more fuel."
> "ok, ill stay here and look after our stereo. there have been news report of steres being stolen"

"good idea. keep the doors locked no matter what. I love you sweaty"

so the guy left to get full for the car. after two hours the girl say "where is my baby, he was supposed to be back by now." then the girl here a scratching sound and voice say "LET ME IN"

the girl doesn't do it and then after a while she goes to sleep. the next morning she wakes up and finds her boyfriend still not there. She gets out to check and man door hand hook car door[13]

"The Hook" is now so familiar a legend that it rarely has the opportunity to circulate as potentially plausible the way that Slender Man now does.[14] The epically bad delivery of a familiar text only serves to reinforce the failure of this as a successful "scary story" in the context of the Internet. Parodies of other classic legends have been portrayed similarly, as in the crappypasta known as "who was phone?":

So ur with ur honey and yur making out wen the phone rigns. U anser it n the vioce is "wut r u doing wit my daughter?" U tell ur girl n she say "my dad is ded." THEN WHO WAS PHONE?[15]

While this story does appear on Creepypasta.com, the first comment seems to set the tone for its reception from the community: ***facepalm***. The popularity of "top ten"–type lists of crappypastas indicates that we enjoy watching the unsuccessful outcomes of the creepypasta process as much as the successful ones. There's also an educational quality in these examples—lots of comments on early creepypasta attempts are encouraging, offering advice and suggestions for how to make the story better.

The message from the creepypasta community seems to be that the quality of frightening content must be stepped up on the Internet. Of course, new (and newly frightening) legends are still circulating offline, but the creative ability to mimic reality finds new outlets through technology, and often a good story succeeds best when accompanied by good pictures, videos, and discursive elements. Of course, there are parodies of Slender Man, too. Their existence is perhaps one of the best pieces of evidence that people have been truly frightened by the original. As Russell Frank explains in his examination of parody photoshops of Tourist Guy that surfaced in the wake of 9/11, the joke photos were speaking to the horror of the original image's sentiment: "As horrific as it was, we had come through other horrific events. We would come through this one as well" (2011, 81).[16] Thus, we can see the threat of Slender Man being mitigated in various ways online, as when a timely post noting the similarities between a blank-faced mannequin and Slender Man led to the latter's acquisition of a brother,

Trenderman, and then an entire extended family, including Splendorman and Offenderman (figure 0.5).[17]

While the offline world has had to cope with the very real crime committed in Waukesha, the online world has appropriated Slender Man, and his mythos, into something not always so threatening.

SLENDY'S SUCCESS

While Slender Man is not the only creepypasta character that has inspired ostensive behavior, both benign and violent, he is definitely the most prominent. Perhaps motivated by the Wisconsin stabbing, other crimes involving young people, ranging from similar interpersonal violence to self-harm, have been attributed to the Slender Man, heightening his perceived influence beyond the realms of fiction and legend. Shortly after the Wisconsin stabbing, a thirteen-year-old in Ohio who was later discovered to have been deeply interested in Slender Man stabbed her mother. In September 2014, a fourteen-year-old girl in Port Richey, Florida, set fire to her family's house using bleach- and rum-soaked linens. Investigators reported that the teenager was "fixated" on Slender Man, presenting it as obvious that there was a connection (Moran 2014).

While the connection to Slender Man in the Florida and Ohio cases was drawn by investigators and the girl's mother respectively, it's not always external supposition that ties the character to troubled youths, many of whom, like the girls involved in the Wisconsin stabbing, report their own sightings of or beliefs in him. Instances of interpersonal violence are certainly frightening, but perhaps more worrisome is the connection of Slender Man to a rash of suicides among young people on a Lakota reservation in South Dakota. In May 2015, the *New York Times* reported that in the previous six months there had been nine suicides and over 100 suicide attempts made by youths living on the Pine Ridge Indian Reservation. As reporter Julie Bosman (2015) explains, "Several officials with knowledge of the cases said that at least one of the youths who committed suicide was influenced by Slender Man, a tall, faceless creature who appears in storytelling websites, often as a figure who stalks and kills victims." Prior to Slender Man's creation, there was a local belief in a "suicide spirit," variously known as the Tall Man, the Big Man, or Walking Sam, who would visit people and encourage them to kill themselves.[18] The youth of Pine Ridge, often living with extreme poverty, difficult family situations, and a lack of mental health resources, have made an understandable, if unfortunate, connection between these precursors and the predominant frightening figure of their own time (Bosman 2015).

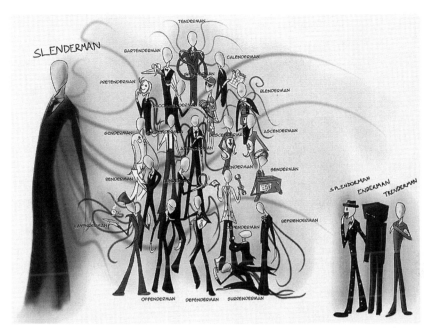

Figure 0.5. A depiction of Slender Man's family. (https://arvata.deviantart.com/art/The
-Slender-Family-321174302.)

What is it about Slender Man that makes him such a successful meme, both online and off? Folklore has no shortage of frightening figures: what leads this one to such prominence? As John Widdowson has noted, "The figures which symbolize or embody man's fears seem to be present in every culture. They differ in name, form and concept from one cultural group to another, but they share a remarkable number of characteristics" (1971, 102). Widdowson divides frightening figures into three general categories: supernatural or invented creatures, human beings with "unusual character-istics," and animals or objects. Slender Man seems to straddle the first and second categories. He is not a known member of the community, but his appearance is one that seems familiar, like a typical businessman in his dress and general form; add in the blank face and suggestion of tentacles instead of arms, and he moves firmly into the category of supernatural creatures.[19] It is perhaps this categorical impermanence that explains the psychological success of Slender Man as a frightening figure—he both fits and breaks the mold, allowing users to adapt and contort the Mythos to suit their own expressive purposes.

Slender Man, for all the terror he provokes, is quite plain in appear-ance. Although he typically has no face, his human-like characteristics are highlighted by his clothing—a distinguished-looking plain black suit and tie. Though stories and images often place him within the woods or wilderness (often the German Black Forest, a nod to traditional folktales), his urbane, bureaucratic mien highlights his uncanniness and distinguishes him from other humanoid monsters of the wilderness like the animalistic Bigfoot or shaggy wild men.[20] Slender Man's calm and tidy appearance provides a counterpoint to the menace that he projects. In many ways, Slender Man's external appearance features markers that contemporary society would suggest are evidence of someone trustworthy and capable: corporate, genteel, composed. And yet the uncanny elements—his lack of distinguishable features, his arms that are too long or too many—eat away at those comforting indices, reminding us that faceless, emotionless corporate powers rarely have our best interests at heart, and are lying in wait to grasp us in their many tentacles. The fact that Slender Man is often believed to target children and adolescents provides a strong commentary on the contradictory ways that young people are forced to perceive adults and institutions today—as caring, capable, and authoritative, but also as a faceless, unified power, manipulative and dangerous. The Slender Man is certainly a frightening figure for our times.

READING IS BELIEVING: THE ROLE
OF FOLKLORISTS IN THE DISCOURSE

The digital tradition surrounding the Slender Man is enough to engage any inquisitive legend scholar, but Slender Man has slipped the confines of the digital context, emerging also as a figure of oral legendry and belief, despite his easily determined fictional origins. Any Internet user who stumbled for the first time across a report of Slender Man would, for several years after the character's initial creation, likely have found as much evidence that Slender Man was a long-standing legendary creature as evidence against it. Several of the chapters in this volume explore the complicated relationship that has grown between online fiction and offline belief.

Considering how folklore proliferates in the fibers of everyday life as a vibrant component of vernacular expression, it is unsurprising to find that a diverse body of people are at least familiar with Slender Man, and often with the legend's accompanying Mythos as well. By virtue of prolonged exposure in mass media and popular culture, general intrigue, the allure of the taboo or sinister, and/or the subtle influence of cultural osmosis, Slender Man has slithered into the peripheries of public discourse while becoming vividly embedded in the mindscapes of creepypasta enthusiasts as well as of media scholars and folklorists. To be sure, the Slender Man phenomenon is greatly indicative of folklore in the digital age, where media convergence and hybridized cultural communication outlets afford individuals greater access to (and dissemination of) information, operational autonomy, and the provision of infinite choice while exploring a vast array of creative avenues, providing a platform to forge communal bonds interchangeably between online and face-to-face communication and blurring the boundaries between corporeality/virtuality as well as between folk, mass, and popular culture (Blank 2013, 2015, 2016; Howard 2008; McNeill 2009; see also Foster and Tolbert 2016).

Though the blogosphere has produced abundant insightful commentary, scholarship on the Slender Man phenomenon hasn't been immense, and what has been done has come from the fields of new media and communications. One of the more prolific early scholars to address Slender Man, media scholar Shira Chess, describes the phenomenon as an open-source horror story:

> This genre is necessarily fictive, involving an unnatural threat to the 'fixed laws of nature' (Sipios 2010, p. 6). While maintaining these genre expectations, in constructing the Slender Man, the Something Awful forums both pulled in older media representations of horror to understand this new space (citing films such as *Phantasm* as well as the works of H. P. Lovecraft), while simultaneously debugging and reforming how to create the most horrific and terrifying monster they could collectively conceive (often, in the process, scaring themselves with their own fiction n.d.). (Chess 2011, 375).

Chess's reference to users "scaring themselves" highlights the role that folkloristics can play here: while Chess is assuming that Slender Man is tied to narrative or literary genres, the character has moved also into the realm of *belief*, and should be considered within that framework as well as the narrative or literary. Several folklorists have published on the Slender Man phenomenon, and it is clear that folklore studies should spearhead academic work in this area, an effort this book hopes to support.[21] The hybridity of the digital context sets folklorists in a prime position to explore the nuances of the Slender Man's emergence and function in contemporary society.

This volume has been several years in the making, beginning with the presentation of select panels and papers at the annual meetings of the American Folklore Society from 2012 to 2015 that spanned the overlapping topics of creepypasta, belief, legend, children's folklore, and the evolving

dynamics of computer-mediated communication. As greater folk awareness of the Slender Man phenomenon began to take shape, particularly
within the realm of popular culture and youth-oriented Internet discourse
(and especially after the stabbing incident in Wisconsin), it became increasingly clear that folkloristic perspectives could bring valuable insights into
the emergent cultural response.[22] Accordingly, folklorist John Bodner organized and chaired a number of community events that culminated in a special panel with invited folklore scholars Trevor J. Blank, Jeffrey A. Tolbert,
and Andrea Kitta, along with two enthusiastic undergraduate students, who
presented "Slender Man Is Coming! Internet Legend, Hoax, and Attempted
Murder" on March 23, 2015, at Memorial University of Newfoundland,
Grenfell Campus, in Corner Brook, Newfoundland, to a lively and numerous audience.[23] In the wake of the presentation and valuable audience feedback that followed, Bodner and the visiting folklorists, along with Lynne S.
McNeill (via Skype), began to hash out the necessary components of a spe-
cialized folkloristic volume on the subject of Slender Man and creepypasta.
These discussions, enlarged by the growing body of metafolklore, cultural
intrigue, and mass-media attention, ultimately brought forth a special issue
of the journal *Contemporary Legend* (2015; Series 3, volume 5), which was the
original iteration of this work.

The opening chapter of this volume, "'The Sort of Story That Has
You Covering Your Mirrors': The Case of Slender Man," is a reprint of
one of the earliest scholarly articles to address Slender Man from a folklorist's perspective (Tolbert 2013). In the essay, Jeffrey A. Tolbert importantly proposes the idea of "reverse ostension" to describe the process
by which a narrative is formed through collective action. In the second
chapter, "The Cowl of Cthulhu: Ostensive Practice in the Digital Age,"
Andrew Peck extends the concept of ostensive action into the more
expansive idea of ostensive practice, a model better suited to the collaborative potential of the digital setting, where individual actions aggregate
into a communally understood body of practice. Through a conscious
awareness of ostension (though not by that term), Internet users who
seek to engage the Slender Man Mythos for themselves learn through
rapid online consensus what kind of activities are considered correct or
successful within the community. Peck emphasizes that most instances of
Slender Man ostension are "fundamentally playful" in nature, in contrast
to the depictions in the popular press.

Following Peck, Andrea Kitta's "'What Happens When the Pictures Are
No Longer Photoshops?' Slender Man, Belief, and the Unacknowledged
Common Experience," explores the reasons Slender Man is so often

reported to "feel real," despite his widely acknowledged fictional roots. Kitta parses the distinct concepts of experience and "an experience," arguing that Slender Man provides an articulable, more tangible way to express what would otherwise be a more abstract, generalized experience.

Jeffrey A. Tolbert's second contribution, "'Dark and Wicked Things': Slender Man, the Folkloresque, and the Implications of Belief," takes on the question of belief in the Slender Man, looking at precursors to this phenomenon in which fiction and reality were similarly muddled. Citing precedents from the 1938 radio drama *War of the Worlds* to the 1999 found-footage horror film *The Blair Witch Project*, Tolbert uses the concept of the "folkloresque" to talk about the thinning barrier between fiction and reality.

Mikel J. Koven's chapter, "The Emperor's New Lore; or, Who Believes in the Big Bad Slender Man?" continues the theme of belief but takes an opposing stance. Koven argues that Slender Man and the narratives about him cannot rightly be classified as contemporary legends, due mainly to the lack of actual belief at their core. They are, he agrees, appropriate for folklorists' study anyway, even if the real fear isn't of the creature himself, but of the susceptibility of our children. Timothy H. Evans, in his "Slender Man, H. P. Lovecraft, and the Dynamics of Horror Cultures," similarly questions the generic placement of the Slender Man Mythos, suggesting that a hybrid of folk and popular culture, specifically "horror culture," is best. He uses the figure of Cthulhu—Lovecraft's popular invention that similarly broke the boundaries of fiction—as a comparison.

Next, Elizabeth Tucker's "Slender Man Is Coming to Get Your Little Brother or Sister: Teenagers' Pranks Posted on YouTube" considers the Slender Man phenomenon through the lens of children's folklore scholarship, looking at teenagers' prank videos as a type of subversive play. Play frames are common in children's folklore, and Tucker provides a comforting message that most children are quite capable of distinguishing the difference between play and reality. In the final chapter, "Monstrous Media and Media Monsters: From Cottingley to Waukesha," Paul Manning picks up the ongoing theme of ostension, seeing it as a sort of semiotic indexicality, a kind of sign that relies on the contiguity of photography. By emerging within the media of verisimilitude, Slender Man has become a perfect media monster.

It is imperative that folklorists embrace the influence of film, television, social media, and other forms of digital technology that continue to challenge and expand our long-standing notions of the field. We see this volume (and the special issue that preceded it) as the first coordinated offering of a concentrated folkloristic response to the Slender Man phenomenon. As such, we welcome dialogue among readers and colleagues alike, and we call upon folklorists to tune their attention toward the murky confines of Internet forums, whispered discussions in hallways, discussions of belief and reality in and outside the classroom (and beyond), and to lend a voice to the unfolding conversation. After all, we wouldn't want to become some faceless character standing ominously at the edge of a cacophonous void. That job appears to have been taken already.

NOTES

1. "Found-footage" films are fictional works that typically purport to be authentic, recovered recordings that were previously "lost" or destroyed. They often involve supernatural phenomena and are usually shot in a documentary or "home movie" style. See Tolbert, chapter 4, for additional perspectives on found-footage films and folklore.

2. The game was originally titled simply *Slender*, but was renamed with the subtitle after version 0.9.7 came out to distinguish it from the sequel. In the game, the player is dropped in a dark forest with a narrow flashlight beam and instructed to collect eight pages. Players search through a foggy landscape, moving past and through mazelike trees and buildings, and tension builds via the soundtrack and the occasional static-laden glimpse of Slender Man himself. If the player takes too long to find the pages, or looks at Slender Man too long, the game ends. Slender Man is often depicted in videos as causing static on screen; thus, static becomes a warning sign of Slender Man's proximity in the video game. See http://the slenderman.wikia.com/wiki/Original_Mythos for an overview of how the Slender Man canon evolved, including a comparison of early and later characteristics popularly associated with the character.

3. Let's Play is a genre of online video in which a gamer plays for an audience. Viewers see the screen as the gamer plays and talks over the experience, sharing their discoveries, observations, and challenges as they go. For a folkloristic application, see Buccitelli 2012.

4. Included within this grouping is the highly intertextual subgenre of creepypasta known emically as the "lost episode" format, which typically employs intricate stories that detail the mysterious or accidental discovery of shocking unreleased, unseen, or underground episodes of either fictional (user-created) or real, *actual* popular television programs in which major franchise characters are brutally harmed, killed, or both. Popular examples include Squidward from *SpongeBob SquarePants* ("Squidward's Suicide"), Bart Simpson from *The Simpsons* ("Dead Simpsons"), Willy Wonka, and even Mickey Mouse ("suicidemouse.avi"; the title's use of ".avi"—audio video interleave—itself alludes to emic knowledge of video file extensions and multimedia preservation, which serves to enhance its look of authenticity). In addition to describing the process of finding these clips within the narrative arc of the stories—many such descriptions taking readers down the proverbial rabbit hole en route to their expected foreboding conclusions—these stories are often, but not always, accompanied by user-created video or image stills for enhanced veracity, much like other forms of creepypasta. While not part of the "lost episode" format, similar motifs appear in other forms of creepypasta, including tales about encountering bizarre glitches or strange occurrences within certain video games, often suggesting or directly calling attention to supernatural forces. For an excellent example,

see "Majora's Mask Creepypasta (BEN DROWNED)" at http://knowyourmeme.com/memes /majoras-mask-creepypasta-ben-drowned.

5. This is not the only killing attempted in the name of a creepypasta character. In November 2015 a twelve-year-old girl from Indiana killed her stepmother, claiming that Laughing Jack, a demonic clown who replaces children's organs with candy, told her to.

6. See Bird 1994; Dégh and Vázsonyi 1983; Ellis 1989; and Lindahl 2005.

7. Note that the example includes explicit language pointing to the purported antiquity of the Der Großmann legend. The demarcation of "1702" and its unverifiability due to age help to heighten the subsequent story's backdrop.

8. We might say that this "feel" carries the "odor of folklore," as described by Foster (2016, 11).

9. As Elliott Oring reminds us, "Participants in legend communication must *entertain* the truth of the account" (Oring 1990, 163).

10. For an elaboration of the Tulpa Effect concept, see http://theslenderman.wikia.com /wiki/The_Tulpa_Effect.

11. In the documentary *Beware the Slenderman* (2017), literary critic Jack Zipes makes the case that Slender Man greatly incorporates some of the traditional motifs found in the Pied Piper tale, namely, the disappearance of children and ambiguity over whether or not the central character—in this case, Slender Man—is benevolent or truly evil.

12. https://www.youtube.com/watch?v=UwzXeqCvY0I.

13. All spelling and grammatical errors in the example are in the original.

14. See Brunvand 2003; Dégh 1968; and Ellis 1994 for additional perspectives on "The Hook" legend.

15. http://www.creepypasta.com/the-original-who-was-phone/.

16. Tourist Guy is an Internet meme that circulated shortly after the events of September 11, 2001. It is a photoshopped image that depicts a young man standing on the observation deck of one of the Twin Towers, with a plane in the background, about to hit the building. The image originally circulated along with a story that it came from an undeveloped film canister found in the rubble.

17. Gothicraft, the creator of a different, but visually similar, image of Slender Man's parodies, commented, "I love the idea that even a scary monster like Slenderman has irritating family members."

18. Before Slender Man, this creature was often connected in appearance and behavior to Bigfoot. See http://cryptomundo.com/cryptozoo-news/walking-sam/ and http://creepy pasta-land.wikia.com/wiki/Walking_Sam.

19. It should be noted, however, that later iterations of Slender Man moved away from describing the character with tentacles.

20. Peter Narváez discusses the liminality of natural spaces in his consideration of fairy lore in Newfoundland. As he explains, "Specific folkloric mechanisms" have "established proxemics boundaries which demarcated geographical areas of purity, liminality, and danger" (Narváez 1991, 337). He goes on to note that spatial liminality distinguishes between "known space (purity) and unknown space (danger) where one might experience the benign or the malignant" (338). Slender Man's presence in the woods, given his cultivated dress, highlights his malign and dangerous presence.

21. For previous work, see Peck 2015 and Tolbert 2013 as well as Tim Evans's (2014) editorial in the *New York Times*.

22. This was made especially clear in the emergence of pseudo-folklore scholarship that misappropriated folkloristic terminology, methodologies, and scholastic identity.

23. See Curlew 2017 for a thoughtful expanded essay stemming from one of the undergraduate presentations. An archived video of the entire panel presentation can be found online at http://research.library.mun.ca/8417.

WORKS CITED

Bird, S. Elizabeth. 1994. "Playing with Fear: Interpreting the Adolescent Legend Trip." *Western Folklore* 53 (3): 191–209. https://doi.org/10.2307/1499808.

Blank, Trevor J. 2013. "Hybridizing Folk Culture: Toward a Theory of New Media and Vernacular Discourse." *Western Folklore* 72 (2): 105–130.

Blank, Trevor J. 2015. "Faux Your Entertainment: Amazon.com Product Reviews as a Locus of Digital Performance." *Journal of American Folklore* 128 (509): 286–297. https://doi.org/10.5406/jamerfolk.128.509.0286.

Blank, Trevor J. 2016. "Giving the 'Big Ten' a Whole New Meaning: Tasteless Humor and the Response to the Penn State Sexual Abuse Scandal." In *The Folkloresque: Reframing Folklore in a Popular Culture World*, ed. Michael Dylan Foster and Jeffrey A. Tolbert, 179–204. Logan: Utah State University Press. https://doi.org/10.7330/97816073 24188.c008.

Bosman, Julie. 2015. "Pine Ridge Reservation Struggles with Suicides among Its Young." *New York Times*, May 1. https://www.nytimes.com/2015/05/02/us/pine-ridge -indian-reservation-struggles-with-suicides-among-young-people.html.

Brunvand, Jan Harold. (Original work published 1981) 2003. *The Vanishing Hitchhiker: American Urban Legends and Their Meanings*. New York: Norton.

Buccitelli, Anthony Bak. 2012. "Performance 2.0: Observations toward a Theory of the Digital Performance of Folklore." In *Folk Culture in the Digital Age: The Emergent Dynamics of Human Interaction*, ed. Trevor J. Blank, 60–84. Logan: Utah State University Press. https://doi.org/10.7330/9780874218909.c03.

Chess, Shira. 2011. "Open Sourcing Horror." *Information Communication and Society* 15 (3): 374–393. https://doi.org/10.1080/1369118X.2011.642889.

Curlew, Kyle. 2017. "The Legend of the Slender Man: The Boogieman of Surveillance Culture." *First Monday* 22 (6). https://doi.org/10.5210/fm.v22i6.6901 http://first monday.org/ojs/index.php/fm/article/view/6901.

Dégh, Linda. 1968. "The Hook." *Indiana Folklore* 1 (1): 92–100.

Dégh, Linda, and Andrew Vázsonyi. 1983. "Does the Word 'Dog' Bite? Ostensive Action: A Means of Legend-Telling." *Journal of Folklore Research* 20 (1): 5–34.

Der Großmann. 2014. Slender Man Connection Wiki. http://slendermanconnection.wikia .com/wiki/Der_Großmann.

Ellis, Bill. 1989. "Death by Folklore: Ostension, Contemporary Legend, and Murder." *Western Folklore* 48 (3): 201–220. https://doi.org/10.2307/1499739.

Ellis, Bill. 1994. "'The Hook' Reconsidered: Problems in Classifying and Interpreting Adolescent Horror Legends." *Folklore* 105 (1-2): 61–75. https://doi.org/10.1080/00155 87X.1994.9715874.

Evans, Timothy H. 2014. "The Ghost in the Machine." *The New York Times*, June 8, SR4.

Foster, Michael Dylan. 2016. "Introduction: The Challenge of the Folkloresque." In *The Folkloresque: Reframing Folklore in a Popular Culture World*, ed. Michael Dylan Foster and Jeffrey A. Tolbert, 3–33. Logan: Utah State University Press. https://doi.org/10 .7330/9781607324188.c000.

Foster, Michael Dylan, and Jeffrey A. Tolbert, eds. 2016. *The Folkloresque: Reframing Folklore in a Popular Culture World*. Logan: Utah State University Press. https://doi.org/10 .7330/9781607324188.

Frank, Russell. 2011. *Newslore: Contemporary Folklore on the Internet.* Jackson: University Press of Mississippi. https://doi.org/10.14325/mississippi/9781604739282.001.0001.

Howard, Robert Glenn. 2008. "Electronic Hybridity: The Persistent Processes of the Vernacular Web." *Journal of American Folklore* 121 (480): 192–218. https://doi.org/10.1353/jaf.0.0012.

Kitta, Andrea. 2019. *The Kiss of Death: Contamination, Contagion, and Folklore.* Logan: Utah State University Press.

Lindahl, Carl. 2005. "Ostensive Healing: Pilgrimage to the San Antonio Ghost Tracks." *Journal of American Folklore* 118 (468): 164–185. https://doi.org/10.1353/jaf.2005.0023.

McNeill, Lynne S. 2009. "The End of the Internet: A Folk Response to the Provision of Infinite Choice." In *Folklore and the Internet: Vernacular Expression in a Digital World,* ed. Trevor J. Blank, 80–97. Logan: Utah State University Press. https://doi.org/10.2307/j.ctt4cgrx5.7.

McNeill, Lynne S. 2015. "Twihards, Buffistas, and Vampire Fanlore." In *Putting the Supernatural in Its Place,* ed. Jeannie Thomas, 126–145. Salt Lake City: University of Utah Press.

Moran, Lee. 2014. "Florida Teen Obsessed with Slender Man Set Fire to Own Home." *New York Daily News,* September 4. http://www.nydailynews.com/news/national/slender-man-obsessed-fla-teen-set-fire-home-cops-article-1.1928945.

Narváez, Peter. 1991. "Newfoundland Berry Pickers 'In the Fairies': Maintaining Spatial, Temporal, and Moral Boundaries through Legendry." In *The Good People: New Fairylore Essays,* ed. Peter Narváez, 336–368. Lexington: University Press of Kentucky.

Oring, Elliott. 1990. "Legend, Truth, and News." *Southern Folklore* 47 (2): 163–177.

Peck, Andrew. 2015. "Tall, Dark, and Loathsome: The Emergence of a Legend Cycle in the Digital Age." *Journal of American Folklore* 128 (509): 333–348. https://doi.org/10.5406/jamerfolk.128.509.0333.

"Slender Man." 2016. Know Your Meme. http://knowyourmeme.com/memes/slender-man.

Smith, Paul. 1997. "Contemporary Legend." In *Folklore: An Encyclopedia of Beliefs, Customs, Tales, Music, and Art,* ed. Charlie T. McCormick and Kim Kennedy White, 493–495. Santa Barbara, CA: ABC CLIO.

Tolbert, Jeffrey A. 2013. "'The Sort of Story That Has You Covering Your Mirrors': The Case of Slender Man." *Semiotic Review,* no. 2: Monsters. https://www.semioticreview.com/ojs/index.php/sr/article/view/19.

Widdowson, John. 1971. "The Bogeyman: Some Preliminary Observations on Frightening Figures." *Folklore* 82 (2): 99–115. https://doi.org/10.1080/0015587X.1971.9716716.

Chapter 1

"The Sort of Story That Has You Covering Your Mirrors"
The Case of Slender Man

Jeffrey A. Tolbert

THIS CHAPTER CONSIDERS ONE CONTEMPORARY permutation of monstrousness, the Internet phenomenon known as the Slender Man. As a monster, Slender Man epitomizes the simultaneous alienness and familiarity that characterize the uncanny. As a self-conscious Internet construct whose backstory has been built up over several years by a massive community of online participants, Slender Man functions metadiscursively to reveal precisely those elements that are popularly conceived of as constituting *monstrousness*. In simplest terms, Slender Man is a distillation of the most frightening images and trends present in contemporary popular culture (primarily, if not exclusively, those of the horror genre) and supernatural folklore. A potent symbol, Slender Man serves as a flexible rhetorical tool, used variously to critique popular trends, instill fear in audiences, and as a self-referential "in-joke" whose significance is intelligible only to those already familiar with the phenomenon. Thus, the figure of the Slender Man indexes at least two separate intellectual strands, two distinct but related conceptual frameworks. First, Slender Man is a sign of abject fear: the ultimate Other, the final evolution of radical alterity. Second, Slender Man subtly references the self-conscious communicative processes that gave rise to the tradition itself and are, in fact, the reason for its continued existence as an Internet icon.

Slender Man stands alongside countless similar phenomena in an area of growing interest for scholars: Internet memes. As Lynne S. McNeill has noted, "The emergence of traditional expressive forms on the Internet,

DOI: 10.7330/9781607327813.c001

Figure 1.1. A fairly typical Slender Man encounter. (Art by *Alheli-delaGarza. http://alheli-delagarza.deviantart.com/.)

and the observation and re-creation of them by other people in new contexts, has not gone unnoticed by the Internet community itself, which has adopted the concept of *memes* to identify what folklorists would call folklore" (McNeill 2009, 84). However, a particularly fascinating aspect of the Slender Man meme is how the figure's backstory deliberately and explicitly mimics the generic conventions typically ascribed to legends (Peck 2015,

335, 338). Michael Kinsella argues, "Legends as a folklore genre represent communal efforts to adapt old customs and beliefs to new situations. Simultaneously, legends frame emergent customs and beliefs by placing them in a historic continuum, thereby connecting the activities, behaviors, and beliefs of individuals and communities in the present to those in the past" (Kinsella 2011, 8). The Slender Man Mythos certainly functions in the ways Kinsella describes.[1] It goes further, though, by containing within itself, from the very outset, a metadiscursive space wherein participants can comment not only on the Slender Man figure but on the nature and significance of the entire legend genre as well.

The present study considers Slender Man from a folkloristic perspective; however, in light of the monster's semiotic potential, Slender Man's interest extends beyond folklore's disciplinary confines. Building on folkloristic work on the concept of ostension—the showing of a thing or experience directly, as opposed to representing it through signs or sign systems such as narratives—I demonstrate how the Slender Man Mythos encapsulates important semiotic processes that are self-consciously, often winkingly, employed by its creators to make a new narrative tradition that deliberately mimics established ones.

Ostension has been famously defined in a folkloristic context as "showing the reality itself instead of using any kind of signification" (Dégh and Vázsonyi 1983, 6), and *ostensive action* as the direct performance of a given action, or its representation through a related action (with the assumption that the ostensive act itself is somehow "real") (8).[2] My primary purpose in this chapter is to demonstrate how Slender Man represents what might be thought of as *reverse ostension*, in that it is an iconic figure produced through a collective effort and deliberately modeled after an existing and familiar folklore genre. If ostension involves the privileging of experience over representation (e.g., acting out the content of a legend text, rather than simply listening to a recitation of it), Slender Man's creators are effectively reversing this process by weaving together diverse strands of "experience" (in the form of personal encounters with the creature, documentary and photographic evidence, etc.) into a more or less coherent body of narratives. Simultaneously, these narratives are consciously modeled on existing, established, "real" ones (specifically, again, the legend genre). Reverse ostension is therefore, in fact, two processes in one: it involves the creation of new objects, new disconnected examples of experience; and it involves the combination of these elements into a corpus of "traditional" narratives modeled on existing folklore (but not wholly indebted to any specific tradition—on which, see Foster 2016).

In considering the Slender Man phenomenon, I examine three of the Mythos's major permutations. The first is the original Internet forum thread that gave rise to the Slender Man and from which it rapidly spread, the "Create Paranormal Images" thread on the Something Awful forums (Gerogerigegege 2009). The forum provides the clearest example of the semiotic process of reverse ostension as a conscious effort to create a specific type of folkloric sign. Second, I consider the YouTube video series Marble Hornets (DeLage, Wagner, and Sutton 2009b), which began as a spinoff of the emerging Slender Man tradition. Marble Hornets depicts the ongoing encounters of a group of individuals with the monstrous Slender Man and is widely regarded as a formative work in the Mythos. And third, to participate directly in one form of ostension set in the Slender Man universe, I played the video game *Slender: The Arrival* (Hadley 2013). The video game represents a move away from reverse ostension back toward a more direct ostensive experience, exemplifying the high degree of adaptability of this contemporary Internet phenomenon. I supplement this material with an interview I conducted with Amanda Brennan, former meme librarian for the website Know Your Meme and self-professed Slender Man fan and participant in the Mythos. Finally, I include responses from members of the Slender Nation forum to a series of questions I posed about the Slender Man Mythos. These sources represent only a small fraction of the entire Mythos, which is expanding every day, but they aptly demonstrate the communicative processes at work among Slender Man's many fans. By emphasizing the experiential, ostensive qualities of these primary sources, I attempt to highlight the workings of reverse ostension and demonstrate its significance as a semiotic process particularly suited to contemporary Internet-based fan culture.

Two other scholarly works on the Slender Man phenomenon have informed this chapter. In the first, Shira Chess argues that Slender Man represents "an 'open-sourcing' of generic horror conventions" (Chess 2011, 375). Chess rightly emphasizes the communal, collaborative nature of the Slender Man Mythos. She writes, "Like Open Source software, the open-sourcing of storytelling involves reuse, modification, sharing of source code, an openness (and transparency) of infrastructure, and the negotiation and collaboration of many individuals" (383)—precisely the concepts with which folklorists have long concerned themselves. Chess goes on to suggest that the nature of online communication makes it possible for scholars to witness the creation and spread of a new tradition like Slender Man in its entirety, something that would have been impossible previously (390).

The second work to consider the Slender Man phenomenon is by folklorist Andrew Peck. Peck argues that Slender Man comprises a "digital legend cycle that combines the generic conventions and emergent qualities of oral and visual performance with the collaborative potential of networked communication" (Peck 2015, 334). Like Chess, Peck notes the Slender Man Mythos' collaborative dimension as well as the unusual opportunity the Mythos affords to study the development of a legend from its creation. He goes further, though, arguing that "[Something Awful] users engaged in performance by referencing existing frameworks which, in turn, gave rise to further shared expectations" (338). These aspects of the early stages of Slender Man's development—the tendency toward collaboration and the appeal to established, recognized genres—are major components of the process of reverse ostension.

MAKING A MONSTER

To make my argument—that Slender Man offers critical commentary on the legend genre by enabling individuals to participate in the creation of a legend through reverse ostension—requires that we turn briefly to that genre and the ways it has been conceptualized.

Scholars differ as to what constitutes a legend, but an influential definition has been that laid out by William Bascom, in which legends are prose narratives taken as true by their tellers and audiences and set in a past less remote than myths (Bascom 1984, 9). The issue of belief, however, is a particularly contentious one.[3] Discussing the ostensive dimensions of legend narratives—that is, their potential to influence reality—Bill Ellis has suggested a more cautious approach: "It seems more accurate to describe legends as normative definitions of reality, maps by which one can determine what has happened, what is happening, and what will happen" (Ellis 1989, 202). Similarly, Michael Kinsella, in his study of legend tripping on the Internet, argues, "Through legends—both supernatural and otherwise—the synergies between narrative and performance can sometimes result in the legend coming to life" (Kinsella 2011, 11).

Regardless of scholarly understandings, the Slender Man Mythos is composed of a number of narratives that, while avowedly fictional, are framed within the narrative tradition as "true" experiences—and the "truth" of the tradition is established in various ways, including by likening it to "real" legends. Peck notes that the Slender Man Mythos "drew upon an existing matrix of belief . . . In other words, the Slender Man was not an entirely new creation and was instead influenced by a vast network of vernacular and institutional performances that had directly and indirectly preceded it" (Peck 2015, 339).[4]

As noted in the introduction to this volume, the Slender Man Mythos began with a post in the Something Awful forums. Something Awful (Kyanka 2016) is a site that hosts a wide range of subject matter, from current events to flash animations to reviews of role-playing games. The site also features forums where users discuss an equally wide array of topics, one of which gave rise to the Slender Man meme. Two pictures posted by user Victor Surge on June 10, 2009, depicted a tall, vaguely monstrous figure looming in the background of otherwise mundane photographs of children.[5] Victor Surge's (2009) original post provides tantalizing hints of a larger narrative involving a terrifying creature—it suggests the being's unique power to induce violence, and indicates that the photographers responsible for the images are missing or dead—and thus sets the stage for the processes that would lead to the communal construction of an entire narrative tradition. Notably, though, the original post leaves the reader with more questions than answers: it points to an underlying story without overtly narrating one. Taken alone, the post is a clear example of ostension: Slender Man is not represented abstractly but presented photographically and "factually." Viewed as the first step in a series of ostensive acts, however, Victor Surge's post represents the beginning of reverse ostension, using fabricated "facts" to create a narrative where none previously existed.

Though the thread in which these images appeared was dedicated to creating fictional "paranormal" images, Slender Man soon became the primary focus of participants. Over the next eight months, forum members continued adding to the emerging Slender Man Mythos, posting their own pictures, videos, audio recordings, and narratives. The creature that resulted from the frantic activity of the Something Awful forum posters was a lanky, black business suit–wearing, faceless monster, sometimes depicted with writhing tentacles sprouting from his back, whose mere proximity is enough to cause insanity in his victims. (Slender Man, as the name suggests, is most often gendered as a male.) In some of the narratives supplied by forum members, Slender Man removes the organs of his victims, placing them in plastic bags before replacing them in their owners' lifeless bodies. In others, he impales his victims in the branches of trees. He is frequently associated with forests, though he appears elsewhere as well.

The monstrous, fearful quality of Slender Man is partly responsible for the massive popularity of the meme, a fact upon which users of the Something Awful forums frequently reflected. User TheRiffie (2009) wrote, "I'm not usually one to get all bandwagony [*sic*] but Slender Man is honestly one of the most inspiring and sinister things I've seen lately. Something about it seems to strike some sort of primal 'wrong' chord." Likewise, Dove from Above (2009) posted,

> Oh, fucky fuck fuck, you people, I have to pee and I can't bring myself to walk through the living room (the only light switch is at the far end) to get to the toilet! Thank God I closed the curtains before it got dark.
>
> This is seriously the sort of story that has you covering your mirrors, and I definitely want to read more, even if I don't sleep well tonight.

And user Soakie (2009), in a post dated June 20, 2009, wrote,

> [Slender Man] is a satisfactory booger [*sic*] man, pressing all the right buttons. Even if we don't really believe in the supernatural, even if our rational minds laugh at such an absurdity . . . we are cutting him out and sewing him together.
>
> We're stuffing him with nightmares and unspoken fears.
>
> And what happens when the pictures are no longer photoshops?

These posts offer explicit commentary on users' conceptions of monsters and the monstrous. But as a consciously constructed sign, Slender Man also reflects important semiotic processes at work among members of the various Internet communities in which his legend has appeared.[6] The most significant of these processes, and perhaps the area that has seen the most fruitful overlap of folkloristic and literary semiotic investigation, is ostension. In turn, the form of ostension most studied by folklorists has been the process of legend tripping, the self-conscious appropriation and enactment of existing legend texts (Koven 2008, 154; Kinsella 2011, x). Legend tripping is well represented in contemporary Internet culture, and the Slender Man Mythos is no exception; however, rather than taking an existing legend text and acting it out through legend tripping, the countless individuals who have contributed to the Slender Man Mythos have taken a wide array of disparate raw materials—often created from scratch and usually of a purportedly experiential nature (e.g., stories of encounters with supernatural beings)—and combined them to form a new narrative tradition that resembles the existing, familiar legend genre. Put differently, a conventional legend about a haunted house might involve a visit to the site to attempt to encounter the ghost. Slender Man inhabits no real-world sites; he is not initially available for direct experience. But narratives of encounters with Slender Man were nevertheless supplied by users. Thus, the Mythos was created from fictional "experiences" of the monster, rather than providing the initial *impetus* for experience. If ostension effectively bypasses the sign (in this case, the narrative) by privileging the direct experience of the object of the sign, then what I am calling reverse ostension implies that a sign is constructed, where none previously existed, by weaving together disparate strands of experience (as well as indexing and mimicking other signs). Reverse ostension is, then, an act of reverse engineering: *an effort to arrive back at the sign*, that is, to create a narrative tradition by correlating and connecting fragmentary narratives (themselves representations of experience, albeit fictional ones).

Although reverse ostension's aim is the construction of a new sign (in this case, a legend text), this would be impossible without the careful and deliberate privileging of—in fact, the insistence upon—the experiential dimension of narratives. Ostension (in either direction) necessitates experience. In his study of ostension in Kamsá myths, John McDowell argues for the existence of an "experiential substrate" underlying narrative genres (McDowell 1982, 122). The experiential substrate is effectively the assumption of the underlying reality of the experience being recounted as well as the chronology of events (as distinct from the chronology of the *telling*). I suggest that the experiential substrate can refer not only to the narrative content of a given text but also, in the case of reverse ostension, to the collective experience of creating the story in the first place. This is particularly true of Internet phenomena such as Slender Man, which are from their inception participatory. As Kinsella argues, "Communication technologies allow us to see more clearly how the reciprocity between experience and tradition results in the ongoing construction of what we call the supernatural" (Kinsella 2011, 147). But Slender Man's interest, and that of phenomena like it, extends beyond its capacity to reveal communicative processes. The experiential emphasis underlying the construction of Slender Man and the careful inclusion of generic markers that indicate its status as a legend enable the monster to remain dynamic, shiftable, and emergent, available to be redeployed by its creators or adopted and adapted by new users (Peck 2015, 334).

These qualities of the Slender Man figure—its carefully maintained vitality and adaptability, and its unsettling capacity to enter, in various ways, into the lived experiences of its creators—merit further attention. By its nature, a sign such as Slender Man, consciously constructed through reverse ostension, moves beyond its immediate purpose of entertainment to provide an ongoing commentary on what constitutes a particular type of folklore (see Peck 2015, 341–344). Put another way, it reveals what people think folklore is, and what it does, and what it looks like. S. Elizabeth Bird has noted that some forms of popular culture succeed specifically because of their resemblance to folklore (Bird 2006, 346). Slender Man's continuing popularity can likewise be attributed at least in part to its folklore-like characteristics. Part of the process of constructing Slender Man out of whole cloth, as it were, consists of working backward from established, known legend texts to create a new one. This is an ostensive act, but it begins where typical ostensive actions end: with experience. Here, the experiential substrate, to use McDowell's term, does not imply an assumed *reality* of experience (meaning an actual encounter with the Slender Man); as I will show in the sections that follow, Slender Man's creators made no such assumption. Instead, the experiential substrate underlying the Slender Man Mythos is the collective action undertaken by its creators: their careful construction of narratives, documentary evidence, audio and video material (all of which relate fictional experiences with the Slender Man). From this basis the legend emerges, a sign ready to be redeployed in new contexts.

"REAL" VERSUS "FAKE"

Ostension, in our sense, involves the intrusion of narrative into reality. Dégh and Vázsonyi (1983) give the example of staged haunted houses at Halloween, which rely to some extent on prior knowledge on the part of their audience about the legends being referenced. They go on to note that even in the absence of an actual legendary background, the resemblance of haunted-house imagery to known legends can be enough to imbue them with a sense of fear: "Paradoxical as it sounds, there are also legends which do not exist but still have a similar effect as the existing ones. Dracula, the most popular among all monsters, has no real folklore . . . The public seems convinced, nonetheless, of the existence of a lush legend realm. The term *fictitious legend* best describes the case of Dracula. Fictitious, not because the story is untrue and the hero of the legend nonexistent, but because the legend itself does not exist" (25).

What Dégh and Vázsonyi term a "fictitious legend" is precisely what has been constructed in the case of Slender Man. It is worth pausing here to address the issue of "real" versus "fictitious" or fictional legends, however. By "real" I simply mean narratives that arise within a community and are accepted as parts of that community's culture (in their connection to places, events, and characters of special significance), regardless of whether they are literally believed. This is in contradistinction to those legends, such as Slender Man, which are consciously crafted as fictions, with no such prior connections to lived culture. It is important to note, too, that the fictional status of Slender Man is an emic distinction, arising from within the group of individuals who originally constructed the Slender Man Mythos. For example, in a post dated October 5, 2009, user rinski observed,

The SM is fascinating to me, because he's such an ideal horror figure for so
many different reasons. I mean, there's the whole "fear of the unknown"
thing, and the "twisting the familiar into something unfamiliar" thing.
There's also the genius of his subtlety: we've trained ourselves to see his
general shape in every photoshop, so now we see him *everywehre* [*sic*].

These factors aren't really unique, though. I think one of SM's more
unique attributes is that he's fake. Not only is he fake, but we know, for a
fact, that he came from a thread on SA. No one is trying to convince us
he's real. (rinski 2009)

This metacommentary by rinski—Slender Man is "fake" but still frightening—serves to emphasize the fictional quality of the Mythos, and does
so from within the community that created it. The term "fake," likewise,
subtly references Slender Man's *resemblance* to something *not fake*—that is,
something real, a real monster of real legend.

Regardless, then, of the "real" or "fictional" status that scholars and others may append to a phenomenon like Slender Man, the monster remains a
conscious expression of a culture shared among a particular group of people,
which bears special significances that depend in part on an understanding of
the group context in which the expressive culture arises.[7] In this sense the
Slender Man legend is as "real" as any other.[8] And as we have seen, the explicit
acknowledgment of Slender Man's fictional status is an important part of the
legend. Mikel Koven (2008) coins the terms *cinematic ostension* and *mass-mediated
ostension* to apply to the forms of ostensive action represented in popular culture texts, and suggests that these forms of ostension "implicitly [recognize]
an audience by encouraging some form of post-presentation debate regarding the veracity of the legends presented. There is also an implicit recognition
of the fictive form of this narration (a fiction film) but equally a recognition
that the stories upon which certain films are based come from 'genuine urban
legends'" (139). This last point—the perceived relationship of a popular
work to "genuine" legend—is the element upon which the process I am calling reverse ostension hinges. Creating a "fictional legend," to use Dégh and
Vázsonyi's term, involves first of all an awareness of what "real" legends are
like: both their structural and formal characteristics as well as their thematic
content, motifs, and other narrative elements. The process of selecting these
elements from existing folklore, or creating new ones that resemble them, is
precisely the inverse of the ostensive action that Dégh and Vázsonyi describe.
Once the necessary elements have been assembled, the new legend text thus
created is available for further ostensive action. In the case of Slender Man,
as Peck suggests, expectations about legend-telling shape the Slender Man
Mythos, but contributors to the legend both adhere to and depart from these

expectations in any given performance of the legend. This process echoes that identified by Henry Jenkins in his now-classic study of television fan culture, where he argues, "Meanings form the basis for the construction and maintenance of the fan community; the expectations and conventions of the fan community also shape the meanings derived from the series and the forms taken by the fan's own artistic creations" (Jenkins 2013, 88).

The significance of the real/fictional dichotomy does not end there, however. Some users attempted to impart a more conventional "reality" to the Slender Man Mythos by explicitly connecting it to "real" folklore, simultaneously increasing its verisimilitude and frightening potential while remaining conscious of the legend's fictional status (they were, after all, its creators). These users hoped, effectively, to shape a legend so compelling that people would be convinced of its veracity *as a legend*. Reacting to other forum members' creation of a Wikipedia page about Slender Man, on June 18, 2009, user Leperflesh posted,

> Going with a wikipedia [*sic*] page up-front was probably a lot of fun . . . but not a good idea.
>
> The right thing to do is establish web resources about the Slender Man first—conspiracy-theory web pages, etc. Then, after there's some cross-pollination and even interest from people outside SA, create a stub Wiki page that just links a source or two, and treats the subject from a skeptical/fact-based standpoint (use words like "myth," "alleged," and "conspiracy theory").
>
> A page like that, that purports only to report on a fringe myth, would have been more likely to survive. An editing history with a lot of different editors, over a long period of time (rather than a goon rush), with multiple references added and removed and edited over time, would have made the page less likely to be deleted.
>
> Now, of course, that's closed off; even if we did all of this, the history of the original page's creation and fast deletion as vandalism will serve as evidence against any future incarnation of the page.
>
> . . . which is OK. I'm thinking we (me?) register slenderman.org, work on it (make it the typical disorganized, slightly unbalanced ranting style typical of the genre—just take a look at websites promoting HHO, 911 Truthers, crop circles, etc. for ideas), and then gradually over time add a selection of stuff from this thread, sticking to the top-quality examples (probably not the supposed secret texts from agencies we've never heard of—don't require someone to believe in an additional conspiracy theory just to accept this one, as that is an implausibility-multiplier). You could even address the subject from a skeptical-believer point of view, showing "obvious forgeries and fakes" on one page and "unable to discount" stuff on another, etc.

> Do it very low-key for a while (a year or more) and eventually it'll creep
> into the 'net's culture, and even have a chance to attract the attention of
> lazy reporters who don't fact-check stuff. (Leperflesh 2009)

Leperflesh makes explicit the desire among some users to form Slender
Man into a real legend (i.e., one people would believe that people believed).
User H. P. Shivcraft took the manipulation of folkloric source material even
further, creating a fictional tale situated (apocryphally) in a real work by a
real folklorist. In a post dated July 1, 2009, H. P. Shivcraft wrote,

> So once the Slender Man began popping up in this thread, I could have
> sworn something about it seemed familiar. I'm an amateur folklorist, so
> I had a few source books lying around. It took me a while, but I finally
> found something in W.K. McNeil's Ghost Stories of the American South.
> Most of the tales collected are transcripts of recordings other folklorists
> made, but McNeil compiles them and offers notes. A really handy book.
> So anyway, this particular story appears in the book's seventh section,
> "Other Supernatural Creatures." (H. P. Shivcraft 2009)

Where Leperflesh offered suggestions for making Slender Man seem
real, H. P. Shivcraft acted directly to accomplish its realization, situating
Slender Man alongside existing legend texts, literally placing it in a collection of "real" narratives. This introductory paragraph is followed by the
text of a legend purportedly collected by McNeil, whose real book, *Ghost
Stories from the American South*, does not in fact contain any such text (McNeil
1985). H. P. Shivcraft even includes, following the legend text, an "analysis"
of the legend supposedly written by McNeil himself, wherein the folklorist
attempts to assign motifs to the narrative. In this way, the reverse ostensive
processes that gave rise to Slender Man are at once emphasized (everyone
knows the user is a user, and everyone in the forum knows the forum is
about a fictional legend) and, conversely, hidden from view, assimilated into
existing American folklore.[9]

An interview with Slender Man's creator, user Victor Surge, posted on
the website Know Your Meme, likewise demonstrates the tremendously
reflexive, savvy, and volitional nature of this meme, and the general awareness of its relationship to more conventional folklore genres:

> INTERVIEWER: What was your reaction when people started creat-
> ing pictures and stories about your newborn myth, in paral-
> lel with yours? Did you think it would get that much popular
> [*sic*] and spread to others [*sic*] websites (4chan, Kongregate,
> Facepunch . . .) as quickly as it did, gaining the status of "Internet
> Urban Legend" and a meme?

VICTOR SURGE: It was amazing to see people create their own little part of Slender Man in order to perpetuate his existance. [*sic*]

I didn't expect it to move beyong [*sic*] the SA forums. And when it did, I found it interesting to watch as sort of an accelerated version of an urban legend. It differs from the prior concept of the urban legend in that it is on the Internet, and this both helps and harms the status of the Slender Man as one. In my personal opinion, an urban legend requires an audience ignorant of the origin of the legend. It needs unverifiable third and forth [*sic*] hand (or more) accounts to perpetuate the myth. On the Internet, anyone is privy to its origins as evidenced by the very public Somethingawful thread. But what is funny is that despite this, it still spread. Internet memes are finicky things and by making something at the right place and time it can swell into an "Internet Urban Legend." (Tomberry 2010)

Here, Victor Surge both acknowledges conservative models of folklore (specifically urban legends) as anonymous, collective works and moves beyond those older models to suggest ways in which the Internet allows users to create new items inspired by well-known genres. Victor Surge's language perfectly reflects the concern in reverse ostension with generating a sign where there was none previously: to "perpetuate the myth," generating a meme with staying power, is the goal. Together with the preceding forum quotes, it plainly echoes Kinsella's assertion that "supernatural legends and occult texts both illustrate attempts to become believable, or better yet, 'real,' by tying themselves to history through blending fiction with fact, infusing everyday reality with elements of the otherworldly and fantastic" (Kinsella 2011, 60). This is the considerable signifying power of reverse ostension, as opposed to its straightforward predecessor: it moves away from reality by creating a sign, but simultaneously moves closer to (a version of) reality by making the sign as much like other, familiar, accepted signs as possible. Reverse ostension indexes a whole realm of preexisting signs (Slender Man exists in intertextual dialogue with other legend texts) and in so doing grants a new legend a different kind of veracity (Slender Man is *believable*).

EXPERIENCING THE LEGEND

One of the earliest offshoots of the original Something Awful thread was the YouTube series Marble Hornets. The first video of the series, *Introduction* (DeLage, Wagner, and Sutton 2009a), was uploaded to YouTube on June 20, 2009, just ten days after Victor Surge's original images were posted to the Something Awful forum. Presented as "found footage," the introduction (in common with the rest of the series) features text captions inserted by protagonist Jay.[10] Jay's narration explains that the footage was shot by his college friend Alex as part of a film project, the eponymous Marble Hornets. During filming, Alex's behavior became strange and he abandoned the project, but eventually agreed to give the tapes to Jay, who explains to the audience through captions that he intends to go through the tapes to determine what may have caused Alex's unusual behavior. Over the course of the series, Jay is pulled into a deepening mystery involving his friend Alex and the monstrous Slender Man (who is never identified as such in the series, but clearly represents the figure created in the Something Awful forum).

Marble Hornets and the related YouTube series totheark (DeLage, Wagner, and Sutton 2009c) illustrate Koven's concept of cinematic ostension, as one Slender Man narrative is presented (albeit in fragmented form) through the videos that Jay collects and films over the course of the series. This is significant in the context of the present discussion because it implies the existence of a sign that can be ostensively experienced: that is, once the Slender Man Mythos was begun by Victor Surge, it was available for direct participation in various forms, including the ostensive action depicted in the fictional Marble Hornets series. To complicate matters further, Marble Hornets and totheark together constitute an alternate reality game (ARG) (Tomberry 2010) that invites users to participate even more directly in the Slender Man Mythos. Totheark's video entries—uploaded by an unknown person or persons from within the Marble Hornets universe—often include coded text that fans have worked to decipher, deepening the mystery and enhancing the ostensive component of the Marble Hornets/Slender Man Mythos (see "Totheark" 2013).

Kinsella notes that "ARGs are open-ended gaming narratives that utilize transmedia storytelling and interweave the ideas and actions of both players and game designers (often called puppet masters) into an unfolding production" (Kinsella 2011, 60). Interestingly, he goes on to argue that "what separates legend-trippers from alternate reality gamers . . . is that the latter are self-consciously aware of their performance and believe in the potency of their play. Legend-trippers, however, generally disavow that it is they who are the cause of the supernatural event. In order to ascribe a supernatural quality to an experience, agency must reside with the otherworldly" (62). Slender Man complicates this point. The Mythos includes both a fan-created legend and a fan-made ARG, *Marble Hornets*, whose primary purpose

Figure 1.2. Slender Man as he appears in *Slender: The Arrival.* (Image used with permission. http://www.slenderarrival.com/images/gallery/forestfog.jpg.)

is to interact with that legend—that is, to legend trip. This suggests that the ostensive action represented by legend tripping is not necessarily undertaken in order to evoke the supernatural; rather, as a semiotic process in which fans consciously and willingly engage, its purpose is to provide direct access to the narrative regardless of its supposed supernatural associations.

Certainly, Marble Hornets is doing something right in terms of its portrayal of and interaction with the Slender Man Mythos and the degree to which this approach resonates with Slender Man fans. As of July 1, 2017, the *Introduction* entry had 4,422,266 views on YouTube—and this is only the first in a series that currently includes ninety-two videos (the most recent of which was released in 2014).[11] A motion picture based on Marble Hornets was released in 2015 (Moran 2015), and the creators of Marble Hornets also contributed to the video game *Slender: The Arrival* (Hadley 2013). The game displays yet another level of ostensive engagement with the Slender Man Mythos, one that derives its efficacy from its adherence to the established rules of that Mythos.

Slender: The Arrival in fact represents a further refining of the meme and, in a sense, its transition from a collective and participatory cultural form to a mass-produced commodity (albeit one developed by an independent studio). The game allows individual players to experience the collectively produced Slender Man legend in a frightening solitary adventure. The frightful images and "historical" knowledge established by the meme tradition are available, in this digital context, for direct engagement (for better or for worse). The game also offers what is arguably the best opportunity for ordinary fans of the Mythos to legend trip in the world of Slender Man.

The game is simple: you control the protagonist, who must navigate several isolated, dark, and potentially dangerous (though essentially mundane) environments to uncover information about her own situation and elude the strange, monstrous figure that seems to be chasing her. The player has no weapons and cannot fight back against Slender Man, whose unpredictable appearances in the game world increase the further you progress in each stage. His presence causes loud static noises and distortion in the game video, and if you remain near him for too long, it will result in a "game over."[12]

The ostension enabled by the Slender Man video game is perhaps unlike that envisioned by earlier generations of folklorists. Despite the obvious differences (it involves a digital "trip" rather than a physical one; the narrative thus explored has been known as a fiction since its beginning), the game nevertheless represents an opportunity for fans to participate directly in the Mythos and to experience the frightful Slender Man figure in a startlingly direct way. It is useful here to consider McDowell's notion of "virtual ostension," which he defines as a type of ostension that occurs during the telling of a narrative, and whose experiential substrate is not available for direct experience by its audience, even though it is invoked in the narrative itself (McDowell 1982, 127). Video game ostension—"virtual" in a different sense—complicates this, because while a story is being told, the player has a high degree of direct influence over its unfolding. Playing the game itself constitutes the experiential substrate, even as it references *other* experiential substrates in the form of the wider legend genre, popular culture portrayals of legend trips, and so on.

EMIC PERSPECTIVES ON SLENDER MAN

One of the first Internet sources I consulted for information about Slender Man was the Know Your Meme database. According to the KYM "About" page, "Know Your Meme is a site that researches and documents Internet memes and viral phenomena" ("Know Your Meme: About" 2013).[13] After perusing the KYM Slender Man page, I contacted the website to ask about using materials from the site. Amanda Brennan, then KYM's meme librarian, responded to my message. We conversed via email, and eventually I asked Brennan if she would be willing to be interviewed on the topic of Slender Man, to which request she graciously agreed. We spoke via Skype; I present excerpts from our conversation here.

I asked Brennan if she felt that Slender Man's success was due to its interactive nature. She responded in the negative; instead, she felt it had to do with the issue of the Mythos's semblance of reality.

> The fact that there's a whole wiki dedicated to this mythos just kind of lets people, lets their imaginations run free. And the Internet is a big facilitator of that, because you have a platform—you can say, "Yeah, I saw Slender Man. Here. Let me tell you about it. Let me show you this picture." It might be—it's photoshopped, but the person you're showing, or the blog you're putting it on—they don't know it's photoshopped. [*JT laughs*] And it's just that question of, oh, is it real? Is it not real? What has science done? [*JT laughs again*]
>
> That definitely feeds into people's curiosity. (Brennan, Skype interview, 2013)

Brennan's comments reflect the concern, noted above, that Slender Man fans have with the Mythos's seeming realness. This point was reiterated by other Slender Man fans whom I questioned about their involvement with the Mythos. In the course of researching the Slender Man phenomenon, I also decided to start an account on the Slender Nation forum. The users of this forum, as the name implies, are well versed in the Slender Man Mythos. I created a thread and asked a series of questions, to which a handful of forum users responded.[14] My main reason for entering into discussion with Slender Man "experts" was to test my ideas about the legendary characteristics of the Slender Man Mythos. In response to a post in which I asked if it was important that the Slender Man Mythos resemble "real" legends, user Voidmaster (2013) posted the following:

I'd never thought of that angle before, but now that you point it out, I would say that it is extremely important.

So much of our desire for knowledge and experience can be immediately placated by things like the internet these days, that it seems we've finally found the boarders [*sic*] of the map. That there are only a few remaining dark areas left on the map, all of which are so extremely esoteric and complicated that, to the common man, they might not as well be there at all.

Simply put, it feels to the layman as if we've learned all there is to know, and all the knowledge in the world is readily available to anyone without training or study via the internet.

And so without any apparent black spots on the map, we seek to draw our own.

Voidmaster went on to discuss the etiological function of traditional folklore, suggesting that Slender Man represents "the idea that, despite all these thousands of years of study and observation, we still have no idea what is going on with this universe. That we are still as woefully in the dark as our ancient counterparts were."

Voidmaster's response emphasized the experiential nature of the Slender Man Mythos. So did that of user sethlapod555 (2013), who wrote, "The Slender Man mythos is one of the only myths that let's [*sic*] you create your own narratives with the story. There are tons upon tons of options that haven't been explored because the myth is so open to innovation and construction that literally anything can be made from it."

I also asked forum members what they thought made Slender Man seem "real." awkwardraptor responded,

> I think it's mostly because, there are just so many pieces of "evidence" in the Mythos (The numerus vlogs/blogs, the woodcuttings, photos, etc.) that makes it seem that Slender Man actually exists, when of course, in real life, Slender Man does not exist. The people who created Slender Man, and the people who continue to add to the legend of The Slender Man, and even a good majority (In my opinion anyway.) of the people who watch the vlogs/read the vlogs, know that Slender Man, in reality at least, does not exist.
>
> But for the people who do not know that The Slender Man is just a creation of somebody's mind, and actually take the "evidence" as fact, that's what makes it real.
>
> In my opinion at least. (awkwardraptor 2013)

This response from awkwardraptor brings to mind Brennan's point about the slippery status of Slender Man's "reality."

When I asked about the video game, user timeobserver2013 (2013) told me that longtime Slender Man fans were unhappy with *Slender: The Eight Pages* (Hadley 2012), which was the predecessor to *Slender: The Arrival*, because it generated a great deal of interest in Slender Man, but the new fans who initially encountered Slender Man via the game were unaware of the complexity of the established Mythos (timeobserver2013 2013). Brennan summed up the importance of the original Mythos during our interview: "I don't know if the original writers had any, like, experience with the mythos prior to writing the game. But—I think, that is—I think—how do I phrase this nicely? [*JT laughs*] I think that the response to the first game caused them to bring on Marble Hornets. Because it was so well received, they wanted someone who was way more knowledgeable about the whole thing."

These responses, and the others I received in the Slender Nation thread, illustrate a number of important characteristics of the fans/creators of the Slender Man Mythos: they are heavily invested in the participatory/experiential dimension of the Mythos (by contributing to this dimension they are actively engaging in the reverse ostension process, ultimately facilitating the expansion of the legend); they possess, and pride themselves on, deep knowledge of the tradition itself; and they are protective of the Mythos as they feel it should be, even as they are open to interpretation and variation. This last point underscores Peck's argument that "each performance is, in and of itself, a statement about what makes for a good performance" (Peck 2015, 335). It also bears out—in a slightly different context—Jenkins's claim that "organized fandom is, perhaps first and foremost, an institution of theory and criticism, a semistructured space where competing interpretations and evaluations of common texts are proposed, debated, and negotiated and where readers speculate about the nature of the mass media and their own relationship to it" (Jenkins 2013, 86).

CONCLUSION

Trevor J. Blank (2009) has suggested that folklorists have tended to avoid Internet-based study due in part to the infamous and unfortunate concept of fakelore (4). Despite this, Blank argues, "The Internet's proclivity for pseudonymous interaction and the ease with which texts can be transmitted makes it the ideal location, instead of oral and journalistic venues, for the resurfacing of narrative texts" (8). Happily, the situation Blank describes is changing. Folklorists, in common with members of allied disciplines, are coming increasingly to recognize that the Internet does indeed provide a forum where processes very much like those attributed to more conventional folkloric media arise and flourish.

Nowhere is this more evident than in the Slender Man Mythos's tendency to invite discussion, interaction, and direct participation. As Andrew Peck (2015) has demonstrated, Slender Man constitutes a digital legend. Legends, in turn, offer opportunities to engage in "metatextual debate about whether such events are *possible*" (Koven 2008, 156). It is interesting that this metatextual function is not diminished even though the process I outline here is the reverse of "ordinary" ostension. In the case of the Slender Man, the metatextual function of the text is not to enable debate about the legend's veracity as experience or historical fact—never in question here, since Slender Man was self-consciously created as a fiction—but to put forward its plausibility *as a representative of the legend genre*. To put it more succinctly, belief in the literal content of the legend is, in most cases, nonexistent and unproblematic; the issue is making the legend *seem like* a legend.[15] This process, what I am calling reverse ostension, *must* be participatory because, as Peck and others have noted, the end result depends on the consensus of the community. The sign that is ultimately produced must live up to a set of shared expectations.

Reverse ostension, in the end, is simply another way to allow direct engagement with legends (or any other narrative genre). It could be argued that, following this model, any act of narration—that is, any conscious construction of a narrative—could constitute reverse ostension. I suggest, however, that this is not the case. Reverse ostension, first of all, is a self-conscious process. It relies on an awareness of the existence of a given semiotic system and a deliberate attempt to mimic or replicate that system, together with its attendant expectations of form, structure, and content. When we narrate the events of a given day in our own lives, linguistic and social norms and expectations of course exert an influence on the form of our narration; but typically, in casual conversation, we are not *consciously* attempting to model our narration on a prior one. Our speech may follow regional patterns or contain idioms unique to our immediate folk groups, and we may alter the types of speech we employ based on our audience and the social context in which they occur; and, of course, any such exchange takes place in the context of a mutually intelligible language; but these elements generally do not reflect an explicit attempt, in ordinary speech, to have our narratives be accepted as belonging to a particular class or genre. Reverse ostension is centrally concerned with this issue of communal acceptance, and operates on the shared understanding that the thing being constructed, the semiotic system being developed, has no experiential grounding: there is no connection to reality beyond the *resemblance* of the system to those already existing.

But then, we *could* label creative acts that construct sign systems based on existing models as reverse ostension. Filmmaking, fiction writing, and the like would clearly fall into this category. However, to do so would overlook the critical participatory nature of phenomena like Slender Man, which more conventional models of mass-mediated or popular culture tend not to exhibit (at the moment, at least). Slender Man became, as Peck demonstrates, an entire legend *cycle*, complete with variants detailing widely different individual "experiences" of the creature, precisely because of the efforts of numerous individuals to create a cohesive but flexible system of signs based on shared understandings of what such a system should look like.

If this insistence on the communal dimension of reverse ostension is reminiscent of early folklorists' insistence on folklore as collective, anonymous expression, it is deliberately so. Popular understandings of what folklore is and how it operates tend to reflect a less problematic, more straightforwardly functionalist orientation, akin to what Catherine Tosenberger has called the "traditionalist" perspective wherein folklore is viewed as something to be collected among conservative folk groups by educated outsiders (Tosenberger 2010, 2.4–2.10; see also Kirshenblatt-Gimblett 1998, 296). Slender Man in particular reflects the desires of its creators to maintain a sign system that is both recognizable (i.e., relatively coherent and stable) and flexible enough to accommodate individual variation. The reason for this is, again, to enable members of the online Slender Man community to engage with the phenomenon on their own terms—something that popular culture often does not do. An important exception to this, of course, is the area of fan culture, which engages in precisely the interactive, communal construction of sign systems that reverse ostension encompasses. Fan fiction, for example, might usefully be regarded as a form of reverse ostension, particularly in its relationship to and critique of the established "canon" within a given fandom.

Through the complex and ongoing process of reverse ostension, members of the various Internet communities who have staked a claim to the Slender Man Mythos have created a fearful symbol, a monster that, according to their own emic standards, is frightening in virtually any context. The appearance of figures like Slender Man is of interest not only because it demonstrates the communicative immediacy of the Internet, which by now is old hat, but also because it demonstrates that the Internet—and indeed, any popular communicative venue—can serve as a vehicle for critical metacommentary from unexpected corners, on unexpected topics. As fan culture emerges around a popular media text, entirely new "stand-alone" texts are created by individuals to respond to changing social trends and the immediacies of everyday life. But even such "new" texts may be carefully placed alongside established ones, wrapped up in the skins of familiar genres and imbued with an air of "traditionality," of continuity, of realness. The interest to scholars should be apparent, and is only increased when these metacommunicative practices are turned toward the areas we regard as part of our disciplinary jurisdictions. Slender Man not only reveals what his creators find frightening: he also demonstrates current trends in popular thinking about the nature of folklore, about how it can be used to achieve specific social ends in uniquely contemporary contexts, and about the kinds of representational strategies and communicative systems that give rise to monsters in the first place.

ACKNOWLEDGMENTS

The author gratefully acknowledges Amanda Brennan, whose help and patience were invaluable, and whose enthusiasm for Slender Man is contagious. Thanks also to the respondents to my thread on the Slender Nation forum. Blue Isle Studios, publisher of the *Slender: The Arrival* game, kindly allowed me to use material from its website and sent me a free copy of the game. Mitsuko Kawabata, Bryan Rupert, Dr. Diane Goldstein, and Dr. Michael Foster read early drafts of this essay and provided invaluable comments and suggestions. I am especially grateful to Andrew Peck of the University of Wisconsin–Madison for the use of a prepublication draft of his own excellent study of Slender Man (since published in the *Journal of American Folklore*). Lastly, thanks to Paul Manning, editor of *Semiotic Review*, for his help in shepherding the original version of this paper to publication and allowing me to reprint it here.

NOTES

This chapter is a revised and updated version of an article that originally appeared in *Semiotic Review*, no. 2: Monsters (Tolbert 2013). The author is grateful for permission to republish it in this form.

1. The relationship of texts in the Mythos parallels similar intertextual relations elsewhere. Otsuka Eiji, discussing a popular anime series, writes, "The greater the number of settings prepared, the greater the sense among audience members that the drama of each episode is real. The ideal is that each one of these individual settings will as a totality form a greater order, a united whole. This accumulation of settings into a single totality is what people in the animation field are accustomed to calling the 'worldview'" (Otsuka 2010, 107). Otsuka coins the term *narrative consumption* to describe the viewing practices of fans (109), a term whose usefulness breaks down in the face of fan practices of active viewing and fan fiction (the latter of which clearly relates to the practices of Slender Man's creators I discuss below). Otsuka himself recognizes this, and anticipates the field of fan studies when he notes that narrative consumption "also bears within it the possibility of a new stage wherein consumers themselves begin to create commodities and consume them on their own terms" (113). Discussing *Star Trek* fandom, Henry Jenkins would later argue that "fandom here becomes a participatory culture which transforms the experience of media consumption into the production of new texts, indeed of a new culture and a new community" (Jenkins 2013, 46).

2. Bill Ellis (1989) gives perhaps the most stirring example of the troubling potential for legend as a model for action, discussing such violent acts as cattle mutilations and human murders potentially patterned on legends of satanic killings. Other contributors to the present volume, including the present author, discuss an attempted murder in Wisconsin predicated on belief in Slender Man.

3. Not only the issue of belief but other aspects of this definition of legend have since been challenged—see especially Georges 1979.

4. In addition to drawing on existing legends, Slender Man has also generally been assimilated into the broader Internet tradition of "creepypasta." Creepypasta are "short

horror fictions and urban legends mainly distributed through word of mouth via online message boards or e-mail" (Frketson 2009). The larger creepypasta genre thus reflects a similar preoccupation with "looking like" legends.

5. The original images are no longer viewable on the Something Awful forums, but they may be viewed on the Know Your Meme Slender Man page, located at http://knowyour meme.com/memes/slender-man#origin. They are also reproduced in the introduction to this volume.

6. Other semiotically inflected folkloristic approaches might see the creation of Slender Man as reflecting, for example, the same process of "semantic staining" that impacted emerging views of putatively "traditional" Japanese monsters (Foster 2015) or, in a psychoanalytic mood, the creative use of folkloric symbols to project unconscious desires and anxieties (Dundes 1976). For a discussion of semiotics in a folkloristic context, see Bauman 1982; Chappell 1999.

7. This is not to say that all folklore is always consciously expressing something—indeed, as Alan Dundes has suggested, there is undoubtedly a great deal that folklore accomplishes unconsciously (1976, 1503). Rather, I mean to suggest that what Slender Man primarily *does*, as an example of reverse ostension, is consciously and overtly express the thoughts and ideas of the communities that created (and continue to create) him.

8. But, interestingly enough, the Wikipedia entry for "fakelore" ("Fakelore" 2016) includes Slender Man in its list of examples of this problematic concept.

9. H. P. Shivcraft's name, a reference to horror author H. P. Lovecraft, is interesting in that it indexes (deliberately or not) the world-building strategies of that author (see Evans 2005). Consider Evans's point about Lovecraft's use of folklore: "The use of folk narratives and beliefs in his stories served to give them an air of verisimilitude; in the same way, Lovecraft's use of material culture, especially architecture, gave his stories a grounding in the real world" (117). Thanks to Paul Manning for pointing out the implications of the Lovecraft connection.

10. Found footage is a cinematic style most often associated with the horror genre. It is usually presented as raw footage documenting the events experienced by the characters. One of the most well-known examples is the film *The Blair Witch Project* (Myrick and Sánchez 1999).

11. This number of YouTube views is a significant increase from that recorded prior to the original publication of this article in 2013, at which time it had 2,748,213 views. If nothing else, this indicates the enduring interest in Slender Man.

12. In the interest of full disclosure, it should be noted that the author was able to complete only the game's first and second levels. It is not only a surprisingly difficult game: it is also terrifying, further testimony to the facility with which its creators adapted the Slender Man Mythos.

13. For a discussion of Know Your Meme's significance in the context of folklore studies, see Kaplan 2013.

14. Space prohibits the inclusion of all responses here, but the thread is viewable in its entirety at this link: http://slendernation.forumotion.com/t3466-experiencing-the-legend-a -scholarly-study-of-slender-man.

15. But see Tolbert 2015, reprinted in this volume (chapter 4), on important exceptions.

WORKS CITED

awkwardraptor. 2013. "Experiencing the Legend: A Scholarly Study of Slender Man." Slender Nation Forum. http://slendernation.forumotion.com/t3466p15-experiencing -the-legend-a-scholarly-study-of-slender-man.

Bascom, William. 1984. "The Forms of Folklore: Prose Narratives." In *Sacred Narrative: Readings in the Theory of Myth*, ed. Alan Dundes, 5–29. Berkeley: University of California Press.

Bauman, Richard. 1982. "Conceptions of Folklore in the Development of Literary Semiotics." *Semiotica* 39 (1–2): 1–20. https://doi.org/10.1515/semi.1982.39.1-2.1.

Bird, S. Elizabeth. 2006. "Cultural Studies as Confluence: The Convergence of Folklore and Media Studies." In *Popular Culture Theory and Methodology: A Basic Introduction*, ed. Harold E. Hinds Jr., Marilyn F. Motz, and Angela M. S. Nelson, 344–355. Madison: University of Wisconsin Press.

Blank, Trevor J. 2009. "Introduction: Toward a Conceptual Framework for the Study of Folklore and the Internet." In *Folklore and the Internet: Vernacular Expression in a Digital World*, 1–20. Logan: Utah State University Press. https://doi.org/10.2307/j.ctt4cgrx5.4.

Chappell, Ben. 1999. "Folklore Semiotic: Charles Peirce and the Experience of Signs." *Folklore Forum* 30 (1–2): 73–93.

Chess, Shira. 2011. "Open-Sourcing Horror: The Slender Man, Marble Hornets, and Genre Negotiations." *Information Communication and Society* 15 (3): 374–393. https://doi.org/10.1080/1369118X.2011.642889.

Dégh, Linda, and Andrew Vázsonyi. 1983. "Does the Word 'Dog' Bite? Ostensive Action: A Means of Legend-Telling." *Journal of Folklore Research* 20 (1): 5–34.

DeLage, Joseph, Troy Wagner, and Tim Sutton. 2009a. *Introduction*. Marble Hornets. YouTube video series. https://www.youtube.com/watch?v=Wmhfn3mgWUI.

DeLage, Joseph, Troy Wagner, and Tim Sutton. 2009b. Marble Hornets. YouTube video series. https://www.youtube.com/user/MarbleHornets?feature=watch.

DeLage, Joseph, Troy Wagner, and Tim Sutton. 2009c. Totheark. YouTube video series. https://www.youtube.com/user/MarbleHornets?feature=watch.

Dove from Above. 2009. "Create Paranormal Images." Something Awful Forums. https://forums.somethingawful.com/showthread.php?threadid=3150591&userid=0&perpage=40&pagenumber=9.

Dundes, Alan. 1976. "Projection in Folklore: A Plea for Psychoanalytic Semiotics." *Modern Language Notes* 91 (6): 1500–1533.

Ellis, Bill. 1989. "Death by Folklore: Ostension, Contemporary Legend, and Murder." *Western Folklore* 48 (3): 201–220. https://doi.org/10.2307/1499739.

Evans, Timothy H. 2005. "A Last Defense against the Dark: Folklore, Horror, and the Uses of Tradition in the Works of H. P. Lovecraft." *Journal of Folklore Research* 42 (1): 99–135. https://doi.org/10.2979/JFR.2005.42.1.99.

"Fakelore." 2016. Wikipedia. https://en.wikipedia.org/w/index.php?title=Fakelore&oldid=743762747.

Foster, Michael Dylan. 2015. "Licking the Ceiling: Semantic Staining and Monstrous Diversity." *Semiotic Review*, no. 2 (June). https://www.semioticreview.com/ojs/index.php/sr/article/view/24.

Foster, Michael Dylan. 2016. "Introduction: The Challenge of the Folkloresque." In *The Folkloresque: Reframing Folklore in a Popular Culture World*, ed. Michael Dylan Foster and Jeffrey A. Tolbert, 3–33. Logan: Utah State University Press. https://doi.org/10.7330/9781607324188.c000.

Frketson. 2009. "Creepypasta." Know Your Meme, August 24. http://knowyourmeme.com/memes/creepypasta.

Georges, Robert A. (Original work published 1971) 1979. "The General Concept of a Legend: Some Assumptions to Be Reexamined and Reassessed." In *American Folk Legend: A Symposium*, ed. Wayland D. Hand, 1–20. UCLA Center for the Study of Comparative Folklore and Mythology—Publications: II. Berkeley: University of California Press.

Gerogerigegege. 2009. "Create Paranormal Images—The Something Awful Forums." *Something Awful*, April 30. https://forums.somethingawful.com/showthread.php ?threadid=3150591.

Hadley, Mark. 2012. *Slender: The Eight Pages.* PC. English. Parsec Productions. http://www .parsecproductions.net/slender/.

Hadley, Mark. 2013. *Slender: The Arrival.* PC. English. Blue Isle Studios. http://www.slender arrival.com/.

Jenkins, Henry. (Original work published 1992) 2013. *Textual Poachers: Television Fans and Participatory Culture.* 2nd ed. New York: Routledge.

Kaplan, Merrill. 2013. "Curation and Tradition on Web 2.0." In *Tradition in the Twenty-First Century: Locating the Role of the Past in the Present,* ed. Trevor J. Blank and Robert Glenn Howard. Logan: Utah State University Press. https://doi.org/10.7330/9780874218992.c05.

Kinsella, Michael. 2011. *Legend-Tripping Online: Supernatural Folklore and the Search for Ong's Hat.* Jackson: University Press of Mississippi. https://doi.org/10.14325/missis sippi/9781604739831.001.0001.

Kirshenblatt-Gimblett, Barbara. 1998. "Folklore's Crisis." *Journal of American Folklore* 111 (441): 281–327. https://doi.org/10.2307/541312.

"Know Your Meme: About." 2013. Know Your Meme, May 17. http://knowyourmeme .com/about.

Koven, Mikel J. 2008. *Film, Folklore, and Urban Legends.* Lanham, MD: Scarecrow.

Kyanka, Rich. 2016. "Something Awful: The Internet Makes You Stupid." http://www .somethingawful.com/.

Leperflesh. 2009. "Create Paranormal Images." Something Awful Forums. https://forums .somethingawful.com/showthread.php?threadid=3150591&userid=0&perpage=40 &pagenumber=14.

McDowell, John H. 1982. "Beyond Iconicity: Ostension in Kamsá Mythic Narrative." *Journal of the Folklore Institute* 19 (2–3): 119–139. https://doi.org/10.2307/3814009.

McNeil, W. K. 1985. *Ghost Stories from the American South.* Little Rock, AR: August House.

McNeill, Lynne S. 2009. "The End of the Internet: A Folk Response to the Provision of Infinite Choice." In *Folklore and the Internet: Vernacular Expression in a Digital World,* ed. Trevor J. Blank, 80–97. Logan: Utah State University Press. https://doi.org/10.2307 /j.ctt4cgrx5.7.

Moran, James, dir. 2015. *Always Watching: A Marble Hornets Story.* Horror.

Myrick, Daniel, and Eduardo Sánchez, dirs. 1999. *The Blair Witch Project.*

Otsuka, Eiji. 2010. "World and Variation: The Reproduction and Consumption of Narrative." Translated by Marc Steinberg. *Mechademia* 5:99–116.

Peck, Andrew. 2015. "Tall, Dark, and Loathsome: The Emergence of a Legend Cycle in the Digital Age." *Journal of American Folklore* 128 (509): 333–348. https://doi.org /10.5406/jamerfolk.128.509.0333.

rinski. 2009. "Create Paranormal Images." Something Awful Forums. https://forums. somethingawful.com/showthread.php?threadid=3150591&userid=0&perpage=40 &pagenumber=39.

sethlapod555. 2013. "Experiencing the Legend: A Scholarly Study of Slender Man." Slender Nation Forum. http://slendernation.forumotion.com/t3466p15-experiencing -the-legend-a-scholarly-study-of-slender-man.

Shivcraft, H. P. 2009. "Create Paranormal Images." Something Awful Forums. https://for ums.somethingawful.com/showthread.php?threadid=3150591&userid=0&perpage =40&pagenumber=25.

Soakie. 2009. "Create Paranormal Images." Something Awful Forums. https://forums. somethingawful.com/showthread.php?threadid=3150591&userid=0&perpage=40 &pagenumber=16.

Surge, Victor. 2009. "Create Paranormal Images." Something Awful Forums. https://for
    ums.somethingawful.com/showthread.php?threadid=3150591&userid=0&perpage
    =40&pagenumber=3.

TheRiffie. 2009. "Create Paranormal Images." Something Awful Forums. https://forums
    .somethingawful.com/showthread.php?threadid=3150591&userid=0&perpage=40
    &pagenumber=4.

timeobserver2013. 2013. "Experiencing the Legend: A Scholarly Study of Slender Man."
    Slender Nation Forum. http://slendernation.forumotion.com/t3466-experiencing
    -the-legend-a-scholarly-study-of-slender-man.

Tolbert, Jeffrey A. 2013. "'The Sort of Story That Has You Covering Your Mirrors': The
    Case of Slender Man." *Semiotic Review*, no. 2: Monsters (November). https://www
    .semioticreview.com/ojs/index.php/sr/article/view/19.

Tolbert, Jeffrey A. 2015. "'Dark and Wicked Things': Slender Man and the Implications of
    Belief." *Contemporary Legend Series 3* 5:38–61.

Tomberry. 2010. "Slender Man." Know Your Meme, January 3. http://knowyourmeme
    .com/memes/slender-man.

Tosenberger, Catherine. 2010. "'Kinda Like the Folklore of Its Day': 'Supernatural,' Fairy
    Tales, and Ostension." *Transformative Works and Cultures*, March. https://doi.org
    /10.3983/twc.2010.0174.

"Totheark." 2013. Marble Hornets Wikidot. March 27. http://marblehornets.wikidot.com
    /totheark.

Voidmaster. 2013. "Experiencing the Legend: A Scholarly Study of Slender Man." Slender
    Nation Forum. http://slendernation.forumotion.com/t3466-experiencing-the-leg
    end-a-scholarly-study-of-slender-man.

Chapter 2

The Cowl of Cthulhu
Ostensive Practice in the Digital Age

Andrew Peck

> *The more you know about him, the closer he gets.*
>
> —The Slender Man, *YouTube* user, January 18, 2013

O<small>N THE LAST DAY OF</small> M<small>AY</small> 2014, <small>TWO</small> twelve-year-old girls stabbed a friend and classmate nineteen times before leaving her to die alone in the woods near their southern Wisconsin home. Their victim crawled, half alive, until she reached the edge of the forest. Lying in a drainage ditch, bleeding badly and barely conscious, she was found by a passing cyclist and rushed to the nearest hospital. Of the nineteen stab wounds, two had penetrated major organs and one was less than a millimeter away from severing a major artery. Six hours in surgery were only the beginning of a long physical and emotional recovery, but on that day in May a young girl survived an encounter with two very real monsters lurking in the woods. Her assailants were quickly apprehended by local authorities. When questioned about their actions, it came to light that the girls committed the crime to win the favor of an entity known as the Slender Man, whom they had learned about online (Effron and Robinson 2014).

Of all the gruesome details of the Wisconsin stabbing, the involvement of Slender Man resonated most in subsequent news coverage. Although relatively unknown offline before the stabbing, Slender Man represents one of the most noteworthy and popular legend cycles to emerge from the digital age (Peck 2015; Tolbert 2013).[1] However, the relative obscurity of the character among the general public and its decontextualized association with the Wisconsin stabbing served to kindle a moral panic narrative. Headlines and sound bites focused on the dangers of unsupervised tween media use

DOI: 10.7330/9781607327813.c002

51

and the corrupting allure of the dark corners of the Internet. By the end
of the summer, national news outlets had linked nearly a half-dozen cases
of violence to Slender Man. In Florida, a teen "obsessed" with the Slender
Man set fire to her family's home (Mauney 2014). A man accused of killing
two police officers in Las Vegas reportedly "often dressed up in costume as
Slender Man," according to one of his neighbors (Murray 2014). After her
daughter donned a white mask and attacked her with a knife, a mother in
Ohio attributed the violence to the influence of Slender Man (Kemp 2014).

During an interview with *ABC News* in the days following the stabbing, I was asked about the Las Vegas case—if it was unusual that someone
would be photographed dressing up as the Slender Man. I explained to the
reporter that it was not unusual; it merely represented a type of behavior
that folklorists call *ostension*—enacting an aspect of a legend cycle in real
life. She proceeded to ask me, oddly hopeful, if attempted murders based
on urban legends were common. I explained they were not (see Lindahl
2005, 181n2). The actions of these young girls did indeed represent ostension, but only at its most unusual and extreme (see Ellis 1989). Hoping
to show the everyday nature of this type of ostension in the digital age,
I offered the reporter a few images from my archive that captured everyday people engaging in various forms of Slender Man ostension—ranging
from Halloween costumes to practical jokes. *ABC News* ran several pictures
from my archive under the headline "Slender Man Now Linked to 3 Violent
Acts" (Murray 2014).

This reporter's assumption that wearing a Slender Man costume was an
unusual, disturbed act resonated with me. It seemed so contrary to my own
experiences and observations that I began wondering how networked communication has affected how legends are performed in everyday life. The
answer, and the element the journalist missed, is that ostension in the digital
age isn't about action, it is about practice.

In this chapter I propose reframing ostensive action as ostensive practice. "Action" suggests an individual expression of volition, ephemeral
and shared on a personal scale; "practice" refers to the collection of many
actions and acknowledges the connectivity, aggregated volition, and self-
awareness enabled by the affordances of networked communication. Such
a move better accounts for how digital documentation and networked sharing raise widespread awareness of ostension in the digital age, and how
this awareness subsequently encourages new dynamics of collaboration,
critique, and reflection among users.

Using everyday performances of the Slender Man legend to illustrate this argument, I begin by suggesting that digital communication has

encouraged the documentation and sharing of everyday behaviors, like ostension, across networks. The result of this affordance is that ostension becomes both more mediated and more visible (Koven 1999, 2007, 2008; Kinsella 2011; Tolbert 2013). This increased visibility creates awareness that, in turn, encourages a sense of collaboration. As users collaborate on ostensive practices, they begin to develop hierarchies of performance that privilege certain types of interaction, creating an atmosphere that facilitates vernacular critique. These dynamics of collaboration and critique enable reflection, the emergence of a "metadiscourse" (Tolbert 2013). This meta-discourse offers a new opportunity for users to reflect not only on the nature of legends but also on the nature of the ostensive practices themselves.

OSTENSIVE PRACTICE IN THE DIGITAL AGE

As discussed in the introduction and first chapter of this volume, Slender Man originated in 2009 as a pair of photoshops and half a dozen lines of text posted to the SomethingAwful.com forums. Details were initially sparse, but as users told stories, shared images, and theorized as to the nature of the nascent Lovecraftian horror, they also participated in its creation. Each performance added to and subtracted from how the entity was imagined by the group. Users critiqued these performances, discussing what elements made them most effective. Successive performances built upon existing performances and discussions. Through social interaction, users collaborated in an ongoing process of performance, interpretation, and negotiation that constructed the details, motifs, and shared expectations of the Slender Man legend cycle (Peck 2015; see also Chess 2012; Tolbert 2013; Chess and Newsom 2015).

In addition to these many forms of online performance, the Slender Man legend cycle is also noteworthy for the many interrelated ways it is performed in offline contexts. The most common offline experiences inspired by this legend cycle include making and wearing Slender Man costumes, playing Slender Man pranks (such as wearing a costume while lurking in a public place or "photobombing"), creating Slender Man graffiti, or going on Slender Man legend trips (such as hunting the creature in a wooded area at night).[2] These playful behaviors represent various forms of Slender Man ostension, and their everyday prevalence stands in direct contrast to many of the moral panic narratives that circulated following the Wisconsin stabbing.

Linda Dégh and Andrew Vázsonyi introduced the term *ostension* into the academic study of folklore to describe real-life occurrences of events described in legends (Dégh and Vázsonyi 1983). Ostensive actions include both conscious choices and unconscious behaviors that emerge from and act out elements of a known legend cycle (Lindahl 2005, 164). These actions range from playful to macabre, with the former category being significantly more common (Ellis 1989, 202; 2001, 163; Lindahl 2005, 181n2). When legends inspire actions like donning a costume (Dégh 1995), traveling to a legend's location (Bird 1994), hunting for supernatural creatures and experiences (Ellis 1981; Kinsella 2011), pranking and hoaxing (pseudo-ostension), attributing natural phenomena to a known legend (quasi-ostension), creating personal experience narratives (proto-ostension; see Ellis 2001), poisoning Halloween candy (Grider 1984), xenophobic violence (Burger 2009), or murder (Ellis 1989), they are inspiring ostensive action. These types of actions, Dégh and Vázsonyi argue, constitute a mode of legend performance that offers an alternative to the field's traditional focus on legends as narrative. As Dégh and Vázsonyi suggest, ostensive actions both express and construct the legend cycles that inspire them.

The intervention I am suggesting here is for a reorientation in terms— shifting from ostensive action to ostensive practice. This move is significant, but it is not radical. In their foundational article, Dégh and Vázsonyi (1983, 27) note that an individual engaging in ostensive action may not identify it as such but "will know its practice." Bill Ellis, whose work greatly expanded upon Dégh and Vázsonyi's, expresses a similar view about the participatory nature of legends, suggesting, "It has therefore been argued that what we should be trying to define is not the style of legend *texts* but rather the style of legend *performance*. In other words, legends are not folk literature, but folk *behavior*" (Ellis 2001, 10). Both views clearly suggest practice is an inherent part of ostension, and I am not disputing this. So, it is not that digital communication turns ostensive action into practice; it is that digital communication *foregrounds* practice.

A shift from ostensive action to ostensive practice more accurately accounts for how ostension is extended by networked communication in the digital age. If action refers to expressions of individual volition, then practice refers to the genres of behavior that come into being as the result of many actions, while—at the same time—guiding and delimiting the potential for further action. What is key here is not simply an acknowledgment of the social nature of ostension (for it has always been social), but instead an acknowledgment of the ways in which digital communication has extended and altered these social dynamics while also enabling new ones. This change is less fundamental and more incremental. By rendering an existing process visible and spreadable, the affordances of digital communication extend and aggregate individual actions on a large scale, creating bodies of practice.

Digital media and networked communication are increasingly common-place in everyday life (see Baym 2010; Hand 2012), and the ability of these technologies to mediate folk practices has been well documented elsewhere (Blank 2009, 2012; Buccitelli 2012; Foote 2007; McNeill 2012). Ubiquitous pocket-sized digital media devices make it easy to document a legend trip or a prank, and networks enable widely sharing the captured media with the click of a button. "The proliferation of visual technologies has become a key aspect of digital culture," writes sociologist Martin Hand. "Digital imaging and photography have become thoroughly *ordinary* accompaniments to com-munication and connection practices in daily life" (Hand 2012, 11). Hand's observation of the mundanity of capturing and sharing everyday experiences on the Internet suggests that digital technologies may enable these practices, but social norms have embraced the affordances of these technologies in ways that make this type of behavior not only possible but *expected*.[3]

This trend toward the convergence of online/offline expression is especially prevalent in adolescents, the group most likely to engage in many ostensive practices.[4] For this age group, much of the identity work they do online feeds back into constructing their offline identities (boyd 2014). This growing imperative for documenting and sharing everyday life sug-gests that modern teenagers and young adults are more likely to record and upload their own ostensive actions. As an example of what such action may look like, let us imagine a legend trip based on the popular "Vanishing Hitchhiker" legend. Picture two friends walking down a stretch of road, in a place where the ghost of a young woman allegedly appears after dark asking for a ride home. One friend decides to play a trick on the other and runs off to hide in the woods, making eerie moans as her friend approaches to look for her. The searcher, initially cocky, gets trepidatious when the moan-ing intensifies and the prankster ignores repeated requests to cut it out. The searcher finally gives up, running back toward the road in fright. The entire exchange is captured by a digital camera on the prankster's phone. Now alone in the woods, the prankster takes a selfie, mockingly pretending to be the phantom from the legend.[5] The prankster posts the video and photo to various social media websites and tags her friend (as well as several mutual friends).[6] The friend, still on the road, receives a notification on her phone that she has been tagged by the missing friend and she, along with their shared social network, realizes she's been pranked and laughs with relief.

Although the scenario above may seem like a solitary, dyadic, or nar-cissistic act, it actually represents a very social ostensive practice. As Mikel J. Koven argues, any dramatized legend text may be construed as osten-sion, "particularly when we are *shown* the narrative through actions rather than having the story retold to us in narration" (Koven 2008, 139). Koven argues for the active role of the audience in mass-mediated ostension, suggesting, "Such a 'cinematic' ostension implicitly recognizes an audience by encouraging some form of post-presentation debate regarding the veracity of legends presented" (139). This debate is dual layered, encompassing the ostensive artifact itself (in Koven's discussion, a cinematic text) as well as the belief represented by that artifact. Mediated ostension is not just textual or a singular instance of expression, it also hails its audience to participate in (and extend) the ostensive experience. In the case of the "Vanishing Hitchhiker" example above, the not-present mutual friends are invited to participate in the ostensive experience via social media and tacitly encouraged to consider and discuss both the artifact and the belief it represents.

Koven's object of study is film, but it is not difficult to extend his ideas to the media-rich landscape of the Internet. As Jeffrey A. Tolbert shows in the preceding chapter, the popular Slender Man YouTube series Marble Hornets serves not only as an example of ostensive practice but also as a text for fan engagement and discussion on other websites. Here we see a concrete record of Koven's implied audience as users participate in a trans-media narrative as part of a larger ongoing alternate reality game centered around Marble Hornets and its related series totheark.[7] The difference from Koven's mass-mediated ostension is that these online ostensive practices both empower and encourage users to create their own interpretations. Unlike in mass media, the creator in vernacular digital interactions does not necessarily speak from a position of privileged authority (Peck 2015), and digital media facilitate the ongoing creation of more participatory expressions using a larger variety of media (Kinsella 2011, 15). The "Vanishing Hitchhiker" example is not just about sharing; it is about taking part in a *culture of sharing*—one that encourages ongoing reciprocal interactions, such as discussion, comment, critique, recirculation, one-upmanship, homage, and play, and is enabled by the affordances of networked communication.

This circulation across networks creates an awareness of ostension as a practice. Digital communication scholar Limor Shifman (2014) observes how such a shift is enabled by networked communication.[8] Using the example of "Kilroy was here" graffiti in the 1940s and 1950s, Shifman notes that seeing or tagging "Kilroy was here" was a fairly rare act, one passed by rumor more than observed in practice. A person was unlikely to see "Kilroy was here" more than a dozen or so times in a lifetime. By documenting and sharing ostensive actions across networks, users make these formerly ephemeral and interpersonal actions more visible across space and more persistent over time. This creates an informal, decentralized catalog of behavior where "it only takes a couple of mouse clicks to see hundreds of versions" (Shifman 2014, 30). The result of this visibility, Shifman argues, is an increase in awareness of the overall sum of these actions (29) and, subsequently, of ostension itself. The circulation and aggregation of ostensive actions across networks lead users to see these actions not as sporadic entities but as parts of a larger set of collective volition (Howard 2011, 19)—as a practice.

PERFORMING SLENDER MAN ONLINE AND OFF: COLLABORATION, CRITIQUE, AND REFLECTION

The greatest change in the shift from ostensive action to ostensive practice comes from the increased visibility brought by digital communication and, subsequently, increased user awareness of ostension as a practice. Having rationalized this reorientation toward a practice-driven framework, I now move to discuss the implications of adopting such a view. Using the case of Slender Man, in this section I demonstrate how this awareness forms the basis for new dynamics of collaboration and discussion that, ultimately, offer the space for "metadiscourse" and reflection on the culture and practices that created them.

When engaging with ostensive practices online, collaboration becomes a more active and varied role for users. Ostension has always been a social activity, passed informally between individuals and practiced in small groups by adolescents. Networked communication extends this dynamic in several notable ways. Most important, the scope of these interactions is no longer bound by geography (Howard and Blank 2013, 10). Legend trippers, cryptid enthusiasts, Slender Man costume makers, and many other individuals are better enabled to seek out others with similar interests and share their experiences (Howard 2011, 17–18). A group that forms around shared interest and experience inspires the creation of further experiences, hailing engagement from other users that further expresses both personal uniqueness and group connectivity (Shifman 2014, 30; Janeček 2014). This engagement emerges collaboratively and through a variety of media and expressions (including creating, viewing, sharing, remixing, and commenting) (Peck 2015) and serves as the basis for further ostensive practices.

Increased engagement (coupled with the rapid speed of digital communication) leads to an increase in potential variants. The sum total of these interactions is cataloged on a variety of web locations, allowing previously uninitiated users to quickly learn about the myriad of variations at play (Kaplan 2013).[9] The result, as Harvard law professor and digital communication scholar Yochai Benkler puts it, is that "the emergence of a new folk culture and of a wider practice of active personal engagement in the telling and retelling of basic cultural themes . . . makes culture more participatory, and renders it legible to all its inhabitants" (Benkler 2006, 299–300). In other words, the digital age facilitates a transition that turns ephemeral small-scale ostensive interactions into collaborative public practices and enables greater user awareness of generic conventions and variants of the practice with which they are engaging.

Certain web locations serve as hubs for these interactions, facilitating the sharing of ostensive practices and encouraging further interaction. Along with more niche websites dedicated to creepypasta, sections of popular websites like Reddit or YouTube are rife with individuals documenting, sharing, and commenting on examples of ostensive practice. As Tolbert notes in chapter 1 of this volume, user consumption of ostensive Slender Man digital media texts (like the video game *Slender: The Arrival* or the YouTube video series Marble Hornets) facilitates further vernacular discussion regarding the legend cycle.[10] Similarly, when users document and share their own ostensive practices online—such as Slender Man costumes, art, hoaxes, or pranks—they are not only demonstrating their own engagement but also hailing further collaboration from other users.

The popular video-sharing website YouTube, for example, plays host to hundreds of thousands of user-produced Slender Man videos. As this sheer volume suggests, a wide range of content is represented, ranging from authentic to playful.[11] A bevy of amateur films and videos purport to have captured the creature in action, sporting eye-catching titles like *[REAL] MAN GET KILLED BY SLENDERMAN 2015!!!*, *HIKER KILLED BY THE SLENDER MAN!!!!! MUST WATCH!!!*, and *Slender Man Caught On Tape (PLEASE HELP FIND THEM)* (McDanser 2015; JAusten Productions 2012; Shmu 2012). Some of these videos strive for authenticity by playing their subject completely straight while others reveal their fictional nature through metadata or by unexpectedly revealing themselves as parodies in their final moments.[12] Video documentation of legend trips and Slender Man hunts are common on the website, as are do-it-yourself costume-making guides, hidden camera pranks, and truth-uncovering hoax videos. Creators range in age from preteens to men and women who appear to be in their twenties.

A video titled *Scariest Real Slender Man Attack Caught on Tape Disturbing NSFW!* posted by user The Slender Man provides a typical example not only of this genre of video but also of the collaborative dynamics enabled by the affordances of the digital age. The video begins with a simple title card that serves as a warning; white text on a black background informs the viewer, "The more you know about him, the closer he gets." After five full seconds of silence, the video begins with a close-up of a woman's hands nervously crumpling and tearing a tissue. Her face is never seen, perpetually out of frame. The room is dimly lit, but a beam of natural light falls on her hands. Between sobs, she informs the viewer that her son died several months ago, and that it was only recently that she was able to overcome her depression and sort through his belongings. She made this video, she tells the viewer, because she needs help: "I took his phone out and . . . and, I was looking through his phone and I don't know what this thing is and . . . and, I don't know where to turn, and so I'm making this video so that maybe somebody will see the images and help me and let me know maybe what you think this is . . ."

The video then cuts to a photograph of a young man with curly hair and a teenage mustache. He's standing in a brightly lit yard. After a few moments, the image zooms in on a shadowy figure lurking near the rear of the yard. Several minutes of phone-shot footage follow, documenting Slender Man consistently lurking on the periphery of this young man's life over a period of months. The final entry is a video from the night of his death. The young man sits in the dark, addled and paranoid. He sees something that we do not. As he collapses and convulses, the video goes dark. Another title card appears, pleading with the viewer, "Please check your photos and videos for sightings of the slender man," followed by a final card, "This is a warning" (The Slender Man 2013).

The video demonstrates collaboration in two major ways. First, many of its elements are constructed to evidence a working knowledge of how ostensive practices surrounding Slender Man are represented. The video uses many stylistic choices present in the popular Marble Hornets videos (the series itself derives from the original Something Awful thread as well as popular found-footage films like *The Blair Witch Project* [Tolbert 2015]). These include things like using white-on-black title cards to provide context and to mask transitions and employing handheld, shaky camerawork that gives a sense of first-person presence to the footage (Koven 2015). As in many other Slender Man stories and videos, the character causes the individual he is stalking to be saddled with nightmares and paranoia.[13] The video's opening title card even references a popular memetic phrase associated with Slender Man, which can be traced all the way back to the original Something Awful thread in 2009 (Peck 2015, 14). Through choices like these—both stylistic and referential—users demonstrate an awareness of a visible constellation of prior ostensive artifacts. This awareness is the heart of the collaborative nature of ostensive practice; it frames how users engage in their own acts of ostension, how they document them, where they share them online, and how those shared artifacts feed back into the larger body of ostensive practice. As a result, through this demonstration of vernacular knowledge, this video is asserting what this user feels makes for a good ostensive document, one worthy of sharing on social media.

Second, in addition to positioning itself as part of a larger, ongoing practice, this video also encourages future collaboration from other users. It begins with a sincere call for help, a mother who is distraught over the loss of her son and wants answers. It also serves as a warning—promoting awareness of Slender Man while at the same time encouraging other users to check their own photos and videos for Slender Man. The implication here is that this user is encouraging others to engage in similar acts of ostension, documentation, and digital sharing. Paradoxically, this plea is positioned as trying to solve a mystery while in practice it actually perpetuates it. In other words, this communication emerges as part of a larger process that serves to dislocate the practice from any single individual who might have a singular answer and instead locate the answer in the digital crowd. Individuals are encouraged to share their own ostensive experiences but are also discouraged from asserting a singular definitive answer.[14] This reinforces the fundamentally collaborative nature of ostensive practice by keeping it firmly in the realm of legend dialectic (Ellis 2001).

The video proved quite popular, drawing in over 350,000 views and nearly 1,900 comments as of January 1, 2017. As is common for YouTube, the majority of user comments were simple sentiments of appreciation, fear, or ridicule (Hess 2009). Several users, however, responded to the video's call by sharing their own experiences and engaging in collaborative communication. For example, when user Shadow Flame commented, "Guys this is real!! I looked at my photos and I saw him! Please believe me!!!" several other users replied with skepticism, asking to see the photos. Shadow Flame then offered to show the photos if anyone wanted to chat on an app and proceeded to explain how she saw Slender Man after school on the playground. While some users called Shadow Flame out as a fake, many others began to engage with her, saying they believed her and offering possible solutions, such as a Bible or Ouija board. When other users began to share their own similar stories, Shadow Flame stopped posting. Roughly a month later, user That Handsome Dude commented on what seemed like an eerily appropriate conclusion to the discussion: "omg what happened to him? is this real or troll? im so worried about him cause after he said that i shall kill myself . . . Im very worried."

This comment thread—which was only about sixty posts long—demonstrates how a single ostensive artifact can hail other users to engage in their own acts of ostension. Shadow Flame took the invitation for collabo-ration provided by the video and used it to share her own story of ostensive action. She got other users to believe her story of being stalked by Slender Man, but more than that, she got others to engage in her story with her, interpolating them into her ongoing act of ostension by asking them for help and discussing possible solutions. This also hailed other users to share their own similar stories, just as the video had gotten Shadow Flame to share hers. In this set of interactions, we can see how the beginnings of col-laborative ostensive action might ripple into wider ostensive practice. Even though many of these communications were quite simplistic, these interac-tions still demonstrate the emergent collaborative possibilities enabled by the affordances of the digital age.[15]

These collaborative affordances go beyond the ability of users to post content and comments; several design choices built into the website itself also support seeing ostension less as an isolated act and more as a piece of a larger practice. For example, YouTube is invested in keeping users view-ing the site. This means that the more effectively it can suggest content a user might be interested in, the more likely it will retain eyeballs for more advertising revenue. As a result, the institution incentivizes exposing users to related content. When a video ends, a list of related videos is displayed. After a few seconds another related video plays automatically. A user's side-bar quickly fills up with recommendations based on their viewing history.[16] All of these small choices add up to a sort of hybrid human/algorithmic curation, wherein new users may find themselves exposed to the vast net-work of existing variants after only a few clicks (Kaplan 2013, 133–134). The result is that users are easily made aware of a wide sample of content available for any given topic and effortlessly enabled to see how all the indi-vidual components of that content relate to each other. In other words, the affordances built into the website create visibility, which, in turn, creates the awareness and hails collaboration.

So, we find the collaborative dynamics that underlie our transition from ostensive action to ostensive practice at every level of the process—arti-fact, discussion, website. These dynamics demonstrate the inherently par-ticipatory nature of ostensive practice in the digital age, with multiple users engaging to appreciate and perpetuate these practices, thereby displaying both their uniqueness and connectivity.

These collaborative expressions of uniqueness and connectivity enabled by networked communication continue to exert influence on ostensive practices, even in primarily offline contexts. To observe offline expressions of this digital practice, on November 1, 2014, I attended a massive public

Figure 2.1. Slender Man costumes on Halloween weekend 2014, Madison, Wisconsin. (Photos by Andrew Peck, Nicky Kurtzweil, and Emily Sauter.)

Halloween celebration in Madison, Wisconsin. Known as Freakfest, the event attracts tens of thousands of college-aged individuals into the State Street area of the city, encompassing half a dozen city blocks between the University of Wisconsin and the State Capitol. Since the Waukesha stabbings had occurred only a few months prior and only about sixty miles away from the city, I was surprised by how many Slender Man appearances I was able to record (see figure 2.1).

While walking near the Langdon Street neighborhood, I passed a young couple on their way to a party.[17] The man wore a black business suit with a red tie; white gloves hid his hands and a white mask obscured the features of his face (see figure 2.2). He was flattered when I stopped him to ask if he was Slender Man. In briefly talking to the couple it became apparent that he had donned the costume because the young woman he was with had shown him several examples of Slender Man legends, including Marble Hornets, *Slender: The Arrival*, and various costumes other users had shared. They were well versed in many of these specific variants. Putting together the costume was easy, they assured me, involving simply combining a mask and gloves with a suit and tie. The couple reveled in being recognized and photographed. They told me that few people had been able to identify the costume as Slender Man, but nonetheless the costume had been freaking out several pedestrians they had encountered, even those unfamiliar with the legend cycle. Although they were not actively documenting the occasion, they hoped the costume would be picked up in the background of photos and videos taken by others. As they left, the young man pulled out a folded scrap of paper, one of many, from the breast pocket of his suit. The couple suggested I was neither the first nor the last to receive such a gift that evening. This crumpled note serves as a memento of our encounter (see figure 2.2).

Figure 2.2. Meeting Slender Man on Langdon Street in Madison (*left*) and a memento from the encounter (*right*). (Photos by Emily Sauter.)

From our short interview, it became evident that this couple saw themselves as engaging with a larger networked practice beyond their immediate surroundings. Digital communication enables practices to emerge from users who are more keenly aware of their permutations. These variants are not just the realm of rumor or word of mouth; they can be directly seen and interacted with. As a result, new ostensive actions emerge in more direct conversation with the myriad variants that preceded them, as exemplified by the litany of Slender Man artifacts this couple acknowledged as their inspiration. This suggests that even a singular ostensive act in the digital age has many collaborative facets influenced by the existence of a large ostensive practice. This young couple, for instance, collaborated not only with each other and all the existing variants they had both viewed, but they also hailed others in their immediate vicinity to engage in the ostensive act—via lurking, jump scares, dropping notes, or even their very presence. They also hoped the ostensive act would be captured on film and recirculated by others, feeding back into the pool of digital variants that had influenced them. Hence, at every level of this process, this couple is co-creating an ostensive experience in dialogue with the constellation of existing online documents that inspired them. This suggests a blurred boundary between online and offline ostension—they are not discrete categories but exist in a continual, mutually constitutive feedback loop wherein one is always considering the other.

Because of this increase in user awareness and shift in collaborative potential, users are also better enabled to engage in the vernacular critique of ostensive practices. As a practice expands to encompass more individuals, those individuals begin to form competing notions about the practice. Although generic conventions may formalize fairly quickly, many users still hold different views as to the most effective way to perform an ostensive act. In contrast to the Halloween costume mentioned above, one of my respondents—Ethan, a male in his mid-twenties and a frequent viewer of Slender Man on Reddit, Imgur, and YouTube—had a different take on creating an effective Slender Man costume:

> ETHAN: I've seen plenty of Slender Man costumes online. The best one I ever saw, the guy wore sheet-rocking stilts so he was actually like ten feet tall. Then he did the blanked-out face, and held onto some poles with hands on the end, and I think he had the tendrils coming off of him as well. And he extended the arms and legs on a suit to cover everything.
>
> ANDREW PECK: That sounds pretty elaborate.
>
> E: Well, if you don't go all out, it's a pretty vague costume.
>
> AP: Just a person in a suit and mask?
>
> E: Pretty much. (Jensen 2014)

This exchange elucidates a tricky tension brought about by the visibility of ostensive practice in the digital age. On one hand, this visibility hails more individuals to view and participate in ostensive practices, but on the other, users can casually sort through so many variations that they begin to create hierarchies of performance. In Ethan's view—based on, as he admits, the many variants he's seen online—a Slender Man costume is something anyone can do because the barrier to entry is so low. Doing it well, then, requires more than mere reference, it requires showing commitment and knowledge of the fine details of the character.

> E: Depends on how well they are playing the part. If they are drinking and laughing and partying and stuff, then I would actually think it's kind of a lame costume. But if they are really into it, I'd probably feel compelled to talk to them, just to be sure.
>
> AP: How would one "play the part" well?

Figure 2.3. Instructions for a simple Slender Man costume posted on Reddit. (xXRofl-FalafelXx 2012.)

E: Keep quiet, stay to the back if you are with a group, while alone keep to the shadows. Watch others.

Many of the qualities that my respondents suggested made for a good Slender Man costume (being homemade, crafting an otherworldly appearance) and proper Slender Man behavior (lurking, sneaking into photos) were elements that made for a more convincing pseudo-ostensive experience. Although individuals differed in their exact preferences, everyone I spoke with had a clear opinion on the matter with no more than minimal hesitation. That motifs exist and that users have different expectations is unsurprising. What is new here is that this critical element emerges naturally in vernacular discourse in a variety of web locations.

Vernacular negotiation and critique are evident in the two very different discussions that emerged surrounding a pair of Slender Man costume threads posted on Reddit in the fall of 2012. The first, which was received poorly, began with an image instructing other users to create the "best halloween costume!" by combining a morph suit with a suit and tie (xXRofl-FalafelXx 2012; see figure 2.3). Amid collaborative suggestions by many users about how to engage in ostensive action while wearing such a costume, several users pushed back against the original post, suggesting this costume lacked effort and authenticity. User Bazofwaz, for example, balked at the terrible quality of the costume and suggested that the original poster should consider ways to add more authentic extras, like using stilts for long legs or adding tendrils made from cloth to "do it right." Many other users shared this sentiment, suggesting that the perceived ease of making a Slender Man costume (and the implied lack of effort) depreciated the character's value through overexposure and a lack of originality. As user Poseidon-SS noted, "If you go to a Halloween party with this, there will be at least five other people with the same costume," to which user Kinomi added, "And none of them will be able to drink. DEFINITELY a well thought out costume." This exchange underlines that the frustration shared by many users was about not only the perceived lack of originality, but also—echoing Ethan's comments—a lack of commitment to the character. As Kinomi's comment reveals, the idea of Slender Man having fun and drinking at a party lies in direct contrast to the expectations held for ostensive practice by many users—and such ostensive *in*action represents the waste of a costume and potential.

Another Slender Man costume discussion thread posted around the same time demonstrates how criticism may emerge differently if the engagement with ostensive practice is received positively (The_Bhuda_Palm 2012). In posting a thread to Reddit titled "I know you guys aren't digging Slender costumes, but I think my buddy was able to pull it off better than the rest," user The_Bhuda_Palm acknowledges the myriad of low-effort variants and rhetorically positions this thread as containing something different and worthwhile.[18] Unlike the "best halloween costume!" thread, this user's original post shares several pictures that document The_Bhuda_Palm's friend getting into an elaborate homemade Slender Man costume and wearing it while sulking around a dark suburb (see figure 2.4). The costume used stilts and wooden planks to provide the illusion of elongated, unnatural limbs. Many users expressed their appreciation for this play toward authenticity, with user Drewboy64 commenting that "the pants are a bit baggy, but finally, someone actually acknowledging the fact that the slenderman is supposed to be slender." Furthermore, the criticism in this post (regarding the baggy pant legs) provided a moment for collaboration, with many users offering suggestions to refine the costume to make it more authentic. According to no_egrets: "They have to fit around his feet. Would have worked a little better if he'd managed to engineer the stilts so his feet were more vertical (a bit like high heels), to allow for slimmer pants." Corbzor suggested, "Or engineer the stilts so the feet can look like knibby knees and

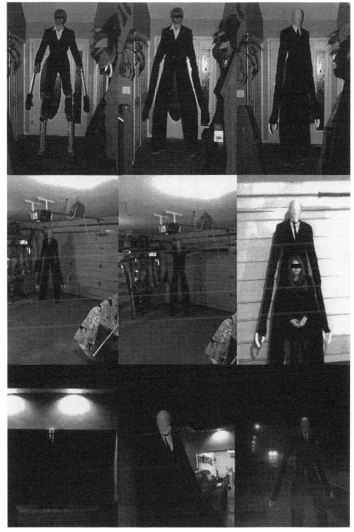

Figure 2.4. Donning and wearing a Slender Man costume. (The_Bhuda_
Palm 2012.)

have tighter pants the [*sic*] widen only at the knee and slim back down. Do
the same at the wrists for knobby elbows, I think that would be more creepy
if done right."

As shown by these comments (and many others like them in the thread),
even well-received instances of ostensive practice offer the space for vernacular critique. These critiques differ from those in the poorly regarded
"best halloween costume!" thread by offering constructive feedback to help

refine the costume. In such instances, a reciprocal relationship between collaboration and criticism emerges. In this positive example of ostensive practice, the vernacular dynamics of collaboration and critique enabled by the affordances of the digital age constitute two parts of a singular whole—here collaboration enables critique while critique facilitates collaboration.

The stakes for these exchanges are social clout, what many of my respondents called a type of Internet prestige or nerd credibility, further underlining the shared nature of ostension in the digital age. As Rob, a twenty-seven-year-old male, put it: "I think 'Internet prestige' is a good word for it. You know, it's something that you could, if you're looking for karma or points or whatever your current forum uses for currency, it would be a safe bet to create content based on the Slender Man if you were, you know, really good at it. And put something out there if it was kinda creepy and people would eat it up" (Finlayson 2014).

When pressed on why this might be the case, Rob suggested that the often insular nature of web communities that engage in these ostensive practices exerted great force on the potential for engagement. Like an inside joke, Slender Man ostension relies on the paradox of simultaneously being known while also being niche. If it strides too far toward either direction, it loses appeal to users, becoming too overdone or too obscure. The dynamics of collaboration and critique enabled by the digital age work to both propagate and police widespread engagement. Hence, by engaging in acts of collaboration and critique in the pursuit of asserting "nerd cred," these users are also self-regulating their own ostensive practices.

Finally, this increased awareness of ostensive practices in the digital age, along with the collaboration and critique such awareness hails, suggests the potential for both self-awareness and reflexivity, constituting—as Tolbert argues in the preceding chapter—a "metadiscourse." If legend metadiscourses provide space for users to engage with each other about the nature and significance of legends, then ostensive metadiscourse enables reflection on the nature and significance of ostensive practice. When users discuss the best way to commit a Slender Man photobomb, for example, they are not only discussing the specific instance they are presented with but also the greater practice that moment represents. Observation of the metadiscourse surrounding Slender Man ostension, then, suggests a practice that emphasizes not only horror but also play.

During our conversation, Rob directed me toward one of his favorite Slender Man videos. The video begins in an empty kitchen/entryway of a small apartment. Disquieting, modulating noise plays in the background (video and audio distortions are common signifiers of Slender Man's presence). A young Australian couple enters and the boyfriend gestures his girlfriend toward another room. The video then cuts to footage of a computer desktop ready to load the *Slender: The Eight Pages* video game. A small inset video on the top left of the screen shows the girlfriend taking her seat in front of the computer while her boyfriend introduces the game.[19] A few minutes of game play footage pass before the girlfriend succumbs to the digital Slender Man. Understandably freaked out by the jump scare at the end of the game, the girlfriend declines to continue playing.

The girlfriend opens the door to leave the room and shrieks—there's something out there. Her boyfriend goes to check, but insists there's nothing in the next room. She is inconsolable. Her boyfriend offers to go and check again, and she begs him not to. He opens the door—still nothing there. He tries to convince her that everything is all right and that she should leave the room. When she moves closer to the door, she sees it again—the Slender Man lurking silently and ominously just past the doorway (ChampChong 2012).

This video sounds a lot like the ones described previously (a man in a costume lurking just out of perception, paranoia, black title cards to orient the viewer), but with one important difference: it is framed as play—a prank. The video doesn't try to hide this from the viewer; the creator's intentions are revealed in its title, "EPIC SLENDER MAN PRANK!!!" Furthermore, at several points the camera cuts from the computer room to the kitchen to show the viewer where Slender Man is hiding and lurking. The video even ends with a dancing Slender Man promoting the channel. So, while the girlfriend is unwillingly given an authentic ostensive experience, the viewer occupies a liminal space between jump scares and japes.

Rob was not alone in liking this video. To date, it has over 7 million views and nearly 10,000 comments on YouTube, making it one of the most watched videos in my archive. It is also far from the only prank video I cataloged: many Slender Man costume and Halloween videos are also framed as pranks. This heavy focus on play might initially seem conceptually tricky to reconcile, but as Koven writes, just because Slender Man frequently uses the trappings of horror movies "we should not be so complacent to assume the intent is to frighten" (Koven 2015, 110; see also Koven's chapter 5 in this volume). I disagree, however, with Koven's assertion that these expressions then represent anti-legends. Instead, it might be more accurate to say, as Elizabeth Tucker does in chapter 7 of this volume, that there is a fine line between play and danger, and ostensive practice frequently evokes both.

And it is this capacity for finding authenticity in a mix of play and horror that the metadiscourse surrounding these ostensive practices illuminates. Individuals engaging in Slender Man ostension—the mother who lost her son, the young couple on the streets of Madison, the costume makers on Reddit, or the prankster couple on YouTube—seek to create an authentic ostensive experience for someone—it just might not be the person currently viewing it. When viewed in other contexts (interviews, costume-planning stages, post-prank videos), these same ostensive actions come off as playful. These backstage behaviors are mediated in the same ways as more traditional acts of ostension, feeding back into the catalog of ostensive practice. The result is that authenticity comes from seeming real while also understanding that Slender Man ostension is an inherently playful act.

THE SIGNIFICANCE OF OSTENSIVE PRACTICE

In this chapter I have advocated for a reorientation toward ostensive practice in order to supplement how we understand the connectedness of ostensive actions in the digital age. By using digital media to document and share ostensive actions on a networked scale, users become more aware of the practice of ostension itself. Although it is unlikely that every case is as robust as that of Slender Man, the dynamics of collaboration, critique, and reflection that undergird ostensive practices are likely to resonate in a broad variety of cases.

And it is this final capacity—social reflection on the nature of ostension itself—that becomes especially evident when the generic expectations for ostensive practice are violated. Although several such examples are discussed in the preceding section, nowhere was this capacity for reaction and reflection more evident than in the discussions sparked by the Wisconsin stabbing. Following news of the stabbing, users on a variety of websites expressed disbelief that Slender Man could be taken seriously and were quick to distance their ostensive practices from this gruesome ostension action. The most common route involved assuming these young girls were mentally ill and using Slender Man as a scapegoat. Reddit user Spycrab_Killer provides a typical example of this sentiment: "They probably have autism or retardation. NOBODY can fucking believe something on the internet so badly to attempt to kill somebody" (Kashito91 2014). In this comment (and many others) ostensive practice is deemed too patently ridiculous to be believable. Other users, such as KennyThePyro, expressed regret and wondered if the play had become too real, "I sincerely hope the kid doesn't die. I almost want to add a disclaimer now that slenderman isn't real" (Kashito91 2014). The use of "almost" in this post expresses the central tension that many of these users are reflecting on—play versus authenticity. Despite generic expectations for authenticity and engrossment in the performance of ostensive acts, the Wisconsin stabbing provided an occasion for digital communities to consider what was most fundamental to this practice and what consequences it might have.

The result of this reflection was a wide-scale reassertion of the fundamentally playful nature of these pseudo-ostensive practices. This sentiment stood in direct contrast to journalistic accounts that portrayed the creature as a refuge for the disturbed and isolated. This coverage, by and large, lacked context and reflection, and as a result was unable to adequately separate play from malice. In effect, by overlooking the wider context of ostensive practice in favor of focusing on extreme and isolated ostensive actions, coverage of the stabbings mistakenly conflated playful practice—such as wearing a Slender Man costume—with grim action. By failing to account for the dynamics of ostensive practice—collaboration, critique, and reflection— enabled by the affordances of digital media and networked communication, scholars of ostension in the digital age risk making a similar mistake.

NOTES

For this project, I conducted recorded interviews with six individuals who identified as fans of Slender Man over the course of three months following the Wisconsin stabbing. In the course of these interviews many of these self-professed fans discussed the web locations they associated with Slender Man and the places where they had seen examples of people wearing Slender Man costumes. Reddit pages were frequently mentioned, as were prank videos posted on YouTube.

Many interview subjects mentioned the Slender Man subreddit, which I observed from June to November 2014, cataloging any thread that involved a Slender Man costume. I then searched the subreddit for examples of Slender Man costumes dating back to 2011. By December 2014 I had documented thirty-five discussion threads involving Slender Man costumes.

Noting a spike in Slender Man costume threads around Halloween, I set out to capture as many Slender Man costumes as possible during the yearly Halloween celebration near the University of Wisconsin–Madison. To that end, I photographed and briefly interviewed five different individuals wearing Slender Man costumes on the evening of November 1, 2014.

Finally, I searched YouTube for user-created videos involving Slender Man, which many of these costumed individuals acknowledged as inspiration. Since search results for Slender Man directed mostly to news stories about the stabbing, it became necessary to add additional terms to refine the search toward vernacular videos. I chose additional search terms based on three factors: (1) common tropes mentioned by my interview subjects, (2) words commonly associated with the legend cycle or used in other videos (for instance, *Halloween* results frequently also contained the word *prank*), and (3) Google auto-complete search recommendations. The resulting searches included: Slender Man caught on tape; Slender Man costume; Slender Man Halloween; Slender Man house; Slender Man hunting; Slender Man parody; Slender Man prank; Slender Man real; Slender Man woods. For each search, I viewed and cataloged all videos on the first two pages of search results (forty videos). I then performed a second search, spelling Slender Man as a single word (a common variant). This change usually resulted in a fairly similar first page and a fairly different second page of search results. New videos resulting from this second search were also added to my archive. In total, I was able to catalog 471 different videos and tens of thousands of comments posted as early as 2009 and as recently as 2016.

1. By the spring of 2014 Slender Man could be found in a variety of digital spaces, including blogs, vlogs, drawings, forums, wikis, stories, photoshops, and augmented reality games. The character was so popular that it had started appearing in a variety of other media. Special monsters in the indie video game *Minecraft* were designed as Slender Man homages. A 2014 episode of the television show *Supernatural* saw the main characters on the trail of a malevolent photo-lurking entity known as the Thin Man. Marble Hornets, a Slender Man web series, has over 55 million views on YouTube, and a Marble Hornets movie entered production in the spring of 2013.

2. *Photobombing* is a colloquial term describing the act of intentionally sneaking into the background of someone else's photograph without their awareness in an effort to disrupt the picture's integrity. In this instance, such an act mimics the "lurking in the background" trope frequently used in visual expressions of the Slender Man legend.

3. Technologies do not dictate how they are used, but they encourage certain uses over others (Winner 1986). A hammer, for example, is better at pounding a nail than cleaning a sink. The Internet is well suited for fast communication unbound by geographical limitations as well as multimediated communication and fluid, selective group interaction. These packages of potentials and constraints constitute what Nancy Baym has called "technological affordances" (Baym 2010, 17). The relationship between technology and society is a reciprocal one (Baym 2010; McNeill 2012). But as a technology becomes a natural part of daily life, certain norms of behavior begin to form around its usage based on these affordances. This is not to suggest that everyone will use a technology in exactly the same way, but it does reflect a social pressure that can help us understand the emergence of expectations that undergird a practice.

4. For adolescent media use, see Baym 2010; boyd 2014. For adolescents and ostension, see Bird 1994; Ellis 1989, 2001; Blank and Puglia 2014.

5. "Selfie" refers to a self-portrait, often taken using a phone's digital camera held at arm's length and at a high angle.

6. "Tags" are a type of metadata commonly used on social media and social networking websites. This information helps sort or identify content and frequently includes names, hashtags, locations, and other relevant topics.

7. There is, of course, still an implied audience in this scenario, as a large percentage of viewers don't actively engage with other users. These users are still, however, engaging with mediated ostension.

8. Shifman's study is about Internet memes, which she acknowledges constitute a type of folklore (Shifman 2014, 15). Several prominent digital folklorists have espoused a similar view, suggesting, "In computer-mediated contexts, the folkloric process of repetition and variation is often identified by emergent patterns of widely disseminated, visually oriented vernacular expression; these constructs are emically referred to as *memes*" (Blank 2012, 8) or "The emergence of traditional expressive forms on the Internet, and the observation and re-creation of them by other people in new contexts, has not gone unnoticed by the Internet community itself, which has adopted the concept of *memes* to identify what folklorists would call folklore" (McNeill 2009, 84). Although the term is still somewhat contentious (see Ellis 2001, 76–80), viewing the practices themselves as digital folklore is more accepted (see also Blank 2015; Foote 2007; Kaplan 2013; McNeill 2012). Indeed, even the Slender Man legend cycle is considered to be a meme under the "creepypasta" genre (Tolbert 2013, 2).

9. For instance, a user making a Slender Man costume may post a video of herself wearing the costume to YouTube, link that video on a creepypasta discussion board, and post a picture of herself in costume to the r/creepy subreddit.

10. Marble Hornets also functions as an "alternate reality game" (ARG), inviting user participation and speculation surrounding the events presented in this found-footage-style web video series.

11. Locating authenticity in contemporary legend performances is often tricky. This issue is exacerbated in the case of Slender Man, as it involves users constructing authenticity around something with a demonstrably fictitious origin point (see Peck 2015 for a more in-depth discussion of the communicative dynamics of this early negotiation). My use of "authentic" here is meant to refer to the performative elements that give the legend cycle a sense of plausibility. These elements might help the audience suspend disbelief or facilitate a blurring of boundaries between the real and the supernatural. As I elaborate in the paragraphs that follow, although my use of *authentic* in this paragraph is juxtaposed with *play*, the reality of ostensive practice is that play and authenticity are often closely linked phenomena.

12. For instance, when a user uploads a video under a name like "JAusten Productions" (2012) or includes "This video is FICTIONAL" in the description (Sam Thrower 2012), that user is acknowledging the fictional nature of the project in a way that allows the video to appear initially authentic until scrutiny is applied. Although this tactic may seem strange, one uploader comment suggests that it is meant to help stem the very common viewer comment that the video looks or seems fake (Sam Thrower 2012).

13. For more details regarding this phenomenon (commonly called "Slender sickness"), see chapters 3 and 4 of this volume.

14. To give a more traditional example, imagine two campers reacting to a scary campfire story. The first gasps in awe, saying, "Whoa, something similar happened to me!" before launching into his own story. The second sneers, rolls his eyes, and says, "That guy probably just killed himself." The second camper, while likely more accurate, violates generic expectations for engrossment and suspension of disbelief, upsetting the collaborative storytelling event. In other words, he's probably getting pushed in the lake tomorrow.

15. It is very likely based on the information these commenters provided that many of them were either in elementary school or middle school. Additionally, a few did not seem to be native English speakers. Based on my research, it seems that preteen and adolescent fans of Slender Man are quite common in digital spaces.

16. In this chapter I intentionally use they/their/them as a gender neutral singular third-person pronoun for individuals whose gender is not specified.

17. Langdon Street is located one block north of State Street (the central venue for Halloween festivities near the University of Wisconsin) and home to most Greek life on campus.

18. Commercial Slender Man costumes were widely available in 2014 (Mejia 2014). I did not find any instances of them in either online or offline observations, but the large amount of costume submissions to this subreddit suggests the separation from commercial costuming is an important rhetorical move.

19. This video-in-video aesthetic is extremely common for individuals who play video games online for audiences, and this video is mimicking the style of the popular Let's Play video genre. Both *Slender: The Eight Pages* and *Slender: The Arrival* have numerous reaction videos and Let's Plays posted to YouTube by a wide variety of users.

WORKS CITED

Baym, Nancy K. 2010. *Personal Connections in the Digital Age.* Cambridge, MA: Polity.

Benkler, Yochai. 2006. *The Wealth of Networks: How Social Production Transforms Markets and Freedom.* New Haven: Yale University Press.

Bird, S. Elizabeth. 1994. "Playing with Fear: Interpreting the Adolescent Legend Trip." *Western Folklore* 53 (3): 191–209. https://doi.org/10.2307/1499808.

Blank, Trevor J., ed. 2009. *Folklore and the Internet: Vernacular Expression in a Digital World.* Logan: Utah State University Press. https://doi.org/10.2307/j.ctt4cgrx5.

Blank, Trevor J. 2012. "Pattern in the Virtual Folk Culture of Computer-Mediated Communication." In *Folk Culture in the Digital Age: The Emergent Dynamics of Human Interaction,* ed. Trevor J. Blank, 1–24. Logan: Utah State University Press. https://doi.org /10.7330/9780874218909.c00.

Blank, Trevor J. 2015. "Faux Your Entertainment: Amazon.com Product Reviews as a Locus of Digital Performance." *Journal of American Folklore* 128 (509): 286–297. https://doi.org/10.5406/jamerfolk.128.509.0286.

Blank, Trevor J., and David Puglia. 2014. *Maryland Legends: Folklore from the Old Line State.* Charleston, SC: History Press.

boyd, danah. 2014. *It's Complicated: The Social Lives of Networked Teens.* New Haven: Yale University Press.

Buccitelli, Anthony Bak. 2012. "Performance 2.0: Observations toward a Theory of the Digital Performance of Folklore." In *Folk Culture in the Digital Age: The Emergent Dynamics of Human Interaction,* ed. Trevor J. Blank, 60–84. Logan: Utah State University Press. https://doi.org/10.7330/9780874218909.c03.

Burger, Peter. 2009. "The Smiley Gang Panic: Ethnic Legends about Gang Rape in the Netherlands in the Wake of 9/11." *Western Folklore* 68 (2–3): 275–295.

ChampChong. 2012. *EPIC SLENDER MAN PRANK!!!* YouTube. https://www.youtube.com /watch?v=JthULY_xS1Y.

Chess, Shira. 2012. "Open-Sourcing Horror: The Slender Man, *Marble Hornets,* and Genre Negotiations." *Information Communication and Society* 15 (3): 374–393. https://doi.org /10.1080/1369118X.2011.642889.

Chess, Shira, and Eric Newsom. 2015. *Folklore, Horror Stories, and the Slender Man: The Development of an Internet Mythology.* New York: Palgrave Pivot. https://doi.org/10.1057 /9781137491138.

Dégh, Linda. 1995. *Narratives in Society: A Performer-Centered Study of Narration.* FF Communications, no. 255. Helsinki, Finland; Bloomington, IN: Suomalainen Tiedeakatemia, Academia Scientiarum Fennica; Distributed in North America by Indiana University Press.

Dégh, Linda, and Andrew Vázsonyi. 1983. "Does the Word 'Dog' Bite? Ostensive Action: A Means of Legend Telling." *Journal of Folklore Research* 20 (1): 5–34.

Effron, Lauren, and Kelley Robinson. 2014. "Slender Man Stabbing Survivor's Parents: 'She's Meant to Do Something Special.'" *ABC News,* September 26. http://abcnews .go.com/US/slender-man-stabbing-survivors-parents-describe-horrific-ordeal/story ?id=25787516.

Ellis, Bill. 1981. "The Camp Mock-Ordeal *Theater as Life.*" *Journal of American Folklore* 94 (374): 486–505. https://doi.org/10.2307/540502.

Ellis, Bill. 1989. "Death by Folklore: Ostension, Contemporary Legend, and Murder." *Western Folklore* 48 (3): 201–220. https://doi.org/10.2307/1499739.

Ellis, Bill. 2001. *Aliens, Ghosts, and Cults: Legends We Live.* Jackson: University Press of Mississippi.

Finlayson, Rob. 2014. Personal interview. Skype. Interview in possession of author.

Foote, Monica. 2007. "Userpicks: Cyber Folk Art in the Early 21st Century." *Folklore Forum* 37 (1): 27–38. https://scholarworks.iu.edu/dspace/handle/2022/3251.

Grider, Sylvia. 1984. "The Razor Blades in the Apples Syndrome." In *Perspectives on Contemporary Legend: Proceedings of the Conference of Contemporary Legend*, ed. Paul Smith, 128–140. Sheffield, UK: CECTAL.

Hand, Martin. 2012. *Ubiquitous Photography*. Cambridge: Polity.

Hess, Aaron. 2009. "Resistance Up in Smoke: Analyzing the Limitations of Deliberation on YouTube." *Critical Studies in Media Communication* 26 (5): 411–434. https://doi.org/10.1080/15295030903325347.

Howard, Robert Glenn. 2011. *Digital Jesus: The Making of a New Christian Fundamentalist Community on the Internet*. The New and Alternative Religions Series. New York: New York University Press. https://doi.org/10.18574/nyu/9780814773086.001.0001.

Howard, Robert Glenn, and Trevor J. Blank. 2013. "Living Traditions in a Modern World." In *Tradition in the Twenty-First Century: Locating the Role of the Past in the Present*, ed. Trevor J. Blank and Robert Glenn Howard, 1–21. Logan: Utah State University Press.

Janeček, Petr. 2014. "Bloody Mary or Krvavá Máři? Globalization and Czech Children's Folklore." *Slovak Ethnology* 62 (2): 221–243.

JAusten Productions. 2012. HIKER KILLED BY THE SLENDER MAN*!!!!!* MUST WATCH*!!!* YouTube. https://www.youtube.com/watch?v=DHp_XteuLEM.

Jensen, Ethan. 2014. Personal interview. Digital correspondence. Interview in possession of author.

Kaplan, Merrill. 2013. "Curation and Tradition on Web 2.0." In *Tradition in the Twenty-First Century: Locating the Role of the Past in the Present*, ed. Trevor J. Blank and Robert Glenn Howard, 123–148. Logan: Utah State University Press. https://doi.org/10.7330/9780874218992.c05.

Kashito91. 2014. "12 Y.o. Girl Murders Friend to Become a Proxy of Slenderman . . . WHAT THE FUCK?!" Reddit. https://www.reddit.com/r/Slender_Man/comments/275t80/12_yo_girl_murders_friend_to_become_a_proxy_of/.

Kemp, Joe. 2014. "Ohio Mom Claims Daughter, 13, Who Attacked Her with Knife Was Obsessed with Slenderman." *Daily News*, June 9. http://www.nydailynews.com/news/national/ohio-mom-claims-daughter-13-attacked-knife-obsessed-slenderman-article-1.1822645.

Kinsella, Michael. 2011. *Legend-Tripping Online: Supernatural Folklore and the Search for Ong's Hat*. Jackson: University Press of Mississippi. https://doi.org/10.14325/mississippi/9781604739831.001.0001.

Koven, Mikel J. 1999. "*Candyman* Can: Film and Ostension." *Contemporary Legend*, n.s., 2: 155–173.

Koven, Mikel J. 2007. "*Most Haunted* and the Convergence of Traditional Belief and Popular Television." *Folklore* 118 (2): 183–202. https://doi.org/10.1080/00155870701337403.

Koven, Mikel J. 2008. *Film, Folklore, and Urban Legends*. Lanham, MD: Scarecrow.

Koven, Mikel J. 2015. "Slender Man: A Dissenting View." *Contemporary Legend* 3 (5): 105–111.

Lindahl, Carl. 2005. "Ostensive Healing: Pilgrimage to the San Antonio Ghost Tracks." *Journal of American Folklore* 118 (468): 164–185. https://doi.org/10.1353/jaf.2005.0023.

Mauney, Matt. 2014. "Florida Teen Obsessed with 'Slender Man' Sets Fire to Home as Family Sleeps." *Orlando Sentinel*, September 5. http://www.orlandosentinel.com/features/gone-viral/os-slender-man-florida-teen-arson-post.html.

McDanser. 2015. *[REAL] MAN GET KILLED BY SLENDERMAN 2015!!!* YouTube. https://www.youtube.com/watch?v=O0Sxb3aefp4.

McNeill, Lynne S. 2009. "The End of the Internet: A Folk Response to the Provision of Infinite Choice." In *Folklore and the Internet: Vernacular Expression in a Digital World*, ed. Trevor J. Blank, 80–97. Logan: Utah State University Press. https://doi.org/10.2307/j.ctt4cgrx5.7.

McNeill, Lynne S. 2012. "Real Virtuality: Enhancing Locality by Enacting the Small World Theory." In *Folk Culture in the Digital Age: The Emergent Dynamics of Human Interaction*, ed. Trevor J. Blank, 85–97. Logan: Utah State University Press. https://doi.org/10.7330/9780874218909.c04.

Mejia, Paula. 2014. "Slender Man Halloween Costume Horrifies Wisconsin Town Where Attack Occured, Pulled from Shelves." *Newsweek*, September 20. http://www.newsweek.com/slender-man-halloween-costume-horrifies-wisconsin-town-where-attack-occurred-271992.

Murray, Rheana. 2014. "Slender Man Now Linked to 3 Violent Acts." *ABC News*, June 9. http://abcnews.go.com/US/slender-man-now-linked-violent-acts/story?id=24058562.

Peck, Andrew. 2015. "Tall, Dark, and Loathsome: The Emergence of a Legend Cycle in the Digital Age." *Journal of American Folklore* 128 (509): 333–348. https://doi.org/10.5406/jamerfolk.128.509.0333.

Sam Thrower. 2012. FRIGHTENING *Slender Man Sighting* (MOVIE) *Hunting in the Woods*. YouTube. https://www.youtube.com/watch?v=ubT510yo7NU.

Shifman, Limor. 2014. *Memes in Digital Culture*. MIT Press Essential Knowledge. Cambridge, MA: MIT Press.

Shmu. 2012. *Slender Man Caught on Tape* (PLEASE HELP FIND THEM). YouTube. https://www.youtube.com/watch?v=jC4DyohGkso.

The_Bhuda_Palm. 2012. "I Know You Guys Aren't Digging Slender Costumes, but I Think My Buddy Was Able to Pull It off Better Than the Rest." Reddit. https://www.reddit.com/r/pics/comments/12g39q/i_know_you_guys_arent_digging_slender_costumes/.

The Slender Man. 2013. *Scariest Real Slender Man Attack Caught on Tape Disturbing NSFW*! YouTube. https://www.youtube.com/watch?v=nYH7bmFgCkY.

Tolbert, Jeffrey A. 2013. "'The Sort of Story That Has You Covering Your Mirrors': The Case of Slender Man." *Semiotic Review*, no. 2: Monsters.

Tolbert, Jeffrey A. 2015. "'Dark and Wicked Things': Slender Man, the Folkloresque, and the Implications of Belief." *Contemporary Legend* 3 (5): 38–61.

Winner, Langdon. 1986. *The Whale and the Reactor: A Search for Limits in an Age of High Technology*. Chicago: University of Chicago Press.

xXRoflFalafelXx. 2012. "Best Halloween Costume!" Reddit. https://www.reddit.com/r/funny/comments/119y40/best_halloween_costume/?sort=old&limit=500.

Chapter 3

"What Happens When the Pictures Are No Longer Photoshops?"
Slender Man, Belief, and the Unacknowledged Common Experience

Andrea Kitta

WHILE ATTENDING A BACKYARD PARTY THAT occurred shortly after the Slender Man stabbing incident, I witnessed a group of children from ages two to thirteen playing together.[1] One child, approximately eight years old, pulled his white T-shirt over his head, shouting, "Look out! I'm Slender Man! I'm coming to get you!" as he began blindly chasing the other (now screaming) children around the yard. Upon catching his first victim, his younger sister, who was approximately five years old, he linked arms with her and the two of them started shrieking and chasing the other children as a team. I later asked the originator of the game who Slender Man was. He shrugged and said, "He's a bad man. He comes and gets you." Further discussion attracted more of the children, all of whom voluntarily contributed to the conversation. As the group debated exactly who Slender Man was and what he looked like, they all were certain of a few things: he watched you, he would take you away (although where or why was much contested), and he was tall, thin, wore a black suit, and didn't have a face. When I asked if they had read anything about him on the Internet, they all reported that they had not, although the older children (whose ages ranged from approximately eleven to fifteen) quickly looked him up on their smartphones. The children also reported that they had not seen anything about him on television.[2] When I asked where they had heard about Slender Man, they all shrugged, stating that everyone knows about Slender Man. One six-year-old girl patiently explained to me that he is "like the Boogeyman, but he lived in the woods, but he could be under your bed or in your closet."[3]

DOI: 10.7330/9781607327813.c003

Slender Man is certainly more than an Internet or popular culture phenomenon.[4] Despite his known origins on the Something Awful forum,
Slender Man has taken on a life of his own. While people continue to
pay Slender Man homage on the Internet, the creature has a life outside
the Internet in children's games, oral storytelling, and belief, highlighting
a specific type of experience: the unacknowledged common experience. I
argue that this supernatural experience, which has been hinted at but never
named, is quite common and rarely discussed except under certain circumstances. Slender Man, however, is one way that people articulate this feeling.

While there certainly is an element of collective subversive collaboration in the creation of Slender Man on the Something Awful forum and in
other venues for creepypasta, there is also a shared aesthetic and, at times,
a shared experience that taps into something deeper than mere play. Just as
Slender Man himself is complicated, so is belief in Slender Man. As Jeffrey
A. Tolbert argues in chapter 1 of this volume, Slender Man may be a type
of reverse ostension in which we have to create both the experience and the
narratives. I would also argue that, at times, Slender Man is the name given
to a shared experience that bridges both the experience-centered hypothesis
used by David Hufford (1989) and the cultural source hypothesis. Clearly
there are incidents where the story comes first and the experience comes
after, but we also see moments where a previous experience is attributed to
Slender Man, a sort of reverse quasi-ostension. I would argue that either
way, the experience still *feels* real.

BELIEF, EXPERIENCE, AND SLENDER MAN

As Hufford (1982) has shown, American society has a "tradition of disbelief"; while it is traditional to believe in certain things, it is also traditional *not*
to believe in certain things. In addition, individuals regard the experiences
of others as up for questioning, while our own experiences are treated as
dogma or, as Hufford states more succinctly, "I know what I know, what
you know, you only believe" (47). These experiences become even more
complicated when a shared belief narrative takes place online, perhaps
more so for digital immigrants than digital natives.[5] To some digital immigrants, anything found online is immediately suspect or thought to be inau-
thentic. In addition, experiences, while they can be shared online, are not
thought to necessarily happen online. This is perhaps best demonstrated
by the use of the abbreviation IRL, or "in real life," in computer-mediated
communication to differentiate between events that have occurred in the
corporeal world as opposed to what happens on the Internet. I would argue

that this distinction between "real life" and what happens online is fading and is, likely, no longer true at all for digital natives. The Internet *is* their real life and Internet transmission is just as real as transmission face-to-face.[6]

As a legend complex, Slender Man has two main issues complicating belief: it is supernatural and it is found on the Internet. In memorates, there can be a sense of anonymity; the line between what has happened online versus IRL is further blurred. As Michael Kinsella states, "Communication technologies allow us to see more clearly how the reciprocity between experience and tradition results in the ongoing construction of what we call the supernatural" (Kinsella 2011, 147). Tolbert asserts that Slender Man is just as real as any other entity found IRL or on the Internet because it is a "conscious expression of a culture shared among a particular group of people, which bears special significances that depend in part on an understanding of the group context in which the expressive culture arises" (see chapter 1 of this volume).

It seems that Slender Man narratives suffer from a double stigma as they are both supernatural and found on the Internet. This stigma is based on the traditions of disbelief. As Hufford rejected the a priori notion that nothing supernatural must be happening because supernatural things do not happen, and Diane Goldstein (2007) rejected the a priori notion that "folk belief expressed in popular or commodified culture is any less serious, any less important, any less rational, or any less a belief than what is expressed more traditionally" (16), I reject the a priori notion that just because something is found on the Internet, created in response to a challenge, or has an individual author, it does not mean that it is not a real experience being expressed in a way that is socially and culturally safer than telling a personal experience narrative. Hufford (1995) states that beliefs are supported by "core spiritual experiences" that are perceptual: these experiences lay the foundation for a belief. Since these experiences may involve emotion or latent cultural values rather than what we consider to be "knowledge," they are often disbelieved. In actuality, these core beliefs do not conflict with knowledge and do use deductive reasoning and scientific methodology (Goldstein 2007, 60–78). However, some may feel that not only are they contrary to knowledge, they are also irrational and have no empirical foundations. By focusing on the subjective experience, Hufford is trying to show that the experience is real and valid. However, even those who accept Hufford's view of experience may not agree that those experiences are as valid when posted online, primarily *because* they are found online. I would argue that, at times, people might be even more honest online than in person since they may feel more anonymous (also see Simmel 1950).

Folklorists seem to accept that experiences *posted* online and *that happen* online can be truthful accounts of actual events. Those who read and participate in these narratives also have experiences with Slender Man. For many, a person's experience reading a Slender Man narrative or watching a video can *feel* just as real as having an actual experience with Slender Man. As one of my participants mentioned: "I know it was probably because I had just been reading Slender Man stories on the Internet, but I was walking home and it was late and I had that feeling that I was being watched. Being followed. And I thought to myself, 'It could be Slender Man,' and I knew that was stupid. I was only thinking about Slender Man because I had just read about it. But I just kept thinking, 'You don't know. Maybe those stories are real. Maybe it is Slender Man.'"[7]

This narrative certainly shows a logical progression: the knowledge that Slender Man is "not real," but also the consideration that the stories written about Slender Man could be based on real experiences. While these potential real experiences do not carry the weight of the individual's own experience, they are a part of the logic used by the individual. I am not arguing that Slender Man is "real" or that those who have contributed to the Slender Man narrative think that he is real or have had an experience with him. Rather, I think there is a core spiritual experience here that connects with others—the feeling of being watched—that has been turned into a narrative about a specific entity since it is a convenient way to discuss an untellable experience. While this was not the original intention of early participants in Slender Man Mythos, the narratives about Slender Man have grown larger than what is merely posted online.[8]

Perhaps Slender Man contains a core experience that many have felt but that does not currently have a name. Slender Man narratives online tap into that core experience, giving those who have had a similar experience a way to discuss these events. Similar to David Hufford's (1989) research with the Old Hag and sleep paralysis, there is perhaps an experience of some kind that "has provided the central empirical foundation from which the supernatural tradition arose" (Goldstein, Grider, and Thomas 2007, 14). Slender Man becomes a "flexible rhetorical tool" (Tolbert 2013, 2) or, more simply, the experience of feeling watched now has a name—and that name is Slender Man.

Victor Surge (Eric Knudsen), the original author of the Slender Man narrative, and the other early participants do not make any claims to the reality of their experience and have overtly stated that their intent was to create a fictional monster. They have never admitted any real experience with Slender Man themselves; however, they have certainly tapped into something that *feels real* to their audience. Even those who contribute to the narrative have an aesthetic sense of the Slender Man story; they understand that while Slender Man is not real, there is an aesthetic that is being created, maintained, and understood. It is an experience that is felt by the participants on some level, even if it is not an actual experience they have encountered. This could be, in part, because the creators of Slender Man understand how to create a character and story that feels like folklore, something that is "folkloresque" (Foster and Tolbert 2016), a concept further explored by Jeffrey A. Tolbert in the next chapter. Perhaps one of the best ways to describe Slender Man is using Michael Dylan Foster's (2014) notion of "fuzzy allusion," where folklore is alluded to in a general way, although there is no specific connection to a particular genre or motif that already exists in folklore. Although Slender Man looks and acts like other liminal creatures, there is no direct connection to those creatures. Slender Man seems to fit in and be part of a long-standing tradition without any real connection to that tradition.

Despite that lack of connection to tradition, there is a shared understanding of who or what Slender Man is, even among those who have not participated in the communal creation of Slender Man on the Internet. When I mention Slender Man to any of my university classes, I rarely have to explain who he is. The students already have a preconceived notion of who or what Slender Man is and many have strong opinions about his appearance and what he does. In one of my classes on the supernatural I asked my students to describe Slender Man while I wrote what they said on the board. The only features the class debated was whether or not Slender Man had tentacles and if he kidnapped people or drove them insane.[9]

While we can ask (and have asked) Eric Knudsen, the creator of Slender Man, what his intentions were, we can now see that Slender Man has transformed into something more through the collective folk process. Perhaps for those engaging in the later Slender Man narratives, Slender Man is not about a specific experience event but rather about a series of events adding up to a cumulative experience.

TYPES OF EXPERIENCE

In past scholarship, academics have primarily described experience in two different ways: as a singular life-changing experience and as everyday experience. The English language typically uses the phrases "an experience" and "mere experience."[10] In the majority of the material that we see concerning an experience and mere experience, we can ascertain that there is a tendency to favor "an" experience over "mere" experience. Mere experience is simply what happens to an individual, whereas an experience, "like a rock in a Zen sand garden, stand[s] out from the evenness of passing hours and years" (Turner 1986, 35). Victor Turner defines "experiences" as instances that are "formative and transformative, that is, distinguishable, isolable sequences of external events and internal responses to them . . . some of these formative experiences are highly personal, others are shared with groups to which we belong by birth or choice" (35). In these shared experiences that Turner mentions, we see that "an experience" can be defined in the terms of a "typical experience" or an experience that is shared with the community and results in sentiments also shared by the community. There is an interaction between what has happened and the feelings related to that experience. In a "typical experience" there is a sense that others have gone through this same thing before, making the experience, although unique to the individual, typical to the community (Abrahams 1986, 60). Perhaps one of the reasons we regard supernatural experience as "less real" than other types of experience is that we don't often share them in the same way we do "typical experiences." While the telling of ghost stories is socially acceptable in certain situations, such as around campfires or near Halloween, ghost stories still belong to traditions of disbelief. Situations in which we engage in a typical experience with the supernatural are still rare, so we do not go through the interaction between the experience and the feelings related to it with others, except in certain circumstances.

I would like to attempt to define these concepts more simply. "An experience" is a unique experience, like Turner's rock in a Zen garden. It stands out and can be told as a singular experience with the option of including other experiences. "Typical experience" is an experience that is shared by a community. It does not go unexamined or untold; rather, it is shared in a way that is socially acceptable and may be assumed to be a part of most people's experience. While I do agree that some experiences are frequent, I would like to argue for another definition of "mere experience," which I think belittles the actual experience. "Mere experiences" are not simple, nor are they trivial; they are just frequent and therefore suffer from the triviality barrier often seen in folkloristics. I would argue that "mere experiences" are not simply what happens to you, but rather what happens to you frequently enough that you may not have an outstanding narrative about it as you would with "an experience." However, unlike typical experiences, they are not always shared. David Hufford tapped into this concept with his term "core experiences," which he defines as those that "form distinct classes with stable perceptual patterns" (Hufford 1995, 31); however, his definition does not include whether or not these consistent patterns are shared by a group (making them "typical experiences") or if they are consistent patterns for the individual (making them "mere experiences"). In addition, Hufford's focus is on the accurate observations made by people, not the sharing of these experiences. He certainly suggests that some experiences are stable, even cross-culturally, because they precisely describe observations that are similar (31), but he has little to say about the sharing of those stories outside of the idea behind the traditions of disbelief.

Diane Goldstein discusses how these experiences are shared, demonstrating that there are typical patterns to memorates, including a defensive structure and the use of logic and reason (Goldstein 2007, 60–78). However, the focus of her work is more on the structure of the stories, in that a story doesn't "exist *in the face of* modern scientific knowledge, but in content and structure it exists *because* of modern scientific knowledge" (78). This concept is certainly important, but it does not yet accurately describe the belief experience.

Certainly, Hufford's (1995) "core experience" is close to what I am attempting to describe; however, it seems that many of the experiences Hufford is talking about are still "an experience" instead of "mere experiences," and he is talking about ones shared within a community ("typical" experiences) and ones that people do not share. While I am tempted to call these experiences "everyday" experiences, I will not, as that indicates that there is a specific frequency to them. I am also tempted to refer to them as "vernacular experiences," like Leonard Primiano's (1995) use of the term *vernacular religion*; however, I also wonder if words like *vernacular* or *common* suffer the same issues as *mere*. I am also reluctant to refer to them as untellable, as they are certainly told, to varying degrees of success. The wording "unexamined experiences" raises a similar issue, as these experiences are examined by the individual; they are just not examined by the community in a way that makes them typical. Although the term suffers from the same issues as "mere," I will call these experiences "unacknowledged common experiences," since I do want to highlight that they are frequent, but also, while sometimes spoken, they are not always accepted by the community.

In this context, I would argue that Slender Man is an unacknowledged common experience that has turned into a "typical experience" on the Internet. This now typical experience is without "an experience," so there is not a single definitive experience, but rather a series of typical experiences. The idea of Slender Man fills in that gap of having "an experience," providing an object to describe this subjective typical experience, heretofore an unacknowledged common experience.

These unacknowledged common experiences are crucial to both experience and the maintenance of belief. "An experience" is not always the most important part of experience, nor is it more valuable than unacknowledged common experience or typical experience. An experience is perceived to be more unusual or interesting, but it is not always what solidifies belief. For example, a close friend told me a series of stories about growing up in a haunted house and, while some of the experiences were exemplary and unique, the convincing aspects to her were the everyday experiences of living in a house that was haunted. She recalled a series of incidents, which she uses as an example of the common experience of living in this house, in which the ghost moved items around:

> So, this used to happen all the time, any time I would leave the room while I was getting dressed. I would lay out all of my clothes on the bed and if I left the room for some reason, because I forgot something in the laundry or because I got distracted, when I came back into the room, my bra would be gone. And I knew I had laid it out on the bed with the rest of my clothes. Well, this would happen every time if I would leave the room while the clothes were out on the bed. It got to be a joke. The second I noticed it and said something about it to my daughter, the bra would reappear. So it got to the point where I would walk back out of the room—it only worked if I wasn't in the room—and I would say out loud, "Oh no! Wherever did my bra go? I swear it was right here!" [*Laughs*] Then it would reappear. It happened all the time.[11]

My informant clearly was no longer frightened by this mysterious disappearance of her clothing because it happened so often; she even describes it as a joke among family members, making it a typical experience for her family.[12] However, the familiar experience of living with this ghost was the most convincing part of this story. Her other narratives about this ghost that detail specific, unique events are described very differently:

> So, there would be sometimes, it was not very often, where, well, he would just get mad. I don't know exactly how to describe it. Jealous, I think. That we were alive and he wasn't. It didn't happen often, but you could feel it. You could feel someone watching you and he was just so angry, you could feel the anger and it was scary. One time I was in my bedroom reading, and I could feel him in the doorway. He was glaring at me. I could actually almost see him and I never saw him before or since. It was weird, because I couldn't actually see him; it was like there was so much energy there that my *feeling* almost turned into *seeing*. Most of the time things just moved around and you knew he was there, but it was nothing bad. But every once in a while, it was bad. He was angry and you felt it.[13]

These singular, unique examples of "an experience" were clearly different. My informant goes on to say that she would often question whether what she had experienced was real, sometimes convincing herself that the events had not happened; other times she wondered if there was a separate entity involved in these incidents—but she never questioned whether or not there was a ghost in the house. She had so many instances of experiences with this particular ghost that she knew he was real.

Slender Man functions in a similar way. The unacknowledged common experience of reading a Slender Man story, playing a game where Slender Man is a character, or otherwise engaging with the narrative is the convincing part of the interaction. Individuals are not having "an experience" with Slender Man; rather, this character is a part of a larger experience with the supernatural. Like legends, which are not literally true but rather "typify life in modern society" (Smith 1999), Slender Man also is a part of the experience of life in the modern world.

In addition, interactions with the supernatural have a certain *feel* to them, which has often been described as a numinous quality. While we might engage our sight and hearing while reading a Slender Man story or watching a video, it is the *feel* of the story that makes the experience real.[14] Since North American culture primarily relies on sight and hearing over touch (Neustadt 1994), the feel of a supernatural experience can be difficult to describe. One of my students, who arrived in my office after our classroom discussion on the topic, was excited to show me some video games with a Slender Man character. He told me: "You have to imagine what this is like. It's different here, now. But if you're up late and there's no one around and you're playing this game, well, it gets to you. This guy will follow you or show up suddenly and when you're home alone playing and it's late at night, it all feels real. It feels like if I just get up to get a drink or go to the bathroom or something, he could be there, for real, in my kitchen or whatever."[15]

I assured him that I understood. Since I had read up on the phenomenon, mostly in the very office where we were discussing his experiences, I knew how convincing some of the narratives and pictures online could be. While I could not understand his exact experience, I understood the unacknowledged common experience (or, if one is fortunate, the typical experience) of being frightened by something I had read about on the Internet. This experience is common, but not often shared. One of my students collected the following narrative from a friend:

> One time, I was out late at night walking down the road to my house from my friend's house (only a few minutes away). Obviously, I was already

scared because I was walking alone but I didn't have another option so I walked as fast as I could to get home. I looked over and on the back of a street sign was a painted picture of Slender Man. I don't think that this would have frightened me in the daylight but since it was night I was really freaked out. I began to convince myself that someone was after me and out to get me. I sprinted the rest of the way home and triple-checked my doors to make sure that they were locked and that I was safely inside without any creepy guy. I heard somewhere that if you looked at Slender Man directly then he would come after you. I had nightmares all night that night. I was being chased by Slender Man.[16]

While the cause of this experience, be it Slender Man or something else, can be individual, it can also be affected by popular culture, further demonstrating the exchange between popular and folk culture. The source of the fear differs; however, the experience of fear, especially unfounded fear, is not uncommon. That being said, it is not always a typical experience since we cannot always discuss it or because we are forced to discuss it in dismissive terms.[17]

Clearly, this experience is not uncommon, but it is not typical either since the narrative alienates rather than incorporates the teller; all of those who admitted they were scared after watching a scary movie knew that it was "stupid" or that they shouldn't feel that way. In instances where the listener also has had a similar experience, the experience can be typical; however, the structure of the story is told in a way that protects the teller from the derision of the listener. If the listener laughs or ridicules the teller, he or she can reiterate a similar belief that the experience was "stupid" in spite of the fact that there is nothing stupid about insomnia or terror.

In addition to Slender Man symbolizing the experientially cross-cultural feeling of being watched, he could certainly be a metaphor for other experiences as well.[18] Perhaps Slender Man is an easier way to express the feeling of being watched on the Internet—where Slender Man was invented—by a faceless entity such as the National Security Administration (NSA). Perhaps he expresses the general feeling that one is being watched or even followed, especially late at night. Since he is often situated in wooded areas, Slender Man may even express our fears about nature, getting lost, or our inability to survive in a world without electronic devices. The possibilities are great and certainly individual, but they all connect with an overall fear that we are not alone and we are being watched, perhaps even stalked.

Although the Slender Man narratives become more specific at times, they do contain overall themes. There is something that has been around for a long time, it watches us, and sometimes it causes people to do terrible things.

The photoshopped "historical" pictures of Slender Man, from the woodcuts to photography, express the perceived longevity of the experience, in particular that this feeling is as old as humankind itself. We are not alone in this expression of fear. However, there are many possibilities as to the function of Slender Man since he does not represent any one thing, but rather fills in for anything frightening, anything that could be watching the individual.

For adults and digital immigrants, Slender Man can also be used to express a fear of unprovoked violence. Much like the Satanic panics or moral panics of the past (see Ellis 1989, 2000), Slender Man has been used as a way of demonstrating or questioning the motives of children and young adults who have engaged in violent acts. While the "Slender Man stabbings" in May 2014 were the most closely associated link between violence and adolescents, later acts of violence, as mentioned in the introduction to this volume, have been linked to interest in Slender Man (also see Murray 2014). Slender Man may also symbolize a fear of the Internet and technology by older adults or those who do not understand Internet usage. For them, the visage of Slender Man represents all the dangers of the Internet in one entity, from dangerous strangers to their fear that digital natives do not understand that there is a difference between the Internet and "real life." This may also express digital immigrants' belief that digital natives do not understand that the Internet and what happens there is not real to the digital immigrant.

Slender Man is not a simple entity that can be looked at as belonging to a single folk group. He is, possibly, an acknowledgment of the unacknowledged common experience of being watched. The reason he "feels real" to so many people is because he helps to give a voice to a real experience that is difficult to articulate otherwise. While an individual can ask another, "Have you ever felt like you were being watched?" and have the other person understand that experience, there is a tradition of disbelief whereby either you are being watched by something human or it is nothing at all. Slender Man offers the possibility that you are being watched—not by anything human but by something that should be taken seriously. Not only does Slender Man give us a place to assign value to these unacknowledged common experiences, he is standing there, acknowledging these experiences.

NOTES

The quote in my essay's title comes from Tolbert (2013, 6), quoting Soakie (2009), "Create Paranormal Images," *Something Awful Forums*, https://forums.somethingawful.com/showthread.php?threadid=3150591&userid=0&perpage=40&pagenumber=16.

1. Diane Goldstein had a similar experience of watching children play that she documents in her book *Once upon a Virus* (Goldstein 2004).

2. I'm fairly sure at least some of them had heard something about the 2014 stabbings from overheard conversations, radios, or televisions left on in the background.

3. Previous to this accidental interaction with this group of children at a party, I was fairly certain that there was a connection between Slender Man and older traditions of supernatural creatures who watch events without interacting with them, such as Mothman and Thunderbirds or, as they have appeared on the television show *Fringe*, "The Watchers." I also saw an association with the Men in Black (MIB) tradition (men or aliens dressed in black suits who attempt to silence recent UFO witnesses), at least in the dress and uncanny appearance. While I do still see the connection to these traditions, until this moment it had not occurred to me that Slender Man could be explained as simply as a boogeyman, a threatening creature who was a "old spirit in a new bottle" (Goldstein, Grider, and Thomas 2007, 1–22) or, in this case, a boogeyman with a new suit.

4. As described above, children play games with Slender Man as "it," while college students (sometimes jokingly, sometimes not) warn of seeing Slender Man in wooded areas or while walking alone. Many examples such as these were provided by my students, who are the inspiration for this work.

5. Digital natives are those who have grown up with technology such as computers and the Internet, whereas digital immigrants have not. For more information, see Blank 2013b and McNeill 2009, 80–97.

6. See Blank 2007, 2013a; Howard 2008; and McNeill 2009 for more on this, especially the notion of hybridity.

7. I have chosen to redact the names of my informants due to the sensitive nature of their stories. For the sake of clarity, I have given them letters instead. Author interview with A., September 17, 2014.

8. For example, the late 2014/early 2015 sightings of Slender Man in Cannock Chase, Staffordshire, UK (Mukherjee 2015).

9. The students in my fall 2014 class on the supernatural came to the consensus that Slender Man kidnapped children and drove adults insane, but they did not reach agreement on whether or not Slender Man had tentacles. The spring 2015 class could not decide either issue.

10. The German language seems to have a better grasp of the concept. The word *Erlebnis*—which is the secondary form of the word *Erleben*, which literally means "to still be alive when something happens"—gives the idea that this type of experience is life changing and important: this experience stands out from other experiences. In contrast, *Erfahrung* gives the idea of mere everyday experience (Gadamer 2004: 60–69, 346–361).

11. Author interview with B., December 18, 2014.

12. Although it is not "an experience" she describes often to those outside her family, making it an unacknowledged common experience in that context.

13. Author interview with B., December 18, 2014.

14. Lynne S. McNeill (2006) finds something similar with her study of ghost hunters, where the numinous quality of the experience trumped scientific proof, either found or not found.

15. Author interview with C., March 15, 2014.

16. Student D interview with F., fall 2014.

17. For example, one student shared in class that they always had to watch something after watching *The Walking Dead* on Sunday nights or they would end up dreaming about zombies chasing them all night. Several others students stated the same thing happened to them and talked about the things they would do after watching *The Walking Dead* in order to fall asleep

and not have nightmares. They all stated they did not believe zombies were real—however, that did not help them sleep. Jeannie Banks Thomas (2007) discusses similar strategies.

18. I've also argued that Slender Man is a way to discuss bullying (Kitta 2019).

WORKS CITED

Abrahams, Roger. 1986. "Ordinary and Extraordinary Experience." In *The Anthropology of Experience*, ed. Victor Turner and Edward Bruner, 45–72. Urbana: University of Illinois Press.

Blank, Trevor J. 2007. "Examining the Transmission of Urban Legends: Making the Case for Folklore Fieldwork on the Internet." *Folklore Forum* 3 (1): 15–26.

Blank, Trevor J. 2013a. "Hybridizing Folk Culture: Toward a Theory of New Media and Vernacular Discourse." *Western Folklore* 72 (2): 105–130.

Blank, Trevor J. 2013b. *The Last Laugh: Folk Humor, Celebrity Culture, and Mass-Mediated Disasters in the Digital Age*. Madison: University of Wisconsin Press.

Ellis, Bill. 1989. "Death by Folklore: Ostension, Contemporary Legend, and Murder." *Western Folklore* 48 (3): 201–220. https://doi.org/10.2307/1499739.

Ellis, Bill. 2000. *Raising the Devil: Satanism, New Religions, and the Media*. Lexington: University Press of Kentucky.

Foster, Michael Dylan. 2014. "The Folkloresque Spiral: Toward a Theory of Allusion, Authority, and Creation." Presentation at the American Folklore Society Annual Meeting, Santa Fe, NM, November 6.

Foster, Michael Dylan, and Jeffrey A. Tolbert, eds. 2016. *The Folkloresque: Reframing Folklore in a Popular Culture World*. Logan: Utah State University Press. https://doi.org/10.7330/9781607324188.

Gadamer, Hans-Georg. 2004. *Truth and Method*. Translation revised by Joel Weinsheimer and Donald G. Marshall. New York: Continuum.

Goldstein, Diane. 2004. *Once upon a Virus: AIDS Legends and Vernacular Risk Perception*. Logan: Utah State University Press. https://doi.org/10.2307/j.ctt4cgmww.

Goldstein, Diane. 2007. "Scientific Rationalism and Supernatural Experience Narratives." In *Haunting Experiences: Ghosts in Contemporary Folklore*, ed. Diane Goldstein, Sylvia Ann Grider, and Jeannie Banks Thomas, 60–78. Logan: Utah State University Press. https://doi.org/10.2307/j.ctt4cgmqg.7.

Goldstein, Diane, Sylvia Ann Grider, and Jeannie Banks Thomas. 2007. "Old Spirits in New Bottles." In *Haunting Experiences: Ghosts in Contemporary Folklore*, ed. Diane Goldstein, Sylvia Ann Grider, and Jeannie Banks Thomas, 1–22. Logan: Utah State University Press. https://doi.org/10.2307/j.ctt4cgmqg.5.

Howard, Robert Glenn. 2008. "Electronic Hybridity: The Persistent Processes of the Vernacular Web." *Journal of American Folklore* 121 (480): 192–218. https://doi.org/10.1353/jaf.0.0012.

Hufford, David. 1982. "Traditions of Disbelief." *New York Folklore* 8:47–55.

Hufford, David. 1989. *The Terror That Comes in the Night: An Experience-Centered Study of Supernatural Assault Traditions*. Philadelphia: University of Pennsylvania Press.

Hufford, David. 1995. "Beings without Bodies. An Experienced-Centered Theory of the Belief in Spirits." In *Out of the Ordinary: Folklore and the Supernatural*, ed. Barbara Walker, 11–45. Logan: Utah State University. https://doi.org/10.2307/j.ctt46nwn8.6.

Kinsella, Michael. 2011. *Legend-Tripping Online: Supernatural Folklore and the Search for Ong's Hat*. Jackson: University Press of Mississippi. https://doi.org/10.14325/mississippi/9781604739831.001.0001.

Kitta, Andrea. 2019. *The Kiss of Death: Contamination, Contagion, and Folklore.* Logan: Utah State University Press.

McNeill, Lynne S. 2006. "Contemporary Ghost Hunting and the Relationship between Proof and Experience." *Contemporary Legend,* n.s., 9: 96–110.

McNeill, Lynne S. 2009. "The End of the Internet: A Folk Response to the Provision of Infinite Choice." In *Folklore and the Internet,* ed. Trevor J. Blank, 80–97. Logan: Utah State University Press. https://doi.org/10.2307/j.ctt4cgrx5.7.

Mukherjee, Ritoban. 2015. "Unveiling the Truth behind the Cannock Chase Slender Man." *Huff Post Weird News,* January 30. https://www.huffingtonpost.com/ritoban-muk herjee/unveling-the-truth-behind_b_6569830.html.

Murray, Rheana. 2014. "Slender Man Now Linked to Three Violent Acts." *ABC News,* June 9. http://abcnews.go.com/US/slender-man-now-linked-violent-acts/story?id =24058562.

Neustadt, Kathy. 1994. "The Folkloristics of Licking." *Journal of American Folklore* 107 (423): 181–196. https://doi.org/10.2307/541079.

Primiano, Leonard. 1995. "Vernacular Religion and the Search for Method in Religious Folklife." *Western Folklore* 54 (1): 37–56. https://doi.org/10.2307/1499910.

Simmel, Georg. 1950. "The Stranger." In *The Sociology of Georg Simmel,* ed. Kurt H. Wolff, 402–408. New York: Free Press. https://www.infoamerica.org/documentos_pdf /simmel01.pdf.

Smith, Paul. 1999. "Definitional Characteristics of the Contemporary Legend." *FOAFtale News* 44. http://www.folklore.ee/FOAFtale/ftn44.htm.

Soakie. 2009. "Create Paranormal Images." Something Awful Forums. Accessed May 17, 2013. http://forums.somethingawful.com/showthread.php?threadid=3150591&user id=0&perpage=40&pagenumber=16.

Thomas, Jeannie Banks. 2007. "The Usefulness of Ghost Stories." In *Haunting Experiences: Ghosts in Contemporary Folklore,* ed. Diane E. Goldstein, Sylvia Ann Grider, and Jeannie Banks Thomas, 25–59. Logan: Utah State University Press. https://doi.org /10.2307/j.ctt4cgmqg.6.

Tolbert, Jeffrey A. 2013. "'The Sort of Story That Has You Covering Your Mirrors': The Case of Slender Man." *Semiotic Review,* no. 2: Monsters. https://www.semioticreview .com/ojs/index.php/sr/article/view/19/19.

Turner, Victor. 1986. "Dewey, Dilthey, and Drama: An Essay in the Anthropology of Experience." In *The Anthropology of Experience,* ed. Victor Turner and Edward Bruner, 33–44. Urbana: University of Illinois Press.

Chapter 4

"Dark and Wicked Things"
Slender Man, the Folkloresque, and the Implications of Belief

Jeffrey A. Tolbert

Behind the success of many great works of fiction is a convincing appeal to "fact," or at least to everyday experience. A case in point: as a Maryland native and an inveterate fan of horror cinema, I look back fondly on that controversial classic of the late 1990s, *The Blair Witch Project* (Myrick and Sánchez 1999a). I confess to being one of many who initially believed in the literal reality of the film's fictional events, which centered on a group of college film students who disappeared while exploring a local legend. I was sixteen when it was released, and the film and its accompanying promotional material—particularly the Sci-Fi Channel companion "documentary" *Curse of the Blair Witch* (Myrick and Sánchez 1999b)—contained precisely the right mix of chilling detail, localness, and sound bites from (apparent) authority figures to convince me that it was all real.[1] And I wasn't alone in this: infamously, believers flooded Burkittsville, Maryland, near which the fictional village of Blair supposedly once stood, in the months following the film's release. These legend trippers (of a fictional legend) vandalized town property and snatched souvenirs in a witch-inspired frenzy that itself seems to have entered the town's folklore (Fiore 2010).[2]

The Blair Witch Project is, of course, far from the only creative work to so effectively confuse fiction and reality. Other notable examples are Orson Welles's infamous radio adaptation of *The War of the Worlds* (Welles 1938) and the 1992 fake BBC news special *Ghostwatch* (Manning 1992). Welles's realistic drama allegedly caused an uproar among listeners (primarily in the New York area), leading him to formally state the day after the broadcast that it was not intended to be taken literally (Heyer 2003, 149–150, 159).[3] Likewise, the initial airing of *Ghostwatch*, which was presented as a primetime

DOI: 10.7330/9781607327813.c004

news special on a haunting in a London suburb, was linked to a subsequent real-world suicide as well as the only known instances of television causing post-traumatic stress disorder in children (Leeder 2013, 174).[4] A further example was the release of the Animal Planet TV mockumentary *Mermaids: The Body Found* (Bennett 2012), which prompted concerned citizens to contact the National Oceanic and Atmospheric Administration (Oremus 2012). In a statement posted to the NOAA's website, the organization wryly pointed out that no evidence exists to support the existence of "aquatic humanoids" (National Oceanic and Atmospheric Administration 2012).

This list is far from exhaustive, but hopefully the point is clear: in each case the "panic" (a term I use loosely) stemmed from the confusion of fiction with reality. None of these broadcasts were "real," but all were presented in ways that mimicked real media conventions and were therefore *convincing* (Harris 2001, 76; Heyer 2003, 150; Leeder 2013, 175). This playful (or cynical) manipulation of the boundaries of fiction and reality—akin to what historian Michael Saler (2012, 14) has called the "ironic imagination"—is discursively powerful, and seems particularly easy to effect when the creators of popular media invoke the conventions of folklore. In this chapter I consider a case with several important parallels to these irruptions of fiction into the real—that is, human, experiential—world. Slender Man, the ubiquitous Internet monster, is not "real" in precisely the way that the Blair Witch, the "aquatic apes" of *Mermaids*, the ghost named Pipes haunting the London family in *Ghostwatch*, and the alien invaders in the *War of the Worlds* broadcast are not real.[5] But like each of these believable fictions, surprising and distressing events have taken place in the "real" world based, at least in part, on alleged failures to recognize Slender Man as "unreal." The most dramatic of these events was the attempted murder of a twelve-year-old girl in Wisconsin.

Beginning with the assumption that all these cases of fiction mistaken for reality do indeed have something in common, there are two organizing principles informing this study: first, the issue of believability, the capacity of self-conscious works of fiction to be convincingly "realistic"; and second, the potential for the savvy manipulation of folkloric forms and conventions—what Michael Dylan Foster (2016b) has called the "folkloresque"—to produce potent rhetorical devices that can in turn be enlisted by others to serve various discursive ends. These themes are inextricably linked. As Foster shows, the folkloresque is a complex process for the creation of new expressive forms and may take many guises, but it always involves an appeal—through vague resemblance or direct imitation—to familiar pre-existing folklore. Through this appeal the folkloresque imbues new texts with cultural authority, but the appeal can be successful only if audiences "buy" the connection between the folkloresque material and established real-world traditions. It must be, in other words, believable. The folkloresque thus imparts one kind of "realness," in this case, the suggestion that a text (such as a Slender Man narrative) might actually exist in traditions that predate its appearance on the Internet.

But particularly where supernatural belief is concerned, this can lead directly into another type of "realness": if there were a preexisting Slender Man tradition, with legends told about it as about any other supernatural being familiar from folklore, then it would be reasonable to assume that the tradition exists in what might be termed an *atmosphere of belief*. By this I mean a context in which tellers and audiences of supernatural narratives may be open to the possibility that a supernatural narrative is real. This is not to say that everyone who hears or tells a legend narrative literally believes in it: as folklorists have long held, legends are always regarded with differing degrees of belief (Dégh 1996; Hufford 1982; Kinsella 2011, 5–6). The point is that by forging connections to real-world belief traditions and thereby attributing the *possibility of belief* to Slender Man narratives, the folkloresque adds another dimension of "realness" to the fictional Slender Man Mythos. The end result of all of these interrelated processes, as we will see, is that the being himself, the supernatural Slender Man, becomes believable in a way that belies his fictional roots.[6] The quality of believability is bolstered by the combination of news accounts about the monster, real-life practices (i.e., ostension, the acting out of a narrative) surrounding the tradition, and the inherently cyclical nature of folkloresque texts, which are created from disparate traditional elements and ultimately form the basis of new traditions (Foster 2016a). Adding another layer of complexity to this discussion is the simple fact that whether one believes in him literally or not, Slender Man *is* real, in that he is present (in countless iterations) throughout our physical and digital worlds.

I suggest that in the discourses emerging after the violence in Wisconsin, belief in Slender Man was often framed as a form of deviance, a view that I attempt to problematize.[7] Folklorists, who make it their business to document the creation and dissemination of such phenomena as Slender Man, are uniquely well positioned to counter the negative or problematic discourses that may arise in their wake (Ellis 1996, 182). In this chapter I focus on these discourses, rather than the texts of the Slender Man Mythos itself, to emphasize that it is human actors, not narratives or characters, that are ultimately responsible for real-world actions. Folklore is emphatically not to blame. In the wake of the Waukesha incident, several folklorists and other scholars argued this and related points in various news outlets.[8] While it is impossible to say whether these voices helped to calm the rumblings of a nascent moral panic, it is nevertheless important and encouraging that they were raised at all.

THE "FACTS" OF THE CASE

As is now common knowledge, Slender Man was created on the Internet as a deliberate fiction, part of an ongoing challenge for users of an online discussion forum to create frightening images. Victor Surge, the online alias of the Something Awful forum user Eric Knudsen, who created the monster, made its origins explicitly clear: "The Slender Man as an idea was made-up [*sic*] off the top of my head, although the concept is based on a number of things that scare me. The name I thought up on the fly when I wrote that first bit" (Surge 2009). But despite its avowedly fictional status, the Slender Man Mythos was tailored to resemble actual legendry (Peck 2015). I have referred to this process as *reverse ostension*, through which some users actually sought to generate narratives that would come to be regarded as real legends by people outside of the original digital community (see chapter 1 of this volume).[9] Despite these aesthetic moves on the part of his creators, though, Slender Man largely remained an amusing, if frightening, fiction.

But the monster was violently shaken from his fictional frame on Saturday, May 31, 2014, when a bicyclist called police after he discovered a twelve-year-old girl lying on the sidewalk outside of David's Park in Waukesha, Wisconsin. The girl had been stabbed—nineteen times, it was later reported—and left for dead. Two other girls of the same age, Morgan Geyser and Anissa Weier, confessed to the attempted murder. They had done it, they said, to gain the favor of Slender Man (Gabler 2014). The victim survived and was released from the hospital on June 6. Weier and Geyser were charged with attempted first-degree intentional homicide (Barton 2014).

Much of the news coverage following the Wisconsin attack focused on the mental health of the accused.[10] Geyser was initially found incompetent to stand trial and ordered to receive psychological treatment; experts testifying on her mental state claimed that she believed she had real-life relationships with other fictional characters as well, including the *Harry Potter* antagonist Voldemort (Vielmetti 2014). She was eventually diagnosed with schizophrenia (Vielmetti 2015a). Another theme that emerged in some discussions of the attack related to perceptions of the Internet as a source of danger. On June 2, 2014, the Waukesha Police Department released a statement, reproduced on the website of the *Los Angeles Times*, outlining the case. In the statement, Police Chief Russell Jack notes, "Both suspects had a fascination in a fictitious character that often posted [*sic*] to a website that is a collection of small stories about death and horror" (Jack 2014). Jack continues:

> Keeping children safe is more challenging than in years past. The Internet has changed the way we live. It is full of information and wonderful sites that teach and entertain. The internet can also be full of dark and wicked things. It is also providing an opportunity for potential child predators to reach children like never before.
>
> Unmonitored and unrestricted access to the internet by children is a growing and alarming problem. This should be a wake up [*sic*] call for all parents. Parents are strongly encouraged to restrict and monitor their children's internet usage. We must also remember that "online" is much more than spending time on the computer. Now smart phones and even video games are completely connected to the outside world.
>
> Parents, please talk to your kids about the dangers that exist online.

Speaking from his position of authority as a law enforcement officer, Jack leaves no doubt as to the source of the problem: the Internet and its "dark and wicked things."[11] Similarly, some writers ran with the notion that people needed to be educated about the reality of Slender Man—that is, about his unreality. An article on *Rolling Stone*'s website featured the telling subtitle, "Everything You Need to Know about the Internet's Disturbing Boogeyman" (Raymond 2014). And CNN's Kelly Wallace wrote, "Warning signs for parents that their children may be having trouble absorbing what they're engaging with online, or differentiating fantasy from reality, include withdrawing from real friends, not engaging with other aspects of their lives, self-injury and injury to others, experts say" (2014).

After the attack, the media attempted to link other stories to Slender Man as well. On June 6, 2014, Cincinnati television station WLWT posted a story to its website detailing another stabbing, this time of a mother by her thirteen-year-old daughter. The mother herself, after learning about the events in Waukesha, suggested there might be a connection to the fictional monster, citing references to Slender Man in her daughter's writings (B. Evans 2014). Two days later a husband and wife in Las Vegas shot and killed three people before killing themselves; a neighbor told reporters that the husband had frequently dressed up as Slender Man (Murray 2014). And in September, a teenaged girl in Pasco County, Florida, set fire to her house with her mother and brother inside (both of whom fortunately escaped). Sheriff Chris Nocco told the press that the girl had visited the site Creepypasta.com and had even written in her journal about the Waukesha stabbing (Orlando 2014).

The flurry of news coverage focusing on Slender Man and real-world violence and the cautionary statements to parents have a whiff of panic about them. In a *Newsweek* piece on the attack, writer Abigail Jones noted "a rising cultural panic this case seems to encapsulate. The response to what these girls are accused of doing reflects our deepest anxieties about girlhood, technology and the growing gulf between parents and their children. And that's why this kind of news story rivets us. We say to ourselves, 'How awful,' while yearning for more" (Jones 2014).[12]

In the next section I consider the implications of the incursion of fictional texts into the real world, and suggest a different, though closely related, cause of the intense interest in the case: the issue of belief.

LEGEND AND BELIEF, DEVIANCE AND MORAL PANIC

Moral panics, as Stanley Cohen outlines in *Folk Devils and Moral Panics*, are responses to perceived deviant acts that are seen as a threat to social norms and that are presented in stereotypical and moralizing ways by the mass media (Cohen 2011, 1). On this point, the case of Slender Man differs from the fictional works mentioned earlier. While the *War of the Worlds* broadcast, *Ghostwatch*, and similar works may have trailed controversy in their wakes and prompted widespread fear among their audiences, those responses notably lacked the element of deviance, of a (perceived) widespread social problem borne out in the actions of a few individuals, which is central to moral panic discourses. In fact, these episodes represent the inverse of the moral panic scenario Cohen describes in at least one important respect: rather than a case of the news media fixating on a real act (or series of acts) of deviance, these fictional works and the panics they induced began *in the media*, with two of the four—*War of the Worlds* and *Ghostwatch*—actually framed diegetically as journalistic reports on current events. (*The Blair Witch Project* and *Mermaids*, meanwhile, both appealed to the documentary film genre to establish authority.) The panics caused were therefore the result of a generalized confusion of fiction with reality: instead of a hyperbolic response to a real event, these "fake" media prompted real (if disproportionate) responses by the viewing/listening public.[13] On the other hand, the media treatment of Slender Man began by fixating on the real-world attack in Waukesha and the subsequent incidents, and the discourses that followed, as we have seen, clearly do reflect concerns with deviance. No one took Slender Man for a "real" being, ironically, except for the young girls accused of an act of terrible violence. The panic that followed that act was a moral panic induced not by the fear of a murderous supernatural being, but by the fear that stories of this being could incite belief (and hence action) in the most vulnerable members of society, its children.

While the fear of alien invasion or angry ghosts, on the one hand, and the fear of young girls behaving violently, on the other, are clearly very different, they are linked in this case by the issue of belief. Paralleling audience responses to the *War of the Worlds* and *Ghostwatch* broadcasts, the seemingly "real" legend of the Blair Witch, and the pseudoscience of *Mermaids*, the fictional Slender Man was interpreted as real and invoked to justify real-world actions (albeit on a far smaller scale). And paralleling conventional moral panics, the media picked up the story, forging tenuous links between it and other current events, because "once a dominant perception is established the tendency is to assimilate all subsequent happenings to it" (Cohen 2011, 273). Despite the questionable connections between the post-Waukesha acts of violence and the Mythos, the mention of Slender Man in this context creates a web of real-life intertextuality, an association between a dark but highly creative and entertaining pastime and a violent reality.

This real-life intertextuality is particularly fascinating because of the processes that gave rise to the Slender Man Mythos. Slender Man is not, after all, of the same order as "real" legendary figures such as Bigfoot or the Chupacabra: unlike legends about these beings, stories about Slender Man did not arise in lived vernacular experience. There was never an atmosphere of belief surrounding the Slender Man creature (at least, not initially), because he was created as an entertaining pastime. But in a statement cited by several news and opinion writers in the wake of the Waukesha stabbing, an administrator for the Creepypasta Wiki (where Weier and Geyser got their information on Slender Man) suggested this might not be entirely the case: "Of course, only a small minority of people (mostly newcomers) on the wiki (and the Internet) truly believe what they read here. And for most people, they will not attempt to replicate atrocities presented in some of the literature on the wiki. Something like this was bound to happen, considering the size of the Creepypasta community. All it takes is one person to do something insane and radical in the name of someone or something" (Sloshedtrain 2014).

It could be argued, then, that from the perspective of the news media and the other sources I consider here, the underlying deviance present in the Waukesha incident and the events following it lay in the act of believing itself. "Normal" people would never believe in the reality of a tradition known from the start to be fictional; in the absence of belief, there would be no cause for the violent actions that have come to be associated with that tradition. Steps must be taken, by this logic, to ensure that children—who are the most vulnerable to such misguided beliefs—are educated about the unreality of Slender Man and related phenomena. The issue of mental health serves to reinforce the perceived deviance of belief: Geyser's belief was a symptom of her early-onset schizophrenia (Vielmetti 2015c).[14] And unlike the *War of the Worlds* broadcast and the other fictional media considered above, which (despite disclaimers announcing their fictional status) were presented in singular form in such a way as to "trick" audiences into believing, the truth of Slender Man's fiction is only a few clicks away. In the case of the broadcasts and films, panic based on belief was in some sense a "normal" response, given the authoritative media presentation style of each fictional work; but in the case of Slender Man, belief was framed as deviant.

Like the Creepypasta Wiki statement, some responses from within the Slender Man community understandably capitalized on this sense of deviance. In my previous study of Slender Man (chapter 1 of this volume) I posted questions on the online Slender Nation discussion forum (Slendernation.forumotion.com) about the process of the monster's creation. I returned to the forum after the Waukesha incident to gauge the reactions of community members. In addition to asking about the impact of the attack on the Mythos, I posed questions to forum members about the reasons Slender Man in particular was invoked by the attackers (The Angry Scholar 2014). Their responses varied, but some themes emerged, including the supposed inevitability of the attack, concerns about mental healthcare, and parental supervision.

Forum user UncleDark (2014) showed a keen awareness of media discourses. He also likened the Waukesha incident to an earlier moral panic:

> My heart goes out to the families of all involved.
>   Too many people will blame "evil influences from the media" or "mental illness," or both, as if that explains everything. I have to wonder what was going on in the lives of these girls that running away to live with Slendy was better than what they had, worth killing for.
>   I remember the 1980's Satanic Panic, which (among other things) included a parental rampage against Dungeons and Dragons. Not HappyFunTimes. I don't want to see something like it again.

UncleDark's mention of the "Satanic Panic" is especially noteworthy. In an important study, Bill Ellis (1989) addresses this widespread fear of Satanic cult–inspired murders in the 1970s and 1980s, and the specific case of two murdered Ohio teenagers that was linked to it. Noting how local events may be assimilated into existing legend complexes, Ellis simultaneously argues that traditional narratives are more than just stories to be analyzed: "They are also maps for action, often violent actions" (218).[15] Discussing another Internet legend complex, the Incunabula Papers, Michael Kinsella argues that "engineered or constructed legends have the capacity to become traditionalized"—that is, their origins may become obscured and they may be accepted as real legends. Once this occurs, people may engage in ostension, the acting-out of their content (Kinsella 2011, 107–108). Legend tripping, the form of ostension wherein people attempt to experience legends directly, enables people to "concurrently discover and create, or perhaps more correctly, *perform into being*, liminal realms bordering between fantasy and reality" (145). Kinsella also points out that individual ostensive experiences may become part of the legends themselves (x, 58, 145).

The alternate reality games (ARGs), creepypastas, video games, and other cross-genre multimedia forms in which Slender Man has appeared all partake, to varying degrees, in ostension, thus contributing to the Mythos's liminal status between reality and fiction.[16] And the crimes committed in Slender Man's name may also be seen as constituting a kind of ostension. This was undoubtedly the case with the girls accused of the stabbing in Wisconsin, who claimed that their actions were motivated by a desire to become "proxies" of Slender Man (a term used within the Mythos to refer to people who are somehow brainwashed into doing the monster's bidding), and to prove that the monster really exists (Gabler 2014). Here is a clear example, then, of a folkloresque tradition being directly engaged with in precisely the same way as "real" folklore, indicating that there has been considerable slippage between the categories of "real" and "fake," both in terms of experience and of cultural expression. If ostension brings legend texts more fully into the real world, it has the same effect on texts that may not match conventional definitions of folklore, but that ultimately operate in identical ways.[17]

Importantly, though, this does not suggest that the Slender Man Mythos is somehow to blame for the tragic uses of its content outlined here. Slender Nation forum user NearTheEnd (2014) felt that the Waukesha attacks were inevitable, and that Slender Man could as easily have been any other supernatural character:

> You have to keep in mind that they were 12. Very easily impressionable. If not Slenderman, it could have been . . . oh, I dunno . . . Henry the flying child-eater that Joe Schmo made up on the internet one day that just so happen to catch attention. So on and so forth. Basically, anything of this genre can easily wiggle its way into and really mess up a child's mind. Anything. Vampires, werewolves, creepy-pastas, fears from the fear mythos . . . Absolutely anything. This time it just so happened to be Slenderman.

Similarly, Magnus96 (2014) wrote:

> I knew that someone would take their obsession to an extreme, I didn't
> think something like this would happen but I knew something extreme
> would happen.
>   Once again I don't wanna anger anyone with this post but I did see
> this coming, it was inevitable with all the fanboys/fangirls obsessing over
> these characters. But I will say that if it wasn't Slendy, then it probably
> would've been something else, like Vampires, Werewolves, or other mythi-
> cal creatures.

On June 8, 2014, user timeobserver2013 posted a link to a story about
the Ohio attack, the second to be associated with Slender Man. User
eudaemon (2014) was the first to respond:

> I have to admit, after this second incident, I did consider pulling my stuff
> down. But that wouldn't actually address the problem at all and really, the
> cat's out of the bag. I think the mythos has a lot of features that could
> appeal to people on the edge. A lot of the characters in the series are,
> themselves, deal[ing] with issues like obsession and feelings of hopeless-
> ness and people reading could identify with that. Unlike vampires, were-
> wolves, ect [*sic*], those deal with giving power to the afflicted in exchange
> for humanity. A lot of Slender Man stuff is the opposite, it's more like a
> sickness that wears the characters down, isolates them. In some of the
> series the characters with the most severe mental issues seem to summon
> or attract Slender Man making things worse for them but also causing
> chaos for those around them. I guess that would be a kind of power to
> inflict some of the pain they are feeling onto those around them. So while
> I agree that if it wasn't Slender Man it would be something else, I can also
> see why Slender Man might be appealing to those suffering from issues
> that make them feel powerless or hopeless.

While not all users agreed that the attacks were "inevitable," several
focused on mental health as a major issue, and some advocated for greater
awareness and sympathy toward people suffering from mental illness. Others
called for increased parental involvement and supervision of Internet use.
There was concern among some forum users about the negative impact the
subsequent events would have on the Mythos, but this was countered by the
emerging discourses of mental health and parental supervision.
    These are sophisticated responses, revealing both forum users' deep
attachment to the Mythos and their awareness of the important social
issues raised by the Waukesha attack and events following it. But importantly, belief is linked, in these responses as well as in the media treatment

of the case, to mental illness and immaturity. On one level this is appropriate enough, as in all but one instance the alleged perpetrators of the violent acts were minors. Further, as we've seen, Slender Man is generally known to be a fiction—unlike, for instance, Satanic cults, the real existence of which is doubtful but which have been surrounded at various points by an atmosphere of belief. But the relationship of fiction to fact is complex, and not only for children. In a study examining how readers process information from fictional sources, psychologists Deborah Prentice and Richard Gerrig write: "We contend that in many or perhaps most of their experiences with fiction, readers assume that authors are attempting to represent real life. The plot of the story may be fictional, and the characters and events may be fabricated, but basic facts about the world should remain true. Thus readers may be vulnerable to fictional information because they have (misplaced) faith in the truth standard to which authors subscribe. Even though a novel is fictional, they may assume that there is no reason to doubt its general assertions about the world" (Prentice and Gerrig 1999, 531).[18]

According to Prentice and Gerrig, the belief that fiction can engender in readers is caused by their unwillingness or inability to critically consider the fictional text. They developed their theory in a series of experiments, each of which involved presenting groups of students with short narratives. The narratives all included various truth claims, some matching real-world facts, some not. In all cases they found that readers "do incorporate fictional information into their real-world knowledge structures, but selectively, with an eye to its potential value for expanding their knowledge base. Compared to fact, fiction seems to be approached with greater credulity and greater abandon, but also with greater selectivity" (Prentice and Gerrig 1999, 542).

One particularly compelling argument Prentice and Gerrig advance is the suggestion that information embedded in narratives labeled as fiction may be more persuasive precisely because, as fiction, these narratives are not subjected to the same critical scrutiny by readers as presumably factual statements (Prentice and Gerrig 1999, 539–540). Moreover, they argue that readers engage actively in narratives by identifying with characters or puzzling out details of the plot; and the more readers engage in these types of activities, the more likely they are to accept the truth claims a narrative makes (543–544). This would seem to suggest that all audiences, regardless of age or mental health, are capable of mistaking fiction for fact—indeed, that this is a relatively normal part of engaging with fiction. It is clear how, in the case of a multimedia, multigenre, participatory phenomenon such as Slender Man, which in some manifestations masquerades as "real" folklore and which deliberately plays with the boundaries between "real" and "fictional" worlds, the potential for believing the fiction increases considerably over "normal" fictional texts.[19] And as media scholar Marjorie Kibby has pointed out, "With computer transmitted stories, the computer screen itself lends instant credibility. There is a lingering perception of the computer's accuracy and a conviction that computers do not make mistakes" (Kibby 2005, 764).

That some individuals incorporate fictional information with less selectivity than in the examples described by Prentice and Gerrig reminds us that age and mental health are important factors in cases like the Waukesha attack, precisely as forum users emphasized. More generally, the situation also calls our attention to the fact that belief in fictional narratives is not as outlandish as it may at first appear. Countering the narrative of deviance can help us avoid the mistake of making a "folk devil"—"a visible reminder of what we should not be"—out of Slender Man or the troubled children who committed violence in his name (Cohen 2011, 2).

CONCLUSION: EMERGING INTO REALITY

Michael Saler (2012) has discussed the capacity of certain works of fiction to effectively transcend their own fictionality, to create imaginary worlds that become, through deliberate inhabitation by their audiences, virtual worlds (4–5). Although Saler is generally optimistic about the creative and critical capacities of these other-than-real worlds, he acknowledges that "imaginary worlds can still become confused with reality when the protections of the ironic imagination are undercut—not only by the desires these worlds fulfill, but also by the security they provide. Unlike the messy contingencies of ordinary experience, imaginary worlds, for all their exoticism, are manageable and safe, appealing sanctuaries from life's uncertainties" (51). Belief is central in the processes Saler outlines, and he distinguishes between "naïve" and "ironic" believers. Naïve believers, in his usage, are those who take fictional worlds, as it were, at face value, accepting them as literally true. Ironic believers, conversely, are those who merely *pretend* to believe—though their pretense may be extremely convincing, as in the case of the Sherlock Holmes fans Saler discusses (113–116).

The Slender Man Mythos unquestionably functions as a virtual world in Saler's sense: it is a fictional universe that countless individuals from around the world have chosen to both inhabit and build upon through creative contributions in the form of videos, games, and written narratives. The overwhelming majority of these contributors and participants also exhibit what Saler would term ironic belief: they know that Slender Man is a fiction, but winkingly create media that pretend otherwise. But as we have seen, not all responses to fictional media are ironic. Despite this, it seems overly reductive to label audience belief in the fictional media considered here—the Slender Man Mythos, *The Blair Witch Project*, *Ghostwatch*, and the rest—as simply naïve. These media exhibit a similar verisimilitude, a characteristic and calculated "realness" that breaks the so-called fourth wall of conventional fiction and enables audiences to become participants. All have also been accompanied by varying degrees of belief on the part of their audiences.[20]

But again, a startling difference is that Slender Man, as a massively participatory online phenomenon, has almost from the moment of his creation been entirely open to dissection and scrutiny by anyone with Internet access.[21] Whereas the more or less straightforward video/audio texts of the other examples are essentially self-contained, inviting testing and criticism only outside their diegetic frames, Slender Man is wholly visible, the monster's entire history laid out for public perusal. The same forums that gave rise to the Slender Man meme criticized and encouraged various aspects of its creation: thus its fictive status was expressed in the same metaphorical breath as the narrative fragments that suggested its reality. And as Slender Man is a monster that resides wholly on the Internet, it seems inevitable that Slender Man's unreality would be discovered almost immediately, as a result of the same search terms that revealed its existence in the first place.

But as an exemplar of the communal processes that constitute what Robert Glenn Howard (2005, 2008, 2009) calls the *vernacular web*, Slender Man is a powerful symbol available for deployment in a wide range of contexts. The participatory nature of the vernacular web amplifies the persuasive power of fictional texts: bombarded with information, much of it presented as truth, readers are left to their own devices to determine what is "real" and what is not. And as Prentice and Gerrig (1999) have shown, distinguishing between fiction and fact is not as straightforward a process as it may seem at first. (The popularity of the website Snopes.com, which seeks to prove or disprove the reality of contemporary legends, chain emails, and other folklore genres, is evidence of the continuing persuasive force of Internet texts.) So perhaps the fictional status of the monster is less obvious than it appears.[22] In a June 2014 article for *Salon*, Andrew O'Hehir wrote:

> Go to absolutely any homemade YouTube video that claims to prove the existence of Slenderman (some of which are highly entertaining) and scan the user comments. (Or start typing "Is Slenderman real" in a search bar.) Without even trying, you'll encounter confused young people by the score, inquiring anxiously whether Slendy really exists or being successfully

trolled by other people's stories about a friend's cousin's classmate who read too much Internet Slendermania—ingeniously, that's how he gets a fix on you—and then disappeared. In a culture where people believe in angels and aliens, believe that 9/11 was an inside job and Sandy Hook a hoax, believe that Barack Hussein Obama is a Muslim socialist, why should 12-year-olds not believe in a rubber-faced, baby-eating monster who looks like a cross between Cthulhu and the villain of an Occupy Wall Street comic book? (When I was that age, my friends and I spent our lunch hours discussing what we would do after we found a portal into Narnia.)

Another reason for this confusion may be the Mythos's overt attempt to mimic "traditional" folklore, as already discussed. In adopting the trappings of legend, the Mythos's creators imbued it with an additional layer of authority. Individual narratives within the Mythos are not only making a kind of truth claim: they are also (supposedly) backed up by many similar experiences, spread through time and space, attested in the folklore record as (fictional) legends and personal experience narratives. It is this folkloresque quality, the strategic appeal to real-world folklore, that makes the Slender Man meme especially participatory, uniquely available for direct experience in numerous forms.

In my previous study of Slender Man I argued, "Reverse ostension is . . . an act of reverse engineering: *an effort to arrive back at the sign*, that is, to create a narrative tradition by correlating and connecting fragmentary narratives (themselves representations of experience, albeit fictional ones)" (Tolbert, chapter 1 in this volume). Following John McDowell (1982, 122), this argument presupposes that traditional narratives have an experiential core: that they relate events supposed to have taken place. Ostensive acts in turn assume that these experiences, or variations or continuations of them, can be repeated; as Kinsella (2011) notes, such ostensive engagement with legend texts can loop back into the legend itself. He coins the term *legend ecologies* to refer to "the interactions between legends, legend-telling situations and communities, the material means and technologies of communication, and the environments throughout which legends circulate" as well as to intertextual connections and debates about legends' veracity by the legend tellers themselves (5).

The idea of legend ecologies is a particularly useful formulation not only in that it calls our attention to the contexts in which legends appear and through which they are communicated, but in that it points to the larger-scale, macro process of "legending" itself, involving not only the creation and performance of individual texts but the elaborate construction of entire legend-oriented communities.[23] The Slender Man Mythos may be primarily a collection of "texts," but the larger Slender Man community constitutes a network of individuals and groups involved in creating and commenting on those texts; thus the "ecology" of Slender Man includes all of the various Internet-based forums and social networks dedicated to him and related phenomena, the individual texts and ARGs hosted on sites such as YouTube, and all of the communicative processes by which human actors tie these locations and texts together. It also includes the violent acts done in Slender Man's name: as O'Hehir observed, "The pathetic notion that those girls would prove their devotion to this imaginary evil god, or prove his existence to skeptics (as one suspect purportedly told the cops), by committing murder was, so to speak, their contribution to the Slenderman mythos" (O'Hehir 2014).

Folkloresque texts, then, can become a part of legend ecologies as surely as "real" folklore. The intertextual links that form between the new text and its real-world analogues may be one source of the potent rhetorical force such texts can muster. For example, the Blair Witch indexes real-world traditions of witches and their curses. *Ghostwatch* likewise echoes any number of haunted-house and poltergeist legends. These are what Michael Dylan Foster (2016b) calls "fuzzy allusions," a central characteristic of the folkloresque and, I suggest, a major reason for its discursive potency. And if the capacity of such texts to challenge the fiction/reality binary remains in doubt, another recent event may tip the scale toward belief: in early 2015 a British paranormal enthusiast linked several ghostly sightings in Staffordshire to Slender Man. Significantly, the sightings occurred in an area called Cannock Chase, a place associated with other supernatural legends as well (Cassady 2015). The fictional status of Slender Man seems lost in this account, but this is precisely the point: whether "real" or not, "believed" or not, the invocation of his name in this context connects this local, physical place and its preexisting legends with the largely digital, but increasingly corporeal, Slender Man Mythos.

The cycle by which folkloresque texts are reabsorbed into vernacular tradition seems to be greatly facilitated by ostensive engagement with the text in the real world.[24] This level of engagement represents the final removal of the apparent barrier between fiction and reality, and between the folkloresque—which begins life as a known product engineered by specific individuals to resemble existing traditions—and folklore.

ACKNOWLEDGMENTS

Many people contributed their time and energy to this chapter. Thanks to Chad Buterbaugh for calling my attention to the Wisconsin attack in the first place. As always, I appreciate Mitsuko Kawabata's comments on an early draft of this paper. Andrea Kitta provided helpful feedback and a much-needed dose of enthusiasm. Michael Dylan Foster also provided helpful comments and suggestions, and pointed me to Andrew O'Hehir's Salon.com article. Bill Ellis and Diane Goldstein independently provided insights into the potential connections between the Slender Man Mythos and real-world violence. Mary Ellen Cadman offered comments, patiently discussed ideas about mental health and supernatural belief, and provided important contextual information. John Bodner deserves special recognition for organizing the public talk in Newfoundland at which I and several other contributors to this volume presented our ideas about Slender Man. Trevor J. Blank and Lynne S. McNeill, the editors of this volume and the special issue on which it is based, were gloriously patient and stupendously helpful throughout the revising process. (Mistakes are, of course, my own.) Lastly, thanks to all the Slender Nation forum users who responded to my questions. Thanks especially to user timeobserver2013 for bringing several of the post-Waukesha incidents to my attention.

NOTES

1. Another part of the film's promotional campaign was the website www.blairwitch.com, which further blurred the fiction/reality border by fleshing out the Blair Witch legend and providing viewers access to fictional "official" documents about the missing filmmakers (Harris 2001, 77–78) This site has since been repurposed to promote the 2016 film *Blair Witch*.

2. For a thorough discussion of the film's truth claims and audience responses, see Harris (2001). See also Goldstein, Grider, and Thomas (2007, 217–219). For my own part, I can't say with any certainty just when I discovered the truth of the film's falsity, but I can say that this discovery in no way lessened my love of *The Blair Witch Project*.

3. Importantly, Hayes and Battles (2011) question the degree to which listeners panicked during the broadcast. In contrast to studies that emphasize listener panic, Hayes and Battles suggest "that the primary audience response was an effort at communication through social and technologically mediated networks. Listeners drew on these networks to interrogate the meaning of the broadcast, share information with others and consult authorities. In this way, they acted as participants in an increasingly interconnected world with multiple nodes of exchange and communication that, while highly centralized, still opened up spaces for public response and intervention" (53). Regardless of the extent of the "panic," the episode illustrates the potential for believable fictions to motivate real-world action and discourse.

4. Notably, Leeder also likens *Ghostwatch* to both *The Blair Witch Project* and the *War of the Worlds* broadcast as well as to contemporary ghost-hunting shows and other films in the found-footage genre.

5. Of course, I am not referring to the actual existence or nonexistence of these types of beings; I am indicating only that these particular works and the specific characters and creatures they contain are fictions.

6. On legends and believability, see Kinsella (2011, 60). On believability and Slender Man in particular, see Tolbert, chapter 1 of this volume. Andrea Kitta explores the ultimate effects of this process in her contribution to this volume, chapter 3.

7. Elsewhere I advance a similar argument in regard to popular treatments of supernatural belief (Tolbert n.d.).

8. Tim Evans (2014) made this point particularly well in a *New York Times* opinion piece. Media scholar Shira Chess argued a similar point in an interview with the *Washington Post* (Dewey 2014), as did the present author in an interview with a BBC reporter (Parkinson 2014).

9. "Real" in this case means, again, having actual traditional existence in real-world folk narratives. This is in contrast to "real" in the sense of the literal reality of the supernatural content of those legends, a shade of meaning that came into play after the creature's creation.

10. Many stories also focused on the recovery of the victim, who was later identified on an episode of the primetime current events program *20/20* (Effron and Robinson 2014).

11. It should be noted that Jack's alarmist tone did not go unnoticed by journalists. *Washington Post* writer Caitlin Dewey (2014) references Jack's "dark and wicked things" comment and argues, "The Internet, truth be told, has very little to do with it." Dewey goes on to claim that blaming the Internet masks real issues such as mental health and parental neglect. Abigail Jones (2014) of *Newsweek* likewise cites the melodramatic passage, suggesting, "Diluted advice to parents and ill-informed attempts at making sense of this case won't get us far. We do not know enough about the two girls' mental states, friendship, families and backgrounds to generalize about their motivations. And their act is so unusual that it tells us little about our daughters."

12. For a pertinent discussion of the broader moral panic surrounding girls' Internet use, see Cassell and Cramer 2008.

13. Though, as Cohen emphasizes, moral panics often do depend on the creation of fake, or at least greatly exaggerated, news accounts. Using the term *inventory* to refer to the media's portrayal of a given deviant individual or group (Cohen 2011, 24), Cohen notes that such portrayals often employ convenient fictions: "Built into the very nature of deviance, inventories in modern society are elements of fantasy, selective misperception and the deliberate creation of news. The inventory is not reflective stock-taking but manufactured news" (41).

14. The relationship between schizophrenia and supernatural belief seems to be well documented by psychologists. See Hergovich et al. 2008 for a review of the literature. Importantly, though, in a somewhat older study Williams and Irwin (1991) argue, "It is tentatively proposed that the endorsement of paranormal beliefs by believers is facilitated by an attempt to structure their world in terms of personally charged and somewhat magical notions of causality. While believers largely reject the notion of chance they do not necessarily 'misunderstand' the operation of randomness. Rather, believers may be exhibiting a distance from their causal ideas that is indicative of mature cognitive functioning; magical causal ideas may thus exist side by side with 'logic'. That is, the appeal to magical notions and their generalisation to paranormal belief systems might well represent a rational (if deviant) attempt to achieve a metacognitive understanding of the world" (1347). Notably, Anissa Weier—who was not diagnosed with schizophrenia—recanted her belief in the monster (Vielmetti 2015b, 2015c). For her part, Geyser's delusions were reduced after she received treatment for her condition (Vielmetti 2016).

15. Indeed, Ellis (1990, 32) elsewhere suggests that panics based on legends are themselves a form of ostension.

16. ARGs are complex game narratives that cut across multiple genres and media and typically require players to take some action in the "real" (nondigital) world (Kinsella 2011, 60–61; McNeill 2012, 88).

17. For more on ostension and its relevance to the Slender Man Mythos, see Andrew Peck's contribution to this volume, chapter 2.

18. But contrast with Currie (1995, 255–256).

19. Significantly, Prentice and Gerrig point out in a footnote that the fantasy genre may be particularly persuasive: "Note that the fantasy elements in children's stories like *Peter Pan* and *The Wizard of Oz* increase their distance from real-world concerns even relative to other forms of fiction, and thus liberate viewers to indulge their emotional responses fully. We expect that animation functions similarly" (Prentice and Gerrig 1999, 544n5). It could be argued that Slender Man and similar supernatural-themed contemporary folklore likewise inspire a more emotional than logical response. On the potential of other forms of Internet folklore to erode the real/virtual or real/fictional distinction, see also Blank (2013, 47–50).

20. In this way they resemble the literary hoaxes by writers such as Edgar Allan Poe that Saler (2012: 61–62) discusses.

21. As Amanda Brennan rightly pointed out in her response to the original version of this chapter (Tolbert 2015), joining the Something Awful forums is not entirely free (Brennan 2015, 93). The onetime membership fee of $9.95 gives users basic access to post to the forums; higher fees unlock additional features (https://secure.somethingawful.com/products/register.php). However, as of this writing, the forums are available to read for free without registering an account, and the archived Create Paranormal Images thread is available to view without a fee or login of any kind (https://forums.somethingawful.com/showthread.php?threadid=3150591).

22. On the interplay of "reality" and "fiction" in scholarly (specifically, sociological) analysis, as well as in the context of schizophrenia and the emergence of the discipline of psychoanalysis, see Gordon (2008, 36–41).

23. Julian Holloway describes a similar "doing of legend" in the context of ghost tours, during which "the affective milieu of the legend trip can assemble a sense of being engrossed in the supernatural possibility of the city" (Holloway 2010, 629).

24. For an example of this process, see Peretti 2016. Peretti discusses how the popular character Superman becomes folklore through fan engagement in such acts as joking and cosplay.

WORKS CITED

Barton, Gina. 2014. "12-Year-Old Stabbing Victim Released from Hospital." *Milwaukee Wisconsin Journal Sentinel*, June 6. http://www.jsonline.com/news/crime/12-year-old-stabbing-victim-released-from-hospital-b99286288z1-262188521.html.

Bennett, Sid, dir. 2012. *Mermaids: The Body Found*. TV movie. USA, Animal Planet. May 27.

Blank, Trevor J. 2013. *The Last Laugh: Folk Humor, Celebrity Culture, and Mass-Mediated Disasters in the Digital Age*. Madison: University of Wisconsin Press.

Brennan, Amanda. 2015. "Response: Slender Man as Meme Machine." *Contemporary Legend* 3 (5): 92–97.

Cassady, Leah. 2015. "Slender Man Spotted in Staffordshire." *Stoke Sentinel*, January 25. https://www.stokesentinel.co.uk/Slender-Man-spotted-Staffordshire/story-25920210-detail/story.html.

Cassell, Justine, and Meg Cramer. 2008. "High Tech or High Risk: Moral Panics about Girls Online." In *Digital Youth, Innovation, and the Unexpected*, ed. Tara McPherson, 57–76. Cambridge, MA: MIT Press.

Cohen, Stanley. 2011 (1972). *Folk Devils and Moral Panics*. London: Routledge.

Currie, Gregory. 1995. "The Moral Psychology of Fiction." *Australasian Journal of Philosophy* 73 (2): 250–259. https://doi.org/10.1080/00048409512346581.

Dégh, Linda. 1996. "What Is a Belief Legend?" *Folklore* 107 (1–2): 33–46. https://doi.org /10.1080/0015587X.1996.9715912.

Dewey, Caitlin. 2014. "Don't Fear the Slender Man." *Washington Post*, June 10. http://www .washingtonpost.com/news/the-intersect/wp/2014/06/10/dont-fear-the-slender -man/.

Effron, Lauren, and Kelley Robinson. 2014. "Out of the Woods." *ABC News*, September 26. http://abcnews.go.com/US/ slender-man-stabbing-survivors-parents-describe-horrific-ordeal/story?id=25787516.

Ellis, Bill. 1989. "Death by Folklore: Ostension, Contemporary Legend, and Murder." *Western Folklore* 48 (3): 201–220. https://doi.org/10.2307/1499739.

Ellis, Bill. 1990. "The Devil-Worshippers at the Prom: Rumor-Panic as Therapeutic Magic." *Western Folklore* 49 (1): 27–49. https://doi.org/10.2307/1499481.

Ellis, Bill. 1996. "Legend-Trips and Satanism: Adolescents' Ostensive Traditions as 'Cult' Activity." In *Contemporary Legend: A Reader*, ed. Gillian Bennett and Paul Smith, 167–186. New York: Taylor & Francis.

eudaemon. 2014. "Slender Man in the News—Page 2." Slendernation.forumotion.com, June 8. http://slendernation.forumotion.com/t4062p15-slender-man-in-the-news#85046.

Evans, Brad. 2014. "Hamilton Co. Mom: Daughter's Knife Attack Influenced by Slender Man." WLWT.com, June 6. http://www.wlwt.com/news/hamilton-co-mom-daugh ters-knife-attack-influenced-by-slender-man/26370588.

Evans, Timothy H. 2014. "The Ghosts in the Machine." *New York Times*, June 7. https://www .nytimes.com/2014/06/08/opinion/Sunday/the-ghosts-in-the-machine.html.

Fiore, Faye. 2010. "A Town's 'Blair Witch' Curse." *Los Angeles Times*, May 31. http://articles .latimes.com/2010/may/31/nation/la-na-blair-witch-20100601.

Foster, Michael Dylan. 2016a. "The Folkloresque Circle: Toward a Theory of Fuzzy Allusion." In *The Folkloresque: Reframing Folklore in a Popular Culture World*, ed. Michael Dylan Foster and Jeffrey A. Tolbert, 41–63. Logan: Utah State University Press. https://doi.org/10.7330/9781607324188.c001.

Foster, Michael Dylan. 2016b. "Introduction: The Challenge of the Folkloresque." In *The Folkloresque: Reframing Folklore in a Popular Culture World*, ed. Michael Dylan Foster and Jeffrey A. Tolbert, 3–33. Logan: Utah State University Press. https://doi.org/10 .7330/9781607324188.c000.

Gabler, Ellen. 2014. "Charges Detail Waukesha Pre-teens' Attempt to Kill Classmate." *Milwaukee Wisconsin Journal Sentinel*, June 2. http://www.jsonline.com/news/crime /waukesha-police-2-12-year-old-girls-plotted-for-months-to-kill-friend-b99282655z1 -261534171.html.

Goldstein, Diane, Sylvia Grider, and Jeannie B. Thomas. 2007. *Haunting Experiences: Ghosts in Contemporary Folklore*. Logan: Utah State University Press. https://doi.org/10 .2307/j.ctt4cgmqg.

Gordon, Avery F. 2008 (1997). *Ghostly Matters: Haunting and the Sociological Imagination*. 2nd ed. Minneapolis: University of Minnesota Press.

Harris, Martin. 2001. "The 'Witchcraft' of Media Manipulation: Pamela and *The Blair Witch Project*." *Journal of Popular Culture* 34 (4): 75–107. https://doi.org/10.1111/j.0022-38 40.2001.3404_75.x.

Hayes, Joy Elizabeth, and Kathleen Battles. 2011. "Exchange and Interconnection in US Network Radio: A Reinterpretation of the 1938 *War of the Worlds* Broadcast." *Radio Journal: International Studies in Broadcast & Audio Media* 9 (1): 51–62.

Hergovich, Andreas, Reinhard Schott, and Martin Arendasy. 2008. "On the Relationship between Paranormal Belief and Schizotypy among Adolescents." *Personality and Individual Differences* 45 (2): 119–125. https://doi.org/10.1016/j.paid.2008.03.005.

Heyer, Paul. 2003. "America under Attack I: A Reassessment of Orson Welles' 1938 *War of the Worlds* Broadcast." *Canadian Journal of Communication* 28 (2): 149–165.

Holloway, Julian. 2010. "Legend-Tripping in Spooky Spaces: Ghost Tourism and Infrastructures of Enchantment." *Environment and Planning. D, Society & Space* 28 (4): 618–637. https://doi.org/10.1068/d9909.

Howard, Robert Glenn. 2005. "Toward a Theory of the World Wide Web Vernacular: The Case for Pet Cloning." *Journal of Folklore Research* 42 (3): 323–360. https://doi.org/10.2979/JFR.2005.42.3.323.

Howard, Robert Glenn. 2008. "The Vernacular Web of Participatory Media." *Critical Studies in Media Communication* 25 (5): 490–513. https://doi.org/10.1080/15295030802468065.

Howard, Robert Glenn. 2009. "Crusading on the Vernacular Web: The Folk Beliefs and Practices of Online Spiritual Warfare." In *Folklore and the Internet: Vernacular Expression in a Digital World*, ed. Trevor J. Blank, 159–174. Logan: Utah State University Press. https://doi.org/10.2307/j.ctt4cgrx5.10.

Hufford, David. 1982. "Traditions of Disbelief." *New York Folklore* 8 (3): 47–55.

Jack, Russell P. 2014. "Waukesha Stabbing News Conference." Latimes.com, June 2. http://documents.latimes.com/waukesha-stabbing-news-conference/.

Jones, Abigail. 2014. "The Girls Who Tried to Kill for Slender Man." *Newsweek*, August 13. http://www.newsweek.com/2014/08/22/girls-who-tried-kill-slender-man-264218.html.

Kibby, Marjorie D. 2005. "Email Forwardables: Folklore in the Age of the Internet." *New Media & Society* 7 (6): 770–790. https://doi.org/10.1177/1461444805058161.

Kinsella, Michael. 2011. *Legend-Tripping Online: Supernatural Folklore and the Search for Ong's Hat*. Jackson: University Press of Mississippi. https://doi.org/10.14325/mississippi/9781604739831.001.0001.

Leeder, Murray. 2013. "*Ghostwatch* and the Haunting of Media." *Horror Studies* 4 (2): 173–186. https://doi.org/10.1386/host.4.2.173_1.

Magnus96. 2014. "Slender Man in the News—Page 2." Slendernation.forumotion.com, June 8. http://slendernation.forumotion.com/t4062p15-slender-man-in-the-news.

Manning, Lesley, dir. 1992. *Ghostwatch*. TV movie. UK, BBC1. October 31.

McDowell, John H. 1982. "Beyond Iconicity: Ostension in Kamsá Mythic Narrative." *Journal of the Folklore Institute* 19 (2–3): 119–139. https://doi.org/10.2307/3814009.

McNeill, Lynne S. 2012. "Real Virtuality: Enhancing Locality by Enacting the Small World Theory." In *Folk Culture in the Digital Age: The Emergent Dynamics of Human Interaction*, ed. Trevor J. Blank, 85–97. Logan: Utah State University Press. https://doi.org/10.7330/9780874218909.c04.

Murray, Rheana. 2014. "Faceless Slender Man Linked to More Slashings, Shootings." *ABC7 Eyewitness News*, June 9. http://abc7ny.com/news/faceless-slender-man-linked-to-more-slashings-shootings-/104215/.

Myrick, Daniel, and Eduardo Sánchez, dirs. 1999a. *The Blair Witch Project*. Motion picture. Lionsgate.

Myrick, Daniel, and Eduardo Sánchez, dirs. 1999b. *Curse of the Blair Witch*. TV documentary. USA, Sci-Fi Network. July 11.

National Oceanic and Atmospheric Administration. 2012. "Are Mermaids Real? No Evidence of Aquatic Humanoids Has Ever Been Found." June 27. https://oceanservice.noaa.gov/facts/mermaids.html.

NearTheEnd. 2014. "Re: Slender Man in the News." Slendernation.forumotion.com, June 7. http://slendernation.forumotion.com/t4062-slender-man-in-the-news.

O'Hehir, Andrew. 2014. "Slenderman: Nightmarish Info-Demon or Misunderstood Cultural Icon?" Salon.com, June 7. https://www.salon.com/2014/06/07/slenderman _nightmarish_info_demon_or_misunderstood_cultural_icon/.

Oremus, Will. 2012. "Federal Agency Wades into Mermaid Debate." *Slate*, July 2. http://www.slate.com/blogs/future_tense/2012/07/02/mermaids_the_body _found_government_agency_noaa_debunks_animal_planet_show.html.

Orlando, Alex. 2014. "Deputies: Pasco Girl Who Set House on Fire Texted Mom an Apology." *Tampa Bay Times*, September 4. http://www.tampabay.com/news/public safety/missing-teen-found-unharmed-after-suspicious-home-fire-in-port-richey /2196079.

Parkinson, Justin. 2014. "The Origins of Slender Man." *BBC News*, June 11. http://www .bbc.com/news/magazine-27776894.

Peck, Andrew. 2015. "Tall, Dark, and Loathsome: The Emergence of a Legend Cycle in the Digital Age." *Journal of American Folklore* 128 (509): 333–348. https://doi .org/10.5406/jamerfolk.128.509.0333.

Peretti, Daniel. 2016. "Comics as Folklore: Various Perspectives." In *The Folkloresque: Reframing Folklore in a Popular Culture World*, ed. Michael Dylan Foster and Jeffrey A. Tolbert, 104–120. Logan: Utah State University Press.

Prentice, Deborah A., and Richard J. Gerrig. 1999. "Exploring the Boundary between Fiction and Reality." In *Dual-Process Theories in Social Psychology*, ed. Shelly Chaiken and Yaacov Trope, 529–546. New York: Guilford.

Raymond, Adam K. 2014. "Meet Slender Man, the Online Phantom That Inspired Attempted Murder." *Rolling Stone*, June 4. https://www.rollingstone.com/culture /news/meet-slender-man-the-online-phantom-that-inspired-attempted-murder -20140604.

Saler, Michael. 2012. *As If: Modern Enchantment and the Literary PreHistory of Virtual Reality*. New York: Oxford University Press.

Sloshedtrain. 2014. "Fiction, Reality, and You." Creepypasta Wiki, June 3. http://creepy pasta.wikia.com/wiki/User_blog:Sloshedtrain/Fiction,_Reality,_and_You.

Surge, Victor. 2009. "Create Paranormal Images." Something Awful Forums. http://for ums.somethingawful.com/showthread.php?threadid=3150591&userid=0&perpage =40&pagenumber=5.

The Angry Scholar. 2014. "Slender Man in the News." Slendernation.forumotion.com, June 6. http://slendernation.forumotion.com/t4062-slender-man-in-the-news.

Tolbert, Jeffrey A. 2015. "'Dark and Wicked Things': Slender Man, the Folkloresque, and the Implications of Belief." *Contemporary Legend Series* 3 (5): 38–61.

Tolbert, Jeffrey A. n.d. *Science, Pop Culture, and Belief: An Unnecessary Antipathy*. Unpublished manuscript, last modified April 1, 2015.

UncleDark. 2014. "Re: Slender Man in the News." Slendernation.forumotion.com, June 6. http://slendernation.forumotion.com/t4062-slender-man-in-the-news#85011.

Vielmetti, Bruce. 2014. "Judge Rules Girl Incompetent, for Now, in Slender Man Trial." *Milwaukee Wisconsin Journal Sentinel*, August 1. http://www.jsonline.com/news/crime /lawyer-for-girl-in-slenderman-case-wants-mental-reports-on-co-defendant-b99319 419z1-269441661.html.

Vielmetti, Bruce. 2015a. "Argues for Keeping Slender Man Case in Adult Court." *Milwaukee Wisconsin Journal Sentinel*, February 25. https://www.jsonline.com/news/crime /prosecutors-seek-to-deflect-move-of-slender-man-case-to-juvenile court-b9945 2024z1-294092321.html.

Vielmetti, Bruce. 2015b. "Expert: Slender Man Defendant Shows Low Risk of Future Crimes." *Milwaukee Wisconsin Journal Sentinel*, May 26. https://www.jsonline.com /news/crime/hearing-begins-on-whether-slender-man-case-belongs-in-juvenile -court-b99507326z1-305047971.html.

Vielmetti, Bruce. 2015c. "Girl Charged in 'Slender Man' Stabbing Isn't Getting Mental-Health Treatment." *Duluth News Tribune*, July 5. http://www.duluthnewstribune.com /news/3779782-girl-charged-slender-man-stabbing-isnt-getting-mental-health -treatment.

Vielmetti, Bruce. 2016. "Judge Denies Bail Reduction for Slender Man Defendants." *Milwaukee Wisconsin Journal Sentinel*, April 15. https://www.jsonline.com/news /waukesha/judge-denies-bail-reduction-for-slender-man-stabbing-defendants -b99707404z1-375855741.html.

Wallace, Kelly. 2014. "Slenderman Stabbing Case: When Can Kids Understand Reality vs. Fantasy?" *CNN*, June 5. http://www.cnn.com/2014/06/03/living/slenderman -stabbing-questions-for-parents/index.html.

Welles, Orson. dir. 1938. *The War of the Worlds*. Mercury Theatre on the Air, October 30. Radio drama. USA, CBS Radio Network. Internet Archive. https://archive.org /details/OrsonWellesMrBruns.

Williams, Leanne M., and Harvey J. Irwin. 1991. "A Study of Paranormal Belief, Magical Ideation as an Index of Schizotypy and Cognitive Style." *Personality and Individual Differences* 12 (12): 1339–1348. https://doi.org/10.1016/0191-8869(91)90210-3.

Chapter 5

The Emperor's New Lore; or, Who Believes in the Big Bad Slender Man?

Mikel J. Koven

THE 2015 PUBLICATION OF *CONTEMPORARY LEGEND*'S special issue on Slender Man brought forth excellent scholarship and persuasive arguments regarding the figure of Slender Man in contemporary legendry, and most of these essays have been revised and are reprinted in the current volume. Along with Chess and Newsom (2015), the essays in the special issue are a central source of scholarly discourse on Slender Man in general, and Slender Man's connection with contemporary legendry and folkloristics specifically. The problem for me is that the evidence presented does not sufficiently engage in the discursive possibilities surrounding belief that are essential to the legend's core (Koven 2015). Slender Man was a consciously fictional construct (in 2009) that sparked a fire of collaborative texts (in creepypastas, photoshopped images, videos and computer games, to name just a few). More distressing is the Waukesha stabbing incident (covered in this current volume), clearly a classic ostension scenario. Slender Man is certainly a figure folklorists are in a key position to study; however, as I discuss below, I am not convinced that it is accurate to label Slender Man and the stories featuring him as contemporary legends. To be sure, legends can be—indeed, *have* been—told regarding the effects of reading Slender Man stories and creepypastas, but this suggests less a belief *in* Slender Man than it does a belief in the media effects and moral panics that surround the spooky figure.

DOI: 10.7330/9781607327813.c005

I WANT TO BELIEVE IN SLENDER MAN:
A SLENDER MAN SURVEY

It is entirely feasible that belief in Slender Man completely passed me by due to age and/or geography. I was in my forties when Slender Man first came on the scene, and I do not tend to read creepypastas or watch videos on YouTube; I tend to find out "what's cool" from either my students or my kids. And what grabs the imagination of children in North America does not necessarily interest British kids. I do not recall the first time I heard about Slender Man, but it was probably from folklorist colleagues in the U.S. who were all abuzz with this particular bogey. Despite being a film academic who specializes in horror movies, or maybe because of this awareness and genre familiarity, I've always found Slender Man to be a rather clumsy construction. I can appreciate a certain uncanniness of Slender Man as a strange figure lurking in the background of photographs, but as the character developed (and grew tentacles!), he became less and less credible for me. The development of the Slender Man Mythos seemed to become more and more absurd, thereby diminishing any credibility or veracity in the monster; this, in turn, diminished any believability in the figure *as a legend*. But just because *I* do not get Slender Man does not mean there are not others for whom Slender Man might be a very real, and very frightening, figure.

In order to understand who might believe in Slender Man, I decided to undertake an informal survey of the key age demographic using the Survey Monkey website. The design of the survey was to be direct, and my questions were to the point:

- Have you ever heard of Slender Man, and if so, what do you know about him?
- Have you ever seen Slender Man, or know someone who has? If so, what happened?
- Do you believe in Slender Man?
- How old are you now, and how old were you when you first heard about Slender Man?
- What general region do you live in (not actual address, but town/county as relevant)?

These last two questions are obviously demographic. Using Facebook, I disseminated the survey to people in certain categories: high school teachers, parents of high schoolers, and high school kids themselves (the children of friends and family members). I tried to cast my net as wide as possible, eliciting responses from across the United Kingdom. Many of the replies I received were from teenagers—which was unsurprising, as I had coerced my son into getting as many of his friends to reply as possible—but I also circulated the survey among my own university students. Overall, the completed survey sample is small (thirty-six completed surveys), but I think sufficient to demonstrate my point regarding belief in Slender Man.

Two samples are not included in these findings: they were "failed" results. These were negative results that yielded no usable data, as noted below. Nonetheless, they were significant in themselves. One teenage respondent in Scotland sent me a message simply saying that neither she nor any of her friends had ever heard of Slender Man or knew anything about him, period. A second sample, from Wales, was stymied from the beginning: I sent the survey to a personal friend who is head of the English department at a high school in Wales. She needed to run the project past her head teacher (principal) for permission to circulate the survey among her students. She was denied permission because of fears that asking *about* Slender Man might give students nightmares and "post-traumatic stress," which the school would not take responsibility for.[1]

The following results are from completed surveys. To begin with, I asked respondents what they knew about Slender Man, assessing their general knowledge of the figure. The question (like all the questions in this survey) was followed by a text box wherein respondents could answer as little or as much as they liked, without prompting from me and with no limits or constrictions on what their answer could include. Seventeen percent of respondents either knew nothing about Slender Man or their answers were too vague to be useful. I have divided the remainder of the responses into three categories: descriptions of Slender Man, his actions, and the sources respondents indicated for this information. Individual respondents were not restricted to the amount of information they could include, so frequently their answers included attributes that fall into more than one category.

In terms of a general description of Slender Man, 42 percent identified the figure as tall, frequently without a face (31 percent). Slender Man was described as wearing a suit (22 percent) and having either very long arms or tentacles (22 percent). Only four people mentioned that he is thin (surely the clue is in his name), and one person said Slender Man is bald. Of those responses that discussed what Slender Man actually *does*, 33 percent said he lurks in the woods and 19 percent said he abducts children. Three people mentioned he chases people, with two saying he causes either paralysis or death. Significantly, only one person stated that he appears in photographs.

It is the third category, the sources of respondents' knowledge, that is most suggestive of belief in Slender Man. Of those who commented where they heard about Slender Man, 36 percent identified Slender Man as fictional, with 25 percent of the entire sample identifying him as a character from a computer game. Only 8 percent identified Slender Man as coming from a "creepypasta," and 8 percent mentioned the Marble Hornets films. One person noted the source of his or her information as the Waukesha stabbing incident. So, we can suggest that there is certain consistency in the description of Slender Man (tall, no face, wears a suit, and has long arms or tentacles) and consistency in his activities (lurks in the woods and sometimes abducts children). It is the source of general knowledge about Slender Man that strikes me as most significant: namely, the recognition that he is an entirely fictional character, with most respondents citing the Slender Man computer games as where they knew him from.

I asked specifically about any respondent experiences with Slender Man or knowledge of anyone who had had such experiences. In hindsight, given the responses discussed above, the question was a poor one; but of course, I did not predict such an overwhelming *disbelief* in the story. Fully 97 percent of survey respondents have not encountered Slender Man, nor do they know anyone who has. Once respondent answered sarcastically, "Yes, he killed me." Other responses mentioned encounters *in* the video games or via cosplay. One respondent identified the "encounter" as being via the news regarding the Waukesha case. Again, these responses support the point made previously about *disbelief* in Slender Man, or at least belief in the character *as* a fictional character.

The straightforward question regarding belief in Slender Man had, I think, some of the most revealing responses. Of the respondents, 78 percent said they did not believe in Slender Man (one noted dismissively, "I'm not 12"). Three said they did believe in Slender Man, and two said they weren't sure. However, I do not propose that these last statistics are evidence of belief *in* Slender Man; I would suggest instead that these exceptions to disbelief are due to respondents assuming a mantle of agnosticism in order to be helpful to the survey collector. The same holds for those who claimed belief in Slender Man: it is likely that they were either trying to be helpful or their answers were sarcastic (as is typical of teenagers); these suppositions are supported by the qualitative analysis of responses as illustrated below.

It is the respondents' qualitative rather than quantitative comments in this regard that are most significant. One noted, "I've never seen him, but I've never seen a million pounds [£1,000,000] either, but it still exists. So I don't see why not." It is difficult to ascertain the sincerity of the agnosticism in this answer: is the person suggesting that Slender Man *might* exist? The answers of those who denied Slender Man's existence are more concrete: "No, he's a computer game." Another person wrote: "I have never considered Slender Man to be anything other than a collective work of fiction," therein identifying, in the Slender Man Mythos, the collective and collaborative authorship of the stories. One last example is certainly the most explicit: "I personally would like to believe in Slender Man as I think it's a very traumatising, but interesting, subject. However, as he was created in 2009 by a guy called Eric Knudsen doesn't help anyone believing he is legitimate." This last comment explicitly notes an awareness of the fictionality of Slender Man, and also of the history of the figure's creation, including referencing Knudsen's *real* name, rather than his nom de plume, Victor Surge. These responses suggest that Slender Man is understood as a multimedia (and multitext) construction by the audience, who believes in him not as real, per se, but as having an independent existence outside of these fictional texts—that is, Slender Man as meme, as discussed below (in creepypastas, YouTube videos, and computer games).

The demographic question about age—how old the respondents were at the time of the survey and how old they were when they first heard about Slender Man—enabled me to see when the stories were in actual circulation. I divided the respondents into age categories: 19 percent were currently high school age (fourteen to seventeen), and 58 percent were university age (eighteen to twenty-two). Four respondents were over twenty-two at the time of responding, and two were under fourteen. Two respondents didn't answer the question.[2] In asking how old respondents were when they first heard about Slender Man, I tried to keep the age divisions comparable: 14 percent first heard the story while in university (aged eighteen to twenty-two) and 36 percent while in high school. Twenty-five percent of respondents said they were between the ages of ten and fourteen, which in the UK means middle school or the early years of high school. Seventeen percent did not (or could not) answer the question. Approximately, then, the year in which the respondents heard about Slender Man was between 2013 and 2014 for 25 percent, and 50 percent heard about him between 2010 and 2012. I think we can conclude from these ages and dates that respondents consistently heard about Slender Man during the period of peak creative output, starting in 2009 with the first photos by Knudsen and the first Marble Hornets videos, and then another period beginning in 2012, coinciding with the release of the computer games. In both cases, respondents were in high school or middle school (or the lower grades at British high schools). The comment I quoted earlier about disbelief in Slender Man because the respondent was not twelve years old has a historical as well as a developmental significance: there may have been some initial belief in the veracity of Slender Man among the younger "kids," but popular culture oversaturation as well as the high rates of pop cultural literacy in teenagers quickly dispels that belief.[3]

"I'M NOT 12": SLENDER MAN AND BELIEVABILITY

As Linda Dégh has noted on numerous occasions, "Belief is inherent in all legends. In fact, legend contextualizes and interprets belief" (Dégh 1996, 34).[4] While I fully accept Slender Man's attraction for folklorists, particularly for the phenomenon's "transmedia storytelling" (Chess and Newsom 2015, 16) and the collaborative context of the "digital campfire" (78), the Slender Man narratives are not, in and of themselves, legendary without a much stronger belief discourse. As folk narrative scholars, if we cannot study these narratives and elicit from them the belief discourse of those who write and circulate them, "legend" appears to be the wrong genre in which to study this phenomenon. As Dégh noted, "Any legend researcher needs to focus on the attitude towards belief expressed by individual participants in the legend process to gain insight into the dialectics by means of which believability, the purpose of any legend communication, are debated" (38). As my small survey suggests, despite awareness and knowledge of the Slender Man Mythos, little actual belief in the ghostly figure exists. Without something to believe in, at their core, the Slender Man stories are meaning-*less*. Belief is, according to Dégh, "the *raison d'être* of the legend as a genre" (44). It simply needs to be there in the mix.

Where the discussion of belief in these stories becomes muddied is in regard to the Waukesha stabbing incident. Peck (2015)[5] makes clear distinctions between the awareness that Slender Man is an entirely fictional construct (not "based on a true story") and the two girls who are accused of stabbing a third in order to become Slender Man "proxies" as an example of ostension; in other words, the stabbing is true, although the reality of Slender Man (allegedly, the motive for the assault) is not.

Any credulity attached to the Slender Man Mythos is due to the stories, videos, and photographs providing the *appearance* of reality; the Slender Man game (of engaging with the Mythos) is intended to be as believable as possible. The (highly problematic) "realness" of Slender Man is in the phenomenon's verisimilitude; it is presented as if it *were* real. David Morrish (2015) notes:

> Even though we can critique an image and come to terms with its probable falseness, we often appreciate its sense of realism and suspend our disbelief with a sense of glee. We often like to be fooled in the same way

we like to be frightened by a horror film, knowing full well it is only a movie. Many want to participate in this game further and create their own narratives. This enters the realm of playful co-creation where images are passed on, altered, . . . reconstructed, recreated, and re-contextualized within a circuit of sharers who ostensibly all know the game and its rules. The narratives are used to heighten the veracity of an image and vice versa. However, when the "fictional" context or "storytelling" intent is not attached to a circulating image, it can be misinterpreted as a document of truth or *something like the truth*. This process seems to especially describe the formation and spread of the Slender Man mythos, but is not restricted to that. Visual artists have often used images and fictional narratives to create artwork that transports a viewer into a world where the borders between fiction and reality are blurred. (87)[6]

Likewise, Tolbert (2015) picks up on how the Slender Man artists aim for maximum veracity by drawing upon other folkloric and popular culture forms, what Michael Dylan Foster calls "fuzzy allusions" (see Foster and Tolbert 2016), that is, vague references to other pop culture sources. For example, Shira Chess and Eric Newsom identify that Victor Surge based the original Slender Man on the figure of the Tall Man (Angus Scrimm) from the *Phantasm* films (1979–2016), the Gentlemen from the episode "Hush" (4.10, 1999) of *Buffy the Vampire Slayer* (1997–2003), and Jack Skellington from *The Nightmare Before Christmas* (1993) (Chess and Newsom 2015, 66): a reasonably eclectic mix of references that Tolbert refers to as "an entertaining pastiche" (Tolbert 2015, 44). It is this very pastiche, however—which, as Morrish noted, is part of the "game" of catching all the fuzzy allusions— that underlines Slender Man's fictionality. The Slender Man narratives emerged just two years after the first of the *Paranormal Activity* (2007) films and coexisted alongside of the then-popular "found-footage" horror films (see Heller-Nicholas 2015). The verisimilitude with which these narratives are presented was simply, at least originally, the style du jour for horror narratives. To this end, Chess and Newsom note, "One of the most interesting subreddits for horror content is /r/nosleep, a subreddit not specifically dedicated to the Slender Man, but for horror fiction in general (although the Slender Man occasionally makes an appearance in posts there). /r/nosleep rules of posting stipulate that participants treat everything as though it were real—posts are required to be written in the first person, as in 'this happened to me,' and must be at least marginally believable" (Chess and Newsom 2015, 105).

While Tolbert wants to call this an "atmosphere of belief" (Tolbert 2015, 40), it is more accurately what Paul Manning refers to as "faux-realist semiotics" (Manning 2015, 118): namely, that the legend-like (or memorate-like) properties of the Slender Man Mythos are affectations of style, not ideology (Dégh uses the term almost synonymously with *belief*). And these affectations are recognized and accepted by the group members who participate within this culture. What this affectation of style is *not*, however, is "a *possibility of belief* [in] Slender Man narratives" (Tolbert 2015, 40). Trevor J. Blank and Lynne S. McNeill, in their introduction to this volume, note explicitly that "the character [Slender Man] has moved also into the realm of *belief*"; but if we look at the actual narratives themselves, there is nothing to be *believed in*, beyond the explicit existence of Slender Man himself. And as indicated above, most of my survey responses *deny* any belief in the Mythos. However, by design, Slender Man is ill defined, and his motives are never fully understood; this is why he is, in the contemporary vernacular of those who engage with the Slender Man Mythos, "creepy as fuck." But "creepy as fuck" is an affectation, and succeeds only within the context of those who understand the codes of production.

For those who engage with Slender Man narratives, I would suggest, the issue is less about belief in the bogey than the pleasure of experiencing feelings of fear and terror in a (relatively) safe way. Slender Man stories (in whatever medium) are *ludic*; one *plays* with being frightened—it is not actual fear. I could further suggest that, again, for *some*, the line between play and real may become confused. However, and this reiterates my central idea here, the legend at the heart of the Slender Man stories is not about Slender Man but about *other people* confusing that line between play and reality. Alexandra Heller-Nicholas (2015), discussing found-footage horror movies, noted a similar dynamic: "Audiences now do not have to believe or even suspect a film is a genuine documentation of something that actually happened to be able to playfully enjoy *pretending* that it might be the case" (113). Seeing Slender Man narratives as ludic dispels the artificial binary between belief/disbelief; the experience of belief is more complicated and more fluid. Belief is ludic; instead of a "suspension of disbelief," perhaps we should refer to "playing with belief."

Since these cross-media narratives and fragment narratives *seem* real, due to the affectations I just discussed, therefore, for some people, Slender Man must *be* real. The Waukesha stabbing seems to confirm this belief. But let me be clear about how I am using "belief": I am not saying people *actually* believe in Slender Man but that, because Waukesha happened, *other people* must believe. The Waukesha incident is evidence that someone *must* believe it, because of the ostensive action that occurred. Such reasoning is cum hoc, ergo propter hoc; because Slender Man "*feels real*" (Kitta 2015,

65), it must be *believed in*. The suggestion here is that this affectation of style is assumed to be a validation of belief. And the assumption is that we must understand this belief, despite the "reality" of Slender Man being an illusion, as the by-product of the style. Andrea Kitta notes, "I am not arguing that Slender Man is 'real' or that those who have contributed to the Slender Man narrative think that he is real or have an experience with him. Rather, I think that there is a core spiritual experience here that connects with others—the feeling of being watched—that has been turned into a narrative about a specific entity since it was a convenient way to discuss an untellable experience" (65).

Kitta's argument about contemporary paranoia regarding the surveillance society—she specifically cites the NSA (Kitta 2015, 71)—or her suggestion that Slender Man is a metaphor for bullying, specifically cyberbullying (Kitta in Norman 2016), requires her to hypothesize about potential beliefs within the narratives. Slender Man's blank face becomes the canvas on which we are enabled to read what we like: including surveillance or cyberbullying. In this regard, to borrow from psychoanalysis, Slender Man becomes a fetish: like the child (in psychoanalytic models) who replaces the trauma of his mother's absent penis with an alternative figure that is less frightening (or at least more controllable), Slender Man is only a little scary, whereas the reality behind the figure—perhaps Kitta's surveillance or cyberbullying discourses—is much more terrifying (Aaron 2005, 213). And because those larger fears behind Slender Man are beyond the individual's control, that same hypothetical individual is able to engage in Slender Man play (returning to the ludic), exerting the necessary illusion of control via the fetishization of the bogey. As scholars, however, we need to be careful not to confuse the fetish with the fear itself. However, sometimes in cases of ostension, that confusion becomes altogether too real.

THE WAUKESHA STABBING AS MORAL PANIC

The facts in the case of the Waukesha stabbing are discussed in the introduction to this volume; here I want to consider the incident as inducing a moral panic, a hysteria that the media fanned in the wake of this tragedy. The moral panic, the fear that these Slender Man stories could provoke "real-world" action, is clearly an example of ostension, as Peck (2015) and Tolbert (2015) in particular discuss. Tolbert's "reverse ostension," wherein the narrative is produced in retrospect to the evidence (Tolbert 2015, 41), is apt.

Although the stabbing victim survived, the violence of the crime made headlines around the world, not least because one of the assailants had claimed, according to media reports, that she wanted to become one of Slender Man's "proxies." In an example of ostension, because of their encounters with the Slender Man Mythos, these two girls were "influenced" by the stories to conduct this horrific crime. While, as I have argued above, the Slender Man stories are not in themselves legendary, the Waukesha stabbing has the potential to be. The legend would run something along the lines of: "Slender Man stories are dangerous to read (let alone write), because they can make you go crazy and try to kill your best friends. I know it is true because I read it in the newspaper/heard it on television/read it online. It happened in Wisconsin, I think."

As Blank and McNeill note in the introduction to this volume, other Slender Man–inspired crimes occurred elsewhere in the United States (see also Peck 2015, 15; Tolbert 2015, 43; Kitta 2015, 72). The ostension lore about Slender Man inevitably mentions Waukesha, but also these other cases. Feeding into the legend matrix, as it were, the suggestion is that while the particular young assailants in Waukesha were diagnosed as insane (Tolbert 2015, 41), this is happening *everywhere*. "This" refers to violent incidents performed by (and on) "kids" directly as a result of reading Slender Man stories, a connection disseminated via the news media. The result was a full-blown moral panic about these very dangerous spooky stories available (to "kids") online. Here, then, is a legend narrative whose core belief is that exposing children to Slender Man stories will harm them psychologically. Kitta notes that not only can Slender Man be used to discuss "the motives of children and young adults who have engaged in violent acts," employing this legend narrative "symbolize[s] a fear of [the] Internet and technology by older adults or those who don't understand Internet usage" (Kitta 2015, 72). Let me be clear here: I am not suggesting that belief in Slender Man causes violence, but rather the belief that the Internet is full of stories/ideas that *could* corrupt the impressionable minds of young people. Slender Man is not the legend; stories *about* Slender Man are.[7] The difference here is between a belief that Slender Man has a real existence and a belief that *stories* about (the very fictional) Slender Man could cause psychological damage that might lead to physical violence. And that latter belief, prompted by the violence in Waukesha and disseminated by news media, caused a moral panic about Slender Man (Tolbert 2015, 44).

Stanley Cohen, in *Folk Devils and Moral Panics*, notes, "The media have long operated as agents of moral indignation in their own right: even if they are not self-consciously engaged in crusading or muck-raking, their very reporting of certain 'facts' can be sufficient to generate concern, anxiety, indignation or panic. When such feelings coincide with a perception that particular values need to be protected, the preconditions for new rule creation or social problem definition are present" (Cohen 2002, 7).

If it were not for the media reportage, the Waukesha stabbing would have been simply a local concern, perhaps disseminated in the context of extreme school bullying. But by making that connection with Slender Man, the story increased its newsworthiness and was circulated globally. Likewise with the other acts of alleged Slender Man–inspired violence. However, as Tolbert notes, Slender Man was not the only inspiration for the Waukesha violence: one of the attackers, subsequently diagnosed with schizophrenia, "believed she had real-life relationships with other fiction characters as well, including the *Harry Potter* antagonist Voldemort" (Tolbert 2015, 41). But the media reports that were most forwarded/ reprinted made the connection with Slender Man, not Voldemort. There was no cry about banning *Harry Potter* because of the influence the story world's evil characters might have on severely disturbed children, at least not in reference to this case. It was the media that grabbed hold of the connection with Slender Man and exploited it for everything they could. The "facts" in the case are reported (and forwarded) not because they are true, but because they make cultural sense within an environment of fear regarding what children have access to online.

In this way, the moral panic about Slender Man reflects the cognitive, emotional, and moral expectations of the audience: it makes sense (for some) that the Internet is full of material that could severely damage impressionable minds, that such materials *out there* are frightening, and that the parents of those children "got what they deserved" for not paying more attention to what their kids were looking at and reading online (see Oring 2008, 157–158). *Here* is the belief at the core of the Slender Man legends: the existence of dangerous and/or psychologically damaging horror stories and images that children have unsupervised access to online. The fear is about media *effects*: the concern regarding what effect reading spooky stories online (unsupervised, unmediated, un*moderated*) might have on children (Hartley 2002, 81–83).

The moral panic about Slender Man has much in common with the moral panic regarding the movie *Child's Play III* (1991). It was proposed that exposure to this film caused Robert Thompson and Jon Venables, two ten-year-old boys, to abduct and beat to death two-year-old James Bulger in Liverpool, England, in 1993. It was widely reported in newspapers that this film had given Venables and Thompson the idea to murder a toddler (presumably as a Chucky substitute). The papers reported that the father of one of the killers had rented *Child's Play III* not long before the murder, thereby creating causation between the film and the crime. While there was never any evidence to support the contention that either of the boys had actually *watched* the film, merely its presence in the house was sufficient to cause the moral panic (Barker 1997, 12; also see Cohen 2002, ix–x). But the film and the murder were inextricably linked in the public's imagination. The moral panic that resulted was about what effects violent movies could have on children who could access these films unsupervised at home. Of course, there are many issues at work in this moral panic, as there are in the Slender Man panic; I merely wish to draw a parallel between these two cases *as* moral panics, to illustrate legend formation around media effects. *Child's Play III* and Slender Man are empty signifiers upon which we project our real fears (Manning 2015, 116); the real monsters are not the Chuckys or the Slendys, but those who make, and make *available*, this material, particularly to children.

CONCLUSIONS

We are, I am sure, more than familiar with the Hans Christian Andersen story "The Emperor's New Clothes." Folklorists, in particular legend scholars, have been very quick to hop on the Slender Man ghost train with both feet, declaring Slender Man *the* new contemporary legend of our age. Using the Andersen fairy tale as a metaphor, I feel a bit like the kid in the story pointing out that the emperor appears to be naked. Slender Man is not a legend, nor is he a legendary figure. There is no belief core in the Slender Man photoshops or creepypastas. And without that core, following Dégh, I have difficulty seeing Slender Man as legend.

Perhaps, as suggested by Chess and Newsom (2015), it is more appropriate to see Slender Man as an Internet meme. *Internet* memes are different from how other folklorists, specifically Jack Zipes (2006), have used the concept originally developed by Richard Dawkins (1976).[8] Internet memes are an appropriation "by Internet culture to similarly describe thoughts and ideas as they occur, are repurposed, changed, and distributed through online spaces" (Chess and Newsom 2015, 19). Chess and Newsom note, "The prevalence of meme culture has fostered the creation of ideas that are easily packaged and spread, which, in the case of Slender Man, helped the legend grow beyond its original author and supported the development of a collective voice capable of yielding an endless supply of variation" (18). While I may quibble over their use of the word *legend* in this context, their point is well taken. Slender Man is an idea: an idea that grabbed the imagination of a variety of creative individuals throughout the Internet who seized onto it, expanded it, developed it, and took it in new directions. But it is not, in itself, a legend.

However, denying Slender Man his role as legend does not mean he is an inappropriate topic for folklorists, specifically legend scholars, to examine. Slender Man's role in the 2013 Waukesha stabbing, as a textbook case of ostension, directly calls for folkloristic interventions. The moral panic spread by the news media created the legend. The fears are not regarding Slender Man himself (the figure is too patently absurd for that); the fears are about our children's susceptibility to this fictional bogeyman and the nefarious intentions of those who create the Slender Man Mythos. To again return to my title, wherein I asked, "Who believes in the big bad Slender Man?" the answer is "Not me!" But who knows what *others* get up to on the Internet?

NOTES

1. To use the contemporary vernacular, "I know, right?"

2. This observation coincides with the comment by Chess and Newsom: "In essence, these most popular of web series [Marble Hornets in particular] about Slender Man feature characters who are at the edge of adulthood yet not fully accepting of a grownup lifestyle. And in this denial or delay in adulthood, the looming presence of Slender Man, watching over them and waiting, seems to take on a new kind of potential eerie significance" (Chess and Newsom 2015, 51). Slender Man's signature suit may also signify adulthood and adult responsibilities that one tries to outrun, but ultimately cannot.

3. It may also be the case that belief in Slender Man is geographically based, and therefore belief outside the U.S. drops considerably. The work of other scholars in this current volume suggesting stronger belief in Slender Man may in part be due to the fact that their samples are American, while the majority of mine are British.

4. I am using Dégh 1996 as an illustrative example of her discussions of belief's role in legend narration; I could just as easily be citing Dégh 1971, Dégh and Vázsonyi 1971, or many others.

5. I cite many of the essays that first appeared in the special issue of *Contemporary Legend* Series 3, vol. 5 (2015). As noted above, this special issue, along with Chess and Newsom (2015), are the keystones of Slender Man scholarship to date, specifically with regards to legend and folkloristics. By necessity, I need to set up the existing scholarship, most of which appeared in that special issue, in order to make my points. Those essays are revised and reprinted in this current volume. However, I have chosen to cite the *Contemporary Legend* version of the papers.

6. Bernadette Flynn refers to this as a "playful, sometimes critical exploration of the *authentic-seeming*" (Flynn 2005, 130; emphasis added).

7. There is perhaps an appropriate parallel story here: actor Charlie Sheen thought *Flower of Flesh and Blood* (1985), a short film in which a man in a samurai costume slowly tortures, dismembers, and murders a young woman in a bizarre ritual, was an actual snuff film (a commercial film wherein the onscreen participant(s) are murdered in reality). The story of snuff movies circulated well in advance of screenwriter/director Hideshi Hino's film, going back at least as far as the mid-1970s. But it is the story of watching the film, not the film itself,

that is the focus of the narrative. Apparently Sheen was sufficiently credulous regarding the film's authenticity that he involved both the police and the FBI in investigating whether it was actually a snuff film. Returning to Slender Man, the stories are about others' beliefs in the figure, not the actual Slender Man texts themselves. And in a parallel to the Waukesha incident, Japanese serial killer Tsutomu Miyazaki re created *The Flower of Flesh and Blood* with at least one of his victims during his spree in the late 1980s as, I guess, an ostensive homage to Hino's film (Carter 2010, 304).

8. The original meme theory is closer to Dundes's (1971) "folk ideas" rather than applicable to Slender Man.

WORKS CITED

Aaron, Michele. 2005. "Looking On: Troubling Spectacles and the Complicitous Spectator." In *The Spectacle of the Real: From Hollywood to Reality TV and Beyond*, ed. Geoff King, 213–222. Bristol, UK: Intellect.

Barker, Martin. 1997. "Newson Report: A Case Study in 'Common Sense.'" In *Ill Effects: The Media/Violence Debate*, ed. Martin Barker and Julian Petley, 11–27. 2nd ed. London: Routledge. https://doi.org/10.4324/9780203465097.

Brennan, Amanda. 2015. "Slender Man as Meme Machine." *Contemporary Legend* 3 (5): 92–97.

Buffy, the Vampire Slayer. 1999. "Hush." Season 4, episode 10. US: Mutant Enemy.

Carter, David Ray. 2010. "It's Only a Movie? Reality as Transgression in Exlpoitation Cinema." In *From the Arthouse to the Grindhouse: Highbrow and Lowbrow Trangression in Cinema's First Century*, ed. John Cline and Robert G. Weiner, 297–315. Lanham, MD: Scarecrow.

Chess, Shira, and Eric Newsom. 2015. *Folklore, Horror Stories, and the Slender Man*. New York: Palgrave Macmillan. https://doi.org/10.1057/9781137491138.

Child's Play 3. 1991. Dir. Jack Bender. US: Universal Pictures.

Cohen, Stanley. 2002. *Folk Devils and Moral Panics: The Creation of the Mods and the Rockers*. 3rd ed. London: Routledge.

Dawkins, Richard. 1976. *The Selfish Gene*. Oxford: Oxford University Press.

Dégh, Linda. 1971. "The Belief Legend in Modern Society: Form, Function, and Relationship to Other Genres." In *American Folk Legend: A Symposium*, ed. Wayland D. Hand, 55–68. Berkeley: University of California Press.

Dégh, Linda. 1996. "What Is a Belief Legend?" *Folklore* 107 (1–2): 33–46. https://doi.org/10.1080/0015587X.1996.9715912.

Dégh, Linda, and Andrew Vázsonyi. 1971. "Legend and Belief." *Genre* (Los Angeles) 4:281–304.

Dundes, Alan. 1971. "Folk Ideas as Units of World View." *Journal of American Folklore* 84 (331): 93–103. https://doi.org/10.2307/539737.

Flower of Flesh and Blood (Giní piggu 2: Chiniku no hana). 1985. Dir. Hideshi Hino. JP: Sai Enterprise.

Flynn, Bernedette. 2005. "Docobricolage in the Age of Simulation." In *The Spectacle of the Real: From Hollywood to Reality TV and Beyond*, ed. Geoff King, 129–138. Bristol, UK: Intellect.

Foster, Michael Dylan, and Jeffrey A. Tolbert, eds. 2016. *Folkloresque: Reframing Folklore in a Popular Culture World*. Logan: Utah State University Press. https://doi.org/10.7330/9781607324188.

Hartley, John. 2002. *Communication, Cultural and Media Studies: The Key Concepts*. 3rd ed. London: Routledge. https://doi.org/10.4324/9780203449936.

Heller-Nicholas, Alexandra. 2015. *Found Footage Horror Films: Fear and the Appearance of Reality*. Jefferson, NC: McFarland.

Kitta, Andrea. 2015. "'What Happens When the Pictures Are No Longer Photoshops?' Slender Man, Belief, and the Unacknowledged Common Experience." *Contemporary Legend* 3 (5): 62–76.

Koven, Mikel J. 2015. "Slender Man: A Dissenting View." *Contemporary Legend* 3 (5): 105–111.

Manning, Paul. 2015. "Monstrous Media and Media Monsters." *Contemporary Legend* 3 (5): 112–123.

Morrish, David. 2015. "Interpreting Photographic Evidence." *Contemporary Legend* 3 (5): 77–91.

The Nightmare Before Christmas. 1993. Dir. Henry Selick. US: Touchstone Pictures.

Norman, Mark. 2016. "Episode 1: Slender Man." *The Folklore Podcast*, July 15. http://www.thefolklorepodcast.com.

Oring, Elliot. 2008. "Legendry and the Rhetoric of Truth." *Journal of American Folklore* 121 (480): 127–166. https://doi.org/10.1353/jaf.0.0008.

Paranormal Activity. 2007. Dir. Oren Peli. US: Blumhouse Productions.

Peck, Andrew. 2015. "At the Modems of Madness: The Slender Man, Ostension, and the Digital Age." *Contemporary Legend* 3 (5): 14–37.

Phantasm. 1979–2016. Dir. Don Coscarelli and David Hartman. US: various production companies.

Tolbert, Jeffrey A. 2015. "'Dark and Wicked Things': Slender Man, the Folkloresque, and the Implications of Belief." *Contemporary Legend* Series 3 (5): 38–61.

Zipes, Jack. 2006. *Why Fairy Tales Stick: The Evolution and Relevance of a Genre*. London: Routledge.

Chapter 6

Slender Man, H. P. Lovecraft, and the Dynamics of Horror Cultures

Timothy H. Evans

Slender Man began as a tall, faceless, and preternaturally slim human figure but rapidly acquired tentacles, a phenomenon reminiscent of (and probably inspired by) H. P. Lovecraft's extraterrestrial god Cthulhu (see Peck, chapter 2 in this volume). This connection led me to the idea of "horror cultures," participatory cultures surrounding specific bodies of horror narrative—not only Slender Man and Lovecraftian horror but Gothic novels, vampires, zombies, "slasher" narratives, and many others. This essay will examine horror cultures with reference especially to Lovecraftian horror and to Slender Man, and the correlations between them.

Slender Man is often described as an Internet legend. Unlike most narratives that are classified as legends, Slender Man has an identifiable creator. He also has an identifiable time and place of creation, although the place is in cyberspace.[1] As is true of many older webpages, the original Slender Man images can still be found on the Internet, which gives them a quality of timelessness and placelessness in relation to the material world. In addition, Slender Man is not in the public domain, although he is generally treated as though he were (Chess and Newsom 2015, 128). Slender Man certainly has characteristics of folklore, such as variation and often anonymity in specific texts and performances (generally through the use of Internet pseudonyms), and has characteristics of Internet folklore specifically—for example, visuality (Bronner 2009, 23; Howard 2015, 100). He also has many characteristics of what Michael Dylan Foster and others have called the folkloresque—that is, "popular culture's own (emic) performance of folklore" (Foster and Tolbert 2016, 5; Tolbert, chapter 4 of this volume). Whether he can be

DOI: 10.7330/9781607327813.c006

narrowly classified as folklore or as a legend is less important than whether he *seems* like folklore or like a legend within the community that participates in the narratives, beliefs, and images that surround him.

Another way to look at Slender Man (and at many similar examples of Internet culture) is that he is not easily classifiable as either folklore or popular culture—he is both, or at least has characteristics of both. He is passed on via anonymous Internet memes and in narratives on fanfic websites such as Creepypasta.com, but he also appears in video games and television shows. He is, perhaps, an example of a third, hybrid kind of culture, showing elements of both folklore and popular culture, and modes of transmission that differ from either or that blend the two together.

One way to think about Slender Man is to put him into the context of what might broadly be called horror culture. Horror cultures, participatory cultures that include media and fandom, have been around since well before the Internet (Manning, chapter 8 of this volume).[2] "Horror culture" encompasses not only fans of the horror genre but its creators, producers, scholars, and even, more peripherally, those who don't consider themselves fans but who have casual acquaintance with the genre, expressed in things like zombie memes and Halloween decorations that reference horror films. Horror culture includes not only literature, film, television, comics, video games, and the communities surrounding these, but the shared motifs, conventions, and structures of horror stories in any media form—what Trevor J. Blank has called "cultural inventories," a huge range of references drawn from all kinds of places, including folklore, popular culture, literature, and film (Blank 2013b, 6–7). Horror culture encompasses not only "serious" horror stories but parody and comedy that draw on horror narratives, visual props, and motifs.

Horror narratives and motifs are often manifested in what has been called "media narraforms." Sylvia Grider defines this term: "a symbiotic relationship between the media and oral tradition: the media provides the content, oral tradition provides the situations and format for the performances of these contemporary, hybrid narratives" (Grider 1981, 126). Media narraforms can be contrasted to their equally symbiotic opposites: media forms such as horror films or tabloids, wherein media provide the form and oral tradition provides the content. But it is more complicated than that: folklore and media, or folklore and popular culture, become so intertwined that they are hard to untangle. All of these are integral parts of horror cultures. Indeed, horror narratives present an unusually complicated interplay and interdependence of literature, film, popular culture of various kinds, folklore, and the folkloresque.

The Internet complicates things even more. An Internet legend such as Slender Man is performed digitally, created digitally (using digital tools such as Photoshop, YouTube, meme generators, and various digital media), and transmitted electronically, but it is deliberately fashioned to be folklore (a "textbook" example of the folkloresque). It gradually acquires a "mythos" to give it folkloric or folkloresque depth and significance as well as to mystify its origin, and it acquires folkloric qualities such as anonymity, variation, and an esoteric, generally playful folk group of Slender Man fans. Slender Man is surrounded by his own horror culture, which interacts, influences, and is influenced by other horror cultures.

As mentioned in the introduction to this book, attempts to give Slender Man a Mythos or an origin story have, for example, linked him to a supposed sixteenth-century German legend referred to as "The Great Man" or "The Tall Man," who is said to have haunted the Black Forest and abducted children, reminiscent of Goethe's "Erl-king." This particular variant of the narrative has been the basis of fanfic, visual memes, and YouTube films. Some variants have other historical settings—for example, the Civil War. This creation of a history or Mythos gives ammunition to those who would dispute the recent origins of Slender Man. Interestingly, his twentieth-century suit and tie is a constant in many of these, even in versions whose historical settings make it anachronistic. The (literally) faceless men-in-black quality of Slender Man seems to transcend the need for historical accuracy (Jones 2013).

In this case, the "cultural inventories" and "media narraforms" are part of the broader "horror culture"—or really, "horror cultures" (plural). Paul Manning argues in chapter 8 of this volume that "the connection between media form and the form of monster is an intimate, even constitutive, one"; a substitution of "horror culture" for "media form" in Manning's observation would also be true.

Horror cultures have existed, arguably, since the emergence of horror stories as a distinct genre of literary culture, at least with the culture of Gothic novels and their fans starting in the late eighteenth century. Gothic cultural inventories were created or drawn on in the works of such authors as Horace Walpole, Anne Radcliffe, Matthew Lewis, Edgar Allan Poe, Mary Shelley, and others. Gothic motifs included medieval castles and abbeys, malevolent noblemen, saintly heroines, evil monks, catacombs, cemeteries, ghosts, trap doors, hidden manuscripts, and a host of others. Gothic narratives also included conventions of plot and writing style (Joshi 2015; Lovecraft 2012). While these and other Gothic conventions have continued to run through horror culture in a variety of media (e.g., many of Roger

Corman's films or Guillermo del Toro's), such popular culture trends as the periodic popularity of vampires and zombies have their own sets of narratives, motifs, and visual images that are drawn on by popular culture but have corresponding lives in folklore, whether it be fan fiction and other aspects of fan culture, zombie walks, Halloween traditions, or many other examples. And of course, fan cultures have coalesced not only around vampires or zombies but around particular varieties of vampires or zombies— Anne Rice's vampires, for example, or the zombies from *The Walking Dead* comics or TV series.

Horror culture lends itself particularly well to what Linda Dégh and Andrew Vázsonyi referred to as "fictitious legends," meaning a literary creation presented as a legend and resembling or acting like a legend, but having no actual basis in oral tradition—again, a good example of the folkloresque. Their example is Bram Stoker's *Dracula*. But of course, whatever their origins (and many horror novels, films, comics, and so on do draw on and reshape oral tradition, often in complex ways), such "fictitious legends" take on a life of their own in a variety of media, including oral and Internet traditions (Dégh and Vázsonyi 1983, 25).

Andrew Peck refers to Slender Man as "a crowd-sourced Cthulhu" (Peck 2015, 337). The reference to Cthulhu, and by implication to Cthulhu's creator H. P. Lovecraft, is appropriate, and not just because both Slender Man and Cthulhu are depicted as humanoid figures with tentacles.[3] Lovecraft was an advocate for what he called weird fiction or the weird tale, a form that drew on the Gothic but differed from it. Lovecraft wrote (in a 1930 letter to his friend and colleague Clark Ashton Smith):

> The more I consider weird fiction, the more am I convinced that a solidly realistic framework is needed in order to build up a preparation for the unreal element . . . My own rule is that no weird story can truly produce terror unless it is devised with all the care and verisimilitude of an actual *hoax*. The author must forget all about "short story technique" and build up a stark, simple account, full of homely corroborative details, just as if he were trying to "put across" a deception in real life—a deception clever enough to make adults believe it. My own attitude in writing is always that of a hoax weaver . . . For the time being I try to forget formal literature, and simply devise a lie as carefully as a crooked witness prepares a line of testimony with cross-examining lawyers in his mind. (Lovecraft 1971, 193)

The irruption of the unreal into a strictly realistic setting is at the heart of the weird tale as conceived by Lovecraft, and, as Paul Manning points out in chapter 8, this is precisely what happens with Slender Man and indeed,

with much of creepypasta and Internet horror generally, although creators
of Internet horror have a range of media tools (Photoshop, for example)
that Lovecraft never imagined. In a weird tale, the narrative is successful if
readers are made to suspend disbelief through the accumulation of realistic detail. This is similar to what Jeffrey Tolbert, in reference to Slender
Man, refers to in chapter 1 of this book as "reverse ostension, using fabricated 'facts' to create a narrative where none previously existed." Ultimately,
the purpose is to go beyond the mere temporary suspension of disbelief
into the realm of legends, wherein belief and disbelief are in an ongoing
dialogue. This is what Lovecraft means by "an actual hoax." Cthulhu and
Slender Man both accumulate belief through this process. Lovecraft was
limited to words on a page, but the effectiveness of his creations led to the
development of an extraliterary and participatory horror culture. Slender
Man was built from the start using the inherently participatory tools of
digital technology and the Internet.

In his stories, Lovecraft created realistic settings through the pains-
taking accumulation of details. He drew on, among other things, current
and historical events (e.g., the New England earthquake of 1925 in "The
Call of Cthulhu," and the Vermont floods of 1927 in "The Whisperer in
Darkness"), detailed descriptions of architecture and setting (derived primarily from Lovecraft's extensive antiquarian travels and research), references
(both actual and invented) to scientific and other kinds of scholarly literature, and references to folk narratives and belief (both actual and invented).
Lovecraft had an informed layman's knowledge of much of the intellectual
landscape of his day, including folklore scholarship, and collected many folk
narratives and beliefs while on his travels, as well as borrowing them from
published folklore collections (Evans 2005; Joshi 2013).

Although he made extensive use of folklore in his writing, Lovecraft
was quite critical of those who simply used or valued folklore in literature
for its own sake, without reworking it. He advocated using "folk myths" to
create "new artificial myths," to use his terms (Lovecraft 1971, 293). The
most interesting thing about Lovecraft's use of folklore is not so much the
incorporation of actual items or texts from folklore into his stories but his
invention of tradition, his use of the structures, styles, and devices of folklore in ways that make his inventions seem like folklore. Or to put it another
way, Lovecraft uses texts that are not folklore (i.e., he created them), but
their structure or style builds on established patterns, they use traditional
motifs within an established narrative, or they incorporate believable contexts that give them an air of traditionality (Evans 2004, 2005). This is what
Michael Dylan Foster calls "fuzzy allusion"—"a whole new creation that

is not based on specific tradition but . . . alludes to folkloric elements in a generalized and imprecise way." It "smells of folklore" (Foster 2016, 46). Foster's definition can apply not only to Lovecraft but to Slender Man, and in fact to a great deal of horror fiction, film, and popular culture.

Lovecraft manufactured authenticity in his stories by creating "fictitious legends," to return to Dégh and Vázsonyi's (1983) term, but more than Bram Stoker, Lovecraft was quite self-conscious that he was inventing folklore, aware of the hoax-like quality of his creations. He created spurious books of occult lore and then cited them in faux scholarly articles, such as his 1927 "History of the Necronomicon"; he created genealogies and origin stories for his extraterrestrial gods and histories of his invented New England towns (Lovecraft 1995, 52–53). This influenced later writers who created similar fictional or "hoax" reference materials, from Jorge Luis Borges to Umberto Eco to Neil Gaiman to Mark Danielewski, but for Lovecraft it was all decidedly tongue in cheek.

Lovecraft's mythos was developed through what amounted to a game, a kind of playful interaction with his writer friends—Clark Ashton Smith, Robert E. Howard, Robert Bloch, and many others—in which they shared references to extraterrestrial gods, degenerate cultists, books of occult lore, decayed New England towns, and other elements (Joshi 2008). These became the motifs for Lovecraftian narratives, just as the decayed castles, evil monks, and the like were the motifs of Gothic fiction, but they were also in-jokes within Lovecraft's social group and among informed readers. For example, the authors' names invented by Lovecraft for his forbidden books were often variations of the names of friends—Klarkash-ton for Clark Ashton Smith, Comte d'Erlette for August Derleth, and others. Lovecraft referred to this process as "Yog-Sothothery" (another in-joke referring to one of his extraterrestrials).

Even the use of particular words such as *eldritch, squamous, blasphemous, fungoid, gibber,* and *tenebrious*—words that are both exotic and sensual in a grotesque way and have a quality of hybridity between categories of human and inhuman—became part of the game.[4] In other words, Lovecraftian writers shared elements not only of content but of style. They also shared elements of structure—typical Lovecraftian narrative plots often involve scientists or scholars (including folklorists) whose researches reveal the true nature of reality, driving them to madness, death, or transformation. Structure, style, and content are not really separable in a Lovecraft (or Lovecraftian) story. Generally, they start in an everyday world using straightforward language, and during the course of the story the world and the language both become more fantastic.

Words for Lovecraft have parallels in visuals for Slender Man. The sense of hybridity created by Lovecraft's language is created in the case of Slender Man by visual images and by the use of Photoshop and other technology in ways that hybridize the human (human body, hands, suit) and inhuman (tall, faceless, with tentacles), the everyday (playgrounds, yards, children) with the uncanny, otherworldly or liminal (forests, darkness, Slender Man's ability to appear and disappear instantaneously).

The eccentricity of Lovecraft's vocabulary is linked to his tendency to describe his horrors as indescribable, and to imply (and more than imply) that if we were able to fully perceive them, if we were able to understand the connections between the detailed, realistic fabric of his narratives, the unnerving alterity of his language, and the hybridity of his monsters, it would destroy our sense of reality and therefore our sanity. This is exemplified by the famous opening passage of "The Call of Cthulhu":

> The most merciful thing in the world, I think, is the inability of the human mind to correlate all its contents. We live on a placid island of ignorance in the midst of black seas of infinity, and it was not meant that we should voyage far. The sciences, each straining in its own direction, have hitherto harmed us little; but some day the piecing together of dissociated knowledge will open up such terrifying vistas of reality, and of our frightful position therein, that we shall either go mad from the revelation or flee from the deadly light into the peace and safety of a new dark age. (Lovecraft 1984, 125)

This quality of irreality, of finding the immaterial and uncanny in the everyday, is a link between Lovecraft's monsters and the monsters of the Internet. On the one hand, Internet monsters such as Slender Man share with many fan cultures (including Lovecraftian fan culture) the quality that Anthony Buccitelli described as "temporally extended digital performance"—that is, they are created and varied through interaction that is simultaneously a directly reactive conversation and extended over time and space (Buccitelli 2012, 76). In addition, Internet monsters exist in cyberspace and therefore in a realm that is related to everyday reality but is not everyday reality—a realm that challenges our notion of what is real. Trevor J. Blank refers to this as "the cognitive hybridization of reality . . . the dissolution of the need or ability to separate the material from the virtual" (Blank 2013a, 106, 108). In horror narratives, this dissolution may become a dissolution of sanity. Slender Man, like Cthulhu, can drive those who meet him insane (Chess and Newsom 2015, 31). Narratives about Slender Man, like those about Cthulhu and Lovecraft's other monsters, lead to the death, insanity, or transformation of the narrator. The line between insanity and transformation may itself be dissolved. Has the (unreliable) narrator become insane or accepted a new way of thinking that enables him or her to perceive new and different realities? This question is at the center of much of Lovecraft's fiction, especially his later work (Evans 2005). The transformation of Lovecraft's protagonists may be a degeneration into madness or it may be a cleansing of the doors of perception, to paraphrase Blake, an ability to perceive the universe (and humanity) in new ways.

The list of Lovecraft's favorite words includes *swarthy* and *mongrel*—clearly racially coded—as well as less clearly racial words such as *squamous* and *ichthyous*, which become racially coded when applied to groups of humans. Although racist images were widely used by the writers of pulp thrillers during Lovecraft's lifetime—as can be witnessed by even a cursory survey of popular fiction magazine covers—Lovecraft encoded such words and images into his mythos, creating themes of racial menace, sometimes rather straightforwardly but more commonly through themes of miscegenation and racial and cultural corruption presented through metaphors of extraterrestrial menace and material and mental decay (Evans 2005; Frye 2007). Lovecraft's evocation of fearful others is one thing that gives his stories the power to terrify. Not all contributors to Lovecraft's mythos have shared his racism—and Lovecraft himself arguably moved away from it to at least some degree during his lifetime—but Lovecraft's ability to convey fear of an imagined other through a kind of elaborate hoax that involved the use and creation of folklore and the folkloresque resonates well beyond horror fiction, reaching even into the political arena.

Lovecraft's mythos provides a kind of fantastic but believable discourse about the other in which fear of human aliens is transmuted into narratives of extraterrestrial aliens, fear of cultural and racial mixing is transmuted into narratives of human miscegenation with extraterrestrial monsters, and evil within ourselves is transmuted into narratives of tainted heredity—although during Lovecraft's writing career, his fear of human and cosmic others transmuted into something more like fascination, and the transformation of his characters tended to come across more positively (Evans 2005, 125).

Through a combination of horror motifs and narratives, folklore, and shared invention, members of the Lovecraft circle built a background, a fabric of verisimilitude, a shared mythos that has continued to expand by a process of bricolage into the participatory culture of the present day (Jenkins 1988, 3).

The success of Lovecraft's idea of the weird tale as hoax is exemplified by the life of his ancient book of occult lore, the *Necronomicon*. Not only has it been widely referenced in popular culture—in everything from *The Evil Dead* to *The Simpsons*—but it has been incorporated into rituals, and several hoax *Necronomicons* have been published. A survey of sources on the *Necronomicon*—including hard copy books and articles and Internet sources—shows that its history and reality, much like Slender Man's history and reality, is a topic of ongoing contention (Harms and Gonce 2003; Price 2002). This is further complicated by the use of Lovecraftian elements in magical or occult movements such as Chaos Magic, in which a shift in belief or ritual can bring about a shift in reality—that is, the Lovecraftian supernatural can be believed into existence (Evans 2005; Woodman 2004). This is similar to assertions that Slender Man is a *tulpa*, that is, he is real because of the collective beliefs of those who accept that he is real (The Slender Man Wiki n.d.). Although the concept of ostension is usually applied to the acting out of folklore rather than the acting out of literature or popular culture, it works quite well in describing the ritual use of Lovecraftian materials.

And like Slender Man, the *Necronomicon* has also been linked to real-life tragedy. In 1998, Luke Woodham opened fire at his high school in Hattiesburg, Mississippi, killing several classmates. He was widely reported to be part of an occult or Satanic group that had been reading and carrying out magic spells from the *Necronomicon* and several other occult books (Chalmers 2010, 18).

In Lovecraft's day, this Mythos was relatively nonsystematic. Readers of pulp magazines such as *Weird Tales* would encounter these references in stories by different writers and wonder at the shared Mythos—wonder if these writers knew something they didn't. This was strengthened by the fact that *Weird Tales* and other pulp magazines published stories by many of the clients of Lovecraft's "revision" service; he edited stories by less talented writers, often rewriting them completely and adding references to his Mythos, and then they were published under the clients' names. Later in his life, Lovecraft was bemused by fan letters asking him about the reality of his creations. In the eighty years since his death, the Mythos has been drawn on in a huge amount of writing, most of it fan fiction but some from highly respected writers (such as Jorge Luis Borges, Joyce Carol Oates, Fred Chappell, and Michael Chabon) as well as in films, comics, visual art, cosplay, toys, and many other examples. Notable here are the games—role-playing games, video games, board games—notable because the games, especially the Call of Cthulhu role-playing game, did much to bring Lovecraft and his most famous creation Cthulhu to public consciousness and into popular culture (Smith 2006; Joshi 2008). As Jeffrey Tolbert has asserted about Slender Man in chapter 4 of this volume, "In the case of a multimedia, multigenre, participatory phenomenon such as Slender Man, which in some manifestations masquerades as 'real' folklore and which deliberately plays with the boundaries between 'real' and 'fictional' worlds, the potential for believing the fiction increases considerably over 'normal' fictional texts." This could equally well be said about the Lovecraftian Mythos.

The expansion of Lovecraft's mythos (sometimes called the Cthulhu Mythos) has led various people to try to systematize it or simply to chart it with lexicons, encyclopedias, or wikis. The number of, for example, extraterrestrial gods or monsters appearing in "Cthulhu mythos" stories (including games, films, etc.) is difficult to specify, but it is certainly in the hundreds, if not thousands (Harms 2008). Attempts to systematically describe and categorize these go back to pre-Internet publications, notably by the writers August Derleth and Lin Carter (Joshi 2008), and include more recently multiple editions of *The Cthulhu Mythos Encyclopedia* by Daniel Harms. Although such attempts to systematize the Mythos have often met with derision from other members of the Lovecraftian community, there are nevertheless a number of wikis and online encyclopedias devoted to mapping the Lovecraftian Mythos: for example, the H. P. Lovecraft Wiki (n.d.), the Cthulhu Wiki (n.d.), and the extensive list of monsters and other motifs in the "Cthulhu Mythos Deities" Wikipedia (n.d.) entry). There are also several Cthulhu Mythos archives that are specifically associated with games, including the Call of Cthulhu role-playing game and the Arkham Horror board games. Similarly, Slender Man wikis and other websites that have attempted to systematize Slender Man have been controversial within the Slender Man community (see Tolbert's chapter 1 in this volume).

The Internet era has, of course, changed the dynamics of such cataloguing and systematization. Earlier cataloguers such as Derleth and Carter had personal interpretations of the Mythos; Derleth (who was Catholic) has been widely criticized for attempting to shape the Mythos to resemble the Christian story of the war between the forces of God and Satan (Joshi 2008). The relatively immediate and participatory nature of Internet archives (Kaplan 2013) makes it more difficult for them to be dominated by single individuals and more immediately fractious by nature, with additions, edits, and positive or negative comments appearing soon after entries are posted. To some degree, Internet archives reveal subcultures within the Lovecraftian community—those whose interest is in fan fiction, role-playing games, video games, and so on, and that therefore have different uses for the Lovecraftian motifs being catalogued.

Ultimately the creation, expansion, and cataloguing of such a Mythos does several things, including legitimating the set of narratives or beliefs by creating a background and history for them, offering a kind of playground for fans to exercise their imaginations, and giving fans a chance to demonstrate their in-group knowledge (and critique or support other fans). Of course, even a relatively esoteric-seeming subculture such as Lovecraft fans or Slender Man fans consists of smaller groups: casual versus hard-core fans, fans of different media forms or genres, and the like. Lovecraft fans, for example, can be divided according to how they discovered him: through fiction, role-playing games, video games, comics, or other sources.

If the culture surrounding Lovecraft and Lovecraftiana is an early and still a prime example of the cultures of horror, Slender Man is a fascinating example of how quickly such cultures can become ubiquitous in the Internet era. Lovecraftian culture spread gradually through fanzines and conventions until it burgeoned in the era of role-playing games and then the Internet; Slender Man spread much more quickly. Media studies specialist Shira Chess (2011) argues that Slender Man represents "an open sourcing of generic horror conventions." Internet horror cultures still have many of the characteristics of pre-Internet horror cultures, but they are easily and quickly accessed and changed in ways that complicate and mystify the relationship between folklore, literature, and popular culture, between oral and electronic transmission, between belief, skepticism, and parody, and between the playful creation of fiction and contentious issues of belief, and thus they resonate far beyond the intentions of their creators.

NOTES

1. The origin of Slender Man has been well documented in several publications, including the introduction and chapter 1 of this book and Peck (2015; chapter 2 in this book).

2. The term *participatory culture* has been defined principally by Henry Jenkins (2008). Referring to *Star Trek*, Jenkins writes, "This ability to transform personal reactions into social interaction, spectatorial culture into participatory culture, is one of the central characteristics of fandom. One becomes a 'fan' . . . by joining a community of other fans that share common interests. For fans, consumption naturally sparks production, reading generates writing, until the terms seem logically inseparable" (Jenkins 1988, 41).

3. Depictions of Slender Man vary; depictions of Cthulhu also vary but less so, since he is described rather vividly by Lovecraft. An image of Cthulhu in "The Call of Cthulhu" is described as "a monster of vaguely anthropoid outline, but with an octopus-like head whose face was a mass of feelers, a scaly, rubbery looking body, prodigious claws on hind and fore feet, and long, narrow wings behind" (Lovecraft 1984, 134). When Cthulhu is actually encountered, "The thing cannot be described—there is no language for such abysms of shrieking and immemorial lunacy, such eldritch contradictions of all matter, force and cosmic order. A mountain walked or stumbled" (152). Although Slender Man is not usually depicted in such cosmic terms, there is a suggestion in both Cthulhu and Slender Man of the violation of natural law.

4. For Lovecraft's vocabulary and his use of specific words, see Waugh 2006.

WORKS CITED

Blank, Trevor J. 2013a. "Hybridizing Folk Culture: Toward a Theory of New Media and Vernacular Discourse." *Western Folklore* 72 (2): 105–130.

Blank, Trevor J. 2013b. *The Last Laugh: Folk Humor, Celebrity Culture, and Mass-Mediated Disasters in the Digital Age.* Madison: University of Wisconsin Press.

Bronner, Simon. 2009. "Digitizing and Virtualizing Folklore." In *Folklore and the Internet: Vernacular Expression in a Digital World*, ed. Trevor J. Blank, 21–66. Logan: Utah State University Press. https://doi.org/10.2307/j.ctt4cgrx5.5.

Buccitelli, Anthony Bak. 2012. "Performance 2.0: Observations toward a Theory of the Digital Performance of Folklore." In *Folk Culture in the Digital Age: The Emergent Dynamics of Human Interaction*, ed. Trevor J. Blank, 60–84. Logan: Utah State University. https://doi.org/10.7330/9780874218909.c03.

Chalmers, Phil. 2010. *Inside the Mind of a Teen Killer.* Nashville, TN: Thomas Nelson.

Chess, Shira. 2011. "Open-Sourcing Horror: The Slender Man, Marble Hornets, and Genre Negotiations." *Information Communication and Society* 15 (3): 374–393. https://doi.org/10.1080/1369118X.2011.642889.

Chess, Shira, and Eric Newsom. 2015. *Folklore, Horror Stories, and the Slender Man.* New York: Palgrave Macmillan. https://doi.org/10.1057/9781137491138.

"Cthulhu Mythos Deities." n.d. Wikipedia. Accessed July 3, 2017. https://en.wikipedia.org/wiki/Cthulhu_Mythos_deities.

Cthulhu Wiki. n.d. Accessed July 3, 2017. https://www.yog-sothoth.com/wiki/index.php/Main_Page.

Dégh, Linda, and Andrew Vázsonyi. 1983. "Does the Word 'Dog' Bite? Ostensive Action: A Means of Legend-Telling." *Journal of Folklore Research* 20 (1): 5–34.

Evans, Timothy H. 2004. "Tradition and Illusion: Antiquarianism, Tourism and Horror in H. P. Lovecraft." *Extrapolation* 45 (2): 176–195. https://doi.org/10.3828/extr.2004.45.2.7.

Evans, Timothy H. 2005. "A Last Defense against the Dark: Folklore, Horror, and the Uses of Tradition in the Works of H. P. Lovecraft." *Journal of Folklore Research* 42 (1): 99–135. https://doi.org/10.2979/JFR.2005.42.1.99.

Foster, Michael Dylan. 2016. "The Folkloresque Circle: Toward a Theory of Fuzzy Allusion." In *The Folkloresque: Reframing Folklore in a Popular Culture World*, ed. Michael Dylan Foster and Jeffrey A. Tolbert, 41–63. Logan: Utah State University Press. https://doi.org/10.7330/9781607324188.c001.

Foster, Michael Dylan, and Jeffrey A. Tolbert, eds. 2016. *The Folkloresque: Reframing Folklore in a Popular Culture World.* Logan: Utah State University Press. https://doi.org/10.7330/9781607324188.

Frye, Mitch. 2007. "The Refinement of 'Crude Allegory': Eugenic Themes and Genotypic Horror in the Weird Fiction of H. P. Lovecraft." *Journal of the Fantastic in the Arts* 18 (3): 93–117.

Grider, Sylvia. 1981. "The Media Narraform: Symbiosis of Mass Media and Oral Tradition." *Arv* 37:125–131.

Harms, Daniel. 2008. *The Cthulhu Mythos Encyclopedia.* Lake Orion, MI: Elder Signs.

Harms, Daniel, and John Wisdom Gonce III. 2003. *The Necronomicon Files: The Truth behind the Legend.* Boston: Weiser Books.

Howard, Robert Glenn. 2015. "Taking (Digital) Folklore Seriously." *Contemporary Legend*, ser. 3, 5:98–104.

H. P. Lovecraft Wiki. n.d. Accessed July 3, 2017. lovecraft.wikia.com.

Jenkins, Henry III. 1988. "*Star Trek* Rerun, Reread, Rewritten: Fan Writing as Text Poaching." *Critical Studies in Mass Communication* 5 (2): 85–107. https://doi.org/10.1080/15295038809366691.

Jenkins, Henry. 2008. *Convergence Culture: Where Old and New Media Collide*. New York: New York University Press.

Jones, Justin, dir. 2013. *Fathom*. Written by Alexander Crews. https://www.youtube.com /watch?v=q2duevcUMGw.

Joshi, S. T. 2008. *The Rise and Fall of the Cthulhu Mythos*. Poplar Bluff, MO: Mythos Books.

Joshi, S. T. 2013. *I Am Providence: The Life and Times of H. P. Lovecraft*. 2 vols. New York: Hippocampus.

Joshi, S. T. 2015. *Unutterable Horror: A History of Supernatural Fiction*. New York: Hippocampus.

Kaplan, Merrill. 2013. "Curation and Tradition on Web 2.0." In *Tradition in the 21st Century*, ed. Trevor J. Blank and Robert Glenn Howard, 123–148. Logan: Utah State University Press. https://doi.org/10.7330/9780874218992.c05.

Lovecraft, H. P. 1971. *Selected Letters III, 1929–1931*. Ed. August Derleth and Donald Wandrei. Sauk City, WI: Arkham House.

Lovecraft, H. P. 1984. *The Dunwich Horror and Others*. Ed. S. T. Joshi. Rev. ed. Original edit by Augusr Derleth. Sauk City, WI: Arkham House.

Lovecraft, H. P. 1995. *Miscellaneous Writings*. Ed. S. T. Joshi. Sauk City, WI: Arkham House.

Lovecraft, H. P. 2012. *The Annotated Supernatural Horror in Literature*. Ed. S. T. Joshi. New York: Hippocampus.

Peck, Andrew. 2015. "Tall, Dark and Loathsome: The Emergence of a Legend Cycle in the Digital Age." *Journal of American Folklore* 128 (509): 333–348. https://doi.org/10 .5406/jamerfolk.128.509.0333.

Price, Robert M, ed. 2002. *The Necronomicon: Selected Stories and Essays Concerning the Blasphemous Tome of the Mad Arab*. Ann Arbor, MI: Chaosium Books.

Slender Man Wiki. n.d. The Tulpa Effect. Accessed December 3, 2016. http://theSlender Man.wikia.com/wiki/The_Tulpa_Effect.

Smith, Don G. 2006. *H. P. Lovecraft in Popular Culture*. Jefferson, NC: McFarland.

Waugh, Robert H. 2006. *The Monster in the Mirror: Looking for H.P. Lovecraft*. New York: Hippocampus.

Woodman, Justin. 2004. "Alien Selves: Modernity and the Social Diagnostics of the Demonic in Lovecraftian Magick." *Journal for the Academic Study of Magic* 2 (2): 13–47.

Chapter 7

Slender Man Is Coming to Get Your Little Brother or Sister
Teenagers' Pranks Posted on YouTube

Elizabeth Tucker

On May 31, 2014, I was in Prague, presenting a paper at the annual meeting of the International Society for Contemporary Legend Research. All of us at the conference had free Wi-Fi, courtesy of Charles University. As we checked news headlines, we were shocked to discover that two twelve-year-old girls in Waukesha, Wisconsin, had stabbed a friend of theirs, claiming that they wanted to please Slender Man. Suddenly, a piece of creepypasta that had inspired folklore papers and journal articles had become international news. Since that disturbing moment, analysis of the Slender Man stabbing has proliferated in print and digital journalism and in folklore publications. This chapter, based on a study of YouTube videos, examines concerns about young people's behavior that have appeared in the news and places them in the context of children's folklore studies.

Slender Man reminds us of well-established legend characters, particularly the Pied Piper who enchants and abducts children from a small village and never returns them to their grieving parents; Jack Zipes examines this similarity in the documentary film *Beware the Slender Man* (2016). Wolfgang Mieder makes the point that the Pied Piper legend "is parabolic and serves as a sign for our fears and needs" (Mieder 2007, 29). This point applies to Slender Man as well. He is a versatile, hybrid figure who evokes the central characters of *Men in Black* (1997); his skeletal shape brings to mind He-Man's Skeletor, Dr. Who's The Silence, and the gigantic aliens of *Close Encounters of the Third Kind* (1977). The blankness of his face allows us to imagine all sorts of possibilities. As Andrea Kitta eloquently explains

DOI: 10.7330/9781607327813.c007

141

in chapter 3 of this volume, he is a bogeyman who "has taken on a life of his own."

After the stabbing in Wisconsin in 2014, adults kept asking why two twelve-year-old girls, Anissa and Morgan, had decided to stab their friend Payton. Journalist Lisa Miller (2015) explains that Anissa had seen Slender Man in a video game and had read about him on the Creepypasta Internet site; she told Morgan, and the two of them fantasized about killing Payton so that the two of them could become proxies of Slender Man. After Morgan's birthday slumber party, Morgan and Anissa led Payton into the woods of a nearby park. They scuffled, then played hide and seek; at Anissa's urging, Morgan stabbed Payton with a knife soon after the game began. Although Miller does not specifically interpret what occurred, she mentions close friendships with shifting "best friend" connections over a period of time, fantasy play, fascination with the Internet, and mental illness in Morgan's family.

Shortly after the stabbing, major television and Internet news networks asked questions. *CNN*'s Kelly Wallace (2014) asked questions that were on the minds of parents, educators, and other adults: "How can we be sure our children can truly separate reality from fantasy? What are the warning signs that children are confusing the two? And how on earth can we keep tabs on everything they're consuming online?" Wallace quotes Jacqueline Woolley, a psychology professor at the University of Texas, who "believes children should have as good an ability to differentiate fantasy from reality as adults." She also quotes Jack Levin, a professor of sociology and criminology at Northeastern University, who emphasizes the importance of the relationship between the two girls who stabbed their friend. His focus on the two girls' close friendship and exclusion of the third girl reminds us how influential "best friend" relationships can be, but some of his other observations seem more extreme. "I call some teenagers and preteens temporary sociopaths," Levin states. Wallace's work shows how worried and confused many adults felt after the stabbing took place.

ANSWERS FROM CHILDREN'S FOLKLORE STUDIES

Folklorists of childhood, who have studied children's play since the nineteenth century, can help to explain this troubling situation. First, we should ask why adults seem so poorly informed about children's and adolescents' play. Why do many adults pay little attention to this? Brian Sutton-Smith gave us the answer to this question in 1970, when he coined the term *triviality barrier*. According to Sutton-Smith, adults, preoccupied with their own concerns, may view children's and teenagers' self-directed activities as trivial. Concentrating on what they think their children *should* do, adults may have little interest in observing young people's actual play. Ironically, play provides one of the most eloquent indices of the hopes and fears of our children and adolescents.

Kelly Wallace (2014) and fellow journalists Abigail Jones (2014) and Nicky Woolf (2014) have asked whether the phenomenon of adolescents committing assaults related to the Internet is new or part of an older pattern. Woolf quotes Internet users who wonder how "real" Slender Man is and whether he comes from the human mind. Insight into older patterns comes from children's folklore studies, which examine both perceptions of threatening characters and forms of play. John Widdowson's (1971) study of frightening figures demonstrates the ubiquity of characters feared by children, known as "bogeymen," "boogeymen," or variant terms. In the southern United States, for example, children have learned to fear the "boogerman" and "Bloody Bones." Marina Warner (2007) traces the "boo" in "boogeyman" back to the ancient Indo-European language; she also suggests that this term may originate from Sanskrit (42). It seems clear that children have feared threatening characters since ancient times. Although many of these characters have been male, some have been female. One example of a well-established female character is the Coast Miwok/Pomo American Indian Slug Woman, who threatens to take children away in her basket (Sarris 1993).

Another important part of children's traditions is the complex genre of play. Iona and Peter Opie's (1959) classic study *The Lore and Language of Schoolchildren* presents many examples of children tormenting each other, including tricks that cause embarrassment and nicknames that signal an unattractive physical attribute or behavior ("fatty," "skinny," "nosey parker," "sneak," "swankpot," "clever-dick," and others). They also go into detail about 'tortures," including arm twists, head pulls, hand or finger crushes, and hair twists. A long chapter lists the numerous forms of physical and psychic pain that children can inflict upon other children they do not like (175–205). The Opies did their research long before the advent of the Internet, but their main point holds true now: preadolescents and adolescents find a plethora of creative ways to go after each other.

Studies of girls' play patterns are especially relevant. Folklorists of childhood have documented girls' imaginative play in small groups and in pairs. A few girls playing together may focus intensely upon exploration of something thrilling, subversive, and potentially dangerous, such as a fainting or choking game (Tucker 2014). The social dynamics of girls' groups heavily influence the kind of play they pursue. Illuminating examples of girls' friendship dynamics can be found in Marjorie Harness Goodwin's (2006) *The Hidden Life of Girls: Games of Stance, Status, and Exclusion*. Closely examining examples of girls' conversation and play, Goodwin studies their friendships, conflicts, speech play, and awareness of social order.

There has been a long history of American girls indulging in subversive play that causes trouble. In Salem, Massachusetts, in 1692, witch trials began after girls testified that shapes of evil witches were poking and prodding them. In Hydesville, New York, in 1848, Kate and Margaret Fox claimed they could summon spirits who made their presence known through loud rapping sounds. Later the Fox sisters confessed that the sounds had come from their finger and toe joints, but many people continued to believe in them anyway. In the twentieth and twenty-first centuries, preadolescent and adolescent girls have performed the playful "light as a feather" lifting ritual, used Ouija boards, and tried to get supernatural results in other ways (Tucker 2007–2008, 2011). Dark, dangerous, and exciting, this kind of play has a tremendous appeal for both girls and boys.

In *Playing Dead: Mock Trauma and Folk Drama in Staged High School Drunk Driving Tragedies*, Montana Miller (2012) explains the allure of the "dazzle and darkness of play" for male and female students (100–116). In high school plays that depict the tragic consequences of driving drunk, adolescents can playfully address difficult, forbidden, and potentially dangerous subjects. Miller agrees with Johan Huizinga's argument that play has been a major force in the history of *homo ludens*, "playing man," but suggests that dark play should be recognized as part of this driving force (Miller 2012, 100; see also Huizinga 1950). Having studied this kind of play since the late 1970s, I agree that it is a vital aspect of human behavior.

A leading folklorist of childhood who has helped us understand play is Brian Sutton-Smith. Sutton-Smith's (2001) *Ambiguity of Play* identifies seven rhetorics of play: the ancient concepts of Fate, Power, Community, Identity, and Frivolity and the more recent concepts of Progress, the Self, and the Imaginary. Sutton-Smith suggests that the variability and quirkiness of play may have facilitated natural selection during the many years of human evolution. At times of community tragedy or national crisis, play can become especially important. One noteworthy study of playful adaptation to a stressful event is Anna Richman Beresin's (2002) "Children's Expressive Culture in Light of September 11, 2001." Describing pebble-shooting games and songs based on nursery rhymes, Beresin suggests that "the boundary between the rational and irrational is finer than we often acknowledge, that violence has its rationale for those who perpetuate it, and that children's irrational play indeed makes a lot of sense" (335). As Beresin wisely observes, extreme polarities may not be the best index of people's actual behavior at stressful times.

We can find a similarity to post–September 11 play in Andrea Kitta's account of children playing a Slender Man chasing game shortly after news of the Wisconsin stabbing came out. At the beginning of chapter 3 in this volume, Kitta describes a child wearing a white T-shirt chasing other children around a yard, shouting, "Look out! I'm Slender Man! I'm coming to get you!" Kitta argues that Slender Man represents "a shared aesthetic and, at times, a shared experience that taps into something deeper than mere play." This role-play is brief but important. The child who shouts, "I'm Slender Man!" gains a sense of power, becoming a bogeyman and enacting that frightening figure's pursuit of children. In playing this game, the child enacts what Bill Ellis calls the "Rumpelstiltskin principle," related to a shared experience or unresolved stress: "Language quantifies the experience, and the process of translating it into words exorcises the monster" (Ellis 2003, 62). Besides language, vigorous enactment and pursuit make this monster come to life and become manageable.

Slender Man play that becomes violent reflects violence as a cultural pattern in America. Simon J. Bronner (2011) describes America's legacy of violence, insightfully observing that "the 'taming of the Wild West,' 'outlaws and gangsters,' and rioting [are] recognized by most Americans in their national heritage" (145). School shootings have recently become part of this troubling heritage. The stabbing in Wisconsin may make us wonder whether young people's play will become more violent and destructive in the future.

FRAME ANALYSIS OF SLENDER MAN
PRANKS IN YOUTUBE VIDEOS

YouTube, a video-posting website that has existed since 2005, offers us intriguing glimpses of Slender Man play: chasing games, hiding games, and pranks. What unites all of these forms of play is role-playing. In chasing games, Slender Man runs after everyone else; in hiding games, he gets ready to jump out at seekers. And in pranks, which the victim does not usually expect, he startles the person who finds him. Pranks resemble hiding games but have more potential to surprise and scare others. Of course, Slender Man hiding games can be both surprising and scary. In the video *Game of Slenderman (My Sister Has a Taser!!)*, a preadolescent sister uses a taser to zap the sibling who finds her. Startling in its use of electricity, this game demonstrates children's creativity, their fascination with dangerous forces, and their awareness of Slender Man as a destructive figure (Kitty_Gaming_Wannabes 2016).

In analyzing young people's Slender Man videos, one can easily apply Erving Goffman's (1986) *Frame Analysis*. According to Goffman, people present themselves to others in certain ways, creating "frames" that influence impressions and responses. Self-presentation through frames resembles an actor's portrayal of a character to an audience. Goffman uses the term *theatrical frame* to designate people's self-presentation through quasi-theatrical performance. This term seems appropriate for YouTube's prank videos and comments, both of which involve performance and show evidence of reflection about the nature of fantasy and reality. Bringing up "the folk notion that everyday life is to be placed on one side and the fanciful realms on the other" (155), Goffman challenges this idea, finding that everyday life and fantasy come together in various ways. In my research on adolescents' folklore of the supernatural in relation to the Internet, I have found that fantasy and reality often come together (Tucker 2011). Kelly Wallace's (2014) question "How can we be sure our children can truly separate reality from fantasy?" does not do justice to the interrelationship of these two realms, to which children become habituated through storytelling, films, television, and computers.

Another helpful source is Brenda Danet's (2001) *Cyberpl@y: Communicating Online*, which analyzes college students' playful behavior online as the result of five intersecting frames of interaction: real life, the Internet Relay Chat Game, a party, pretend play, and performance (102). Danet pays particular attention to games identified as *ilinx* games by Roger Caillois: those that cause dizziness or disorientation (Caillois 1961, 23). Provoking laughter, such pursuits—which include both games and pranks—are very popular on college campuses. In my study of adolescents' videos about the lifting ritual known as levitation, I found that both posting such videos and making humorous, startling comments about them constituted satisfying forms of ilinx play. Applying Danet's form of frame analysis, I identified six frames for the levitation videos and their comments: real life, YouTube, virtual slumber party, ilinx play, performance of levitation ritual, and comments (improvised performance) (Tucker 2011, 49–50).

In Slender Man prank performances among siblings, a new but related set of frames emerges. Like levitation, which ends with a person's startling rise from the floor, the prank belongs to the subgenre of ilinx play, which disturbs the players' equilibrium. From the standpoint of a sibling who must compete with younger and/or older brothers and sisters, pranks assert power. Startled and surprised, the victim, generally a younger sibling, is at the mercy of the prank player. Folklorists such as Iona and Peter Opie (1959, 377–392), Marilyn Jorgensen (1995), Sheldon Posen (1974), Richard Tallman (1974), and myself (Tucker 2008, 37–39, 79–82) have chronicled young people's pranks; Sylvia Grider (1973), Marion Bowman (1987), and I (Tucker 2005, 93–96) have studied college students' pranks in relation to legends. Records of pranks played by young siblings are relatively rare. That is not because such pranks are uncommon but because folklorists have tended to gather information at schools and camps and in other institutional settings. Although there are relatively few publications on this subject, many of us who grew up with siblings have vivid memories of pranking the younger ones by warning them that someone scary might come soon. My middle sister and I pranked our youngest sister by telling her that if she picked up the telephone and heard the word *operator*, a witch named Operator would come to get her. We also played other similar pranks. If YouTube had existed then, we would probably have posted those pranks online.

The following set of frames fits siblings' pranks posted on YouTube: real life, competition with siblings, YouTube, ilinx play, pranks, and comments. As Danet (2001) has demonstrated in *Cyberpl@y* and my own research has also shown (Tucker 2011), adolescents love to engage in ilinx play online. YouTube provides an open forum for supernatural rituals, pranks, and other kinds of play that shock and disorient the viewer. Within the frame of competition with siblings, which is an important part of growing up, ilinx play on YouTube becomes quite intense. Prank performances have become especially popular because they generate laughter and give the prank player a sense of power. Once the prank performance appears on YouTube, commenters discuss, dispute, praise, and vilify its contents.

YouTube contains so many videos of Slender Man pranks that it is impossible to do justice to them all in a short chapter. Therefore, I want to explore the pranks' common patterns with the objective of understanding the video-makers' perception of Slender Man and their attempts to shock and embarrass their siblings. I also want to determine why prank players care so much about sharing their pranks with a large audience of viewers online. Those of us who played pranks on our siblings as teenagers before the 1990s did not have an opportunity to broadcast our trickiness; now anyone has the potential to become a star of a widely viewed, applauded prank video. Seeking fame in the form of a large number of viewers and enthusiastic comments is certainly one strong motivator, but further motivation seems to come from the joy of competition with siblings.

Before looking closely at siblings' prank videos, I should acknowledge that there are many Slender Man prank videos generated by adults. To some extent, these videos, many of which are quite polished and well edited, provide models for videos made by adolescents. For example, JOOGSQUAD's (2014) BEST OF SLENDERMAN!!! offers a long compilation of popular Slender Man pranks. Some of the most enthusiastic adolescent prank video creators are boys in their midteens who have decided to play pranks on their very young or preadolescent brothers or sisters. Some video-makers are girls, and occasionally parents offer help. Usually the prank follows a straightforward sequence; the teenager dresses up as Slender Man, pulling a pillow case or other white material over his or her head and dressing up in a suit. Then the teenager stands beside a door or another entrance, waiting patiently to jump out at his or her sibling.

SUCCESSFUL SLENDER MAN PRANKS

As I clicked my way around YouTube, exploring teenagers' Slender Man pranks on their brothers and sisters, I discovered that some prank videos had received much more enthusiastic comments than others. One of the teenaged boys who has received the strongest accolades is Jared, proprietor of the SpintwistVideos channel, who lives in Utah; his family is white, lives in a large house, and seems to be affluent. One of two older siblings who enjoys playing pranks, Jared posted a video, *Scary Slenderman Prank on My Brother!* on August 26, 2012 (SpintwistVideos 2012). By June 24, 2017, his video had been viewed 2,557,792 times. Inspired by his video's growing fame, Jared produced four more videos: *Scary Slenderman Prank on My Brother 2!* on June 29, 2013 (SpintwistVideos 2013a); *Slender Man Prank! GONE WRONG!* on October 1, 2013 (SpintwistVideos 2013b); *Slender Man Prank on Halloween 2013!* on November 11, 2013 (SpintwistVideos 2013c); and *Scary Slenderman Prank on My Brother 3!* on March 10, 2014 (SpintwistVideos 2014). Although none of the later videos have received as much applause as the first one did, the series has made Jared feel very proud; in the Halloween video he explains, "Slender Man pranks are my specialty." Viewers of his 2012 video can click on two links: one for the 2013 Halloween prank video and another for the *Scary Slenderman Prank on My Brother 3!* video. There is also a link for donations to the SpintwistVideos channel.

In the introduction to his 2012 video, Jared explains that he and his brother have decided to play a prank on their younger brother because their brother is "terrified of Slenderman" and has "played Slenderman." We do not know whether the small brother has played a chasing game or a hiding game, but no matter what kind of game it was, it has clearly scared him. Noting his vulnerability, the two older brothers plan to surprise him with a Slender Man prank. One of them dresses up in a dark suit, pulls a white mask over his face, and positions himself by a door. When the little brother opens this door and sees the Slender Man figure, he immediately screams and cries. One of the two older siblings exults, "That was *good*!"

Comments on this video express appreciation for the prank's success. Typical comments are "This was awesome. U just gained a subscriber!" "lol ur little brother was terrified," "lmao that was too good," and "OMG your brother's a pussy." Many of the positive comments acknowledge that the little brother was truly terrified. There is also a substantial number of negative comments about the little boy's reaction: "Poor boy! He's only young ;(" "How was that funny? Poor boy!" "I feel so bad for that kid," and "And the biggest dick award goes to . . ." A few viewers comment on their own love of pranks. One female viewer writes, "I used to do the same thing with my little brother, then he got older and started playing pranks on me. I'm the better prankster lol." Here we see an older sibling tormenting her little brother, then accepting him as a fellow prankster while upholding her own superiority in playing pranks. In this comment both the pleasure and the annoyance of competition with siblings come through.

In Jared's later videos, the little brother seems more blasé. Having survived his two older siblings' first Slender Man prank, he is no longer easy to frighten. Nonetheless, he plays along with the later pranks, helping his brothers make good videos. In *Scary Slenderman Prank on My Brother 2*, he pokes Slender Man, muttering, "Stupid!" This prank involves certain props: a device for producing "scary slender static" and a bench for the older brother to stand on. Although this second video received a substantial 277,012 views by June 24, 2017, comments show that viewers find it less impressive than the first one. Typical comments include "That prank sucked!" "The first one was better," "That was lame," "so mean," and "OMG your brother's a pussy" (a recurrent theme in comments on this series of prank videos).

Of the later videos in this series, the one that has received the most appreciative comments is *Slender Man Prank! GONE WRONG!* With 572,466 views by June 24, 2017, this video has stimulated lively dialogue. The video begins with a warning—"Mimicking the Slender Man can be dangerous"— and ends with the little brother stretched out on the floor, apparently killed by the dangerous Slender Man. In the initial scenes, one of the older brothers takes his younger brother out to the playground, where Slender Man lurks; this setting reminds us of some of the pictures that appeared on the

Creepypasta site shortly after Slender Man's creation (Slender Man 2016). The video warns viewers about danger to children from this frightening figure. Special effects, including the use of red and other colors with an accentuating filter, make the video startling and exciting.

In the "Comments" section of this video, teenagers discuss whether they were scared and whether the video seems real. Accusations of "FAAAKE!" provoke an explanation from Jared: "For all of you who failed to read the description, THIS VIDEO IS NOT REAL, yes, there is no slenderman. I have been making videos of me imitating Slenderman since 2012 and I am still alive. So if you comment FAAAKE the comment will just get automatically filtered out and deleted." In spite of this disclaimer, viewers write about feeling scared by the video and dare each other to watch it. A recent comment states, "I all ready new this was fake because slenderman is just a cartoon thing so if you ever see a video that says slender caught on tape it's fake slenderman never even exist it's just a person they no who is acting for the video." This poignant comment, in which the viewer struggles to stave off feelings of fear, received a brief spelling correction from a fellow viewer: "*Knew.*"

FAILED(?) SLENDER MAN PRANKS

Since the adolescent creators of Slender Man prank videos are not professionally trained videographers, some of their efforts do not succeed as well as they'd hoped. According to commenters, the most important index of success is whether the prank *worked*: did the sibling on whom the prank was played get scared and/or angry? And did the player of the prank feel satisfied with the outcome? Interestingly, failed pranks have gotten much attention from viewers on YouTube; in fact, some of them have had so many views that they seem to have succeeded rather than failed in entertaining their audience. Young people enjoy watching and commenting on videos of pranks that show a struggle to get satisfying results. Watching videos identified as failures, they learn about the process of video-making; awareness of this process will help them make videos themselves, if they choose to do so.

A good early example of a prank identified by its poster as a failure is *FAILED SLENDERMAN PRANK!*, posted by user MrPilot817 on May 30, 2011. Having had 11,844 views by October 10, 2016, this video has become quite popular. As in many such videos, the poster's name and place of residence are not given. Nonetheless, it is evident that the poster is an adolescent white American boy who enjoys playing the video game *Halo*, making videos, and playing pranks on his younger teenaged sister. Their family seems to be fairly affluent. Since we do not know the teenaged prankster's name, I will call him a shortened version of his screenname, MrPilot.

At the beginning of this video, MrPilot explains that his younger sister is about to come back from a trip and that the two of them have watched the Slender Man series [*Marble Hornets*] together. Having noticed how much Slender Man has scared his sister, he expects to scare her with his prank. Nervously, with great excitement, he hangs a suit such as Slender Man wears outside his sister's bedroom window. Then he turns out the lights and waits; the screen stays dark for a while. His little sister bursts through the door with a smiling friend or sibling. She tries without success to turn on the light but finally manages to turn it on. "What happened here? Oh, my God!" she shouts. Although she does not notice the Slender Man suit hanging outside her window, she quickly spots her brother, and the prank fails.

Comments on this video do not mince words about the video's defects. One viewer suggests, "I can't even see him, you need to do it more obvious, open the blinds a bit more and have a faint light behind it so she notices it better." Another notes, "You should of dress like him and waited until she comes in. XD [emoticon signifying hearty laughter]." A few commenters develop a parody of Slender Man called Stonerman: "Stoner laugh much?"; "I immediately laughed at *Stonerman.*" As in comments on other prank videos, some viewers criticize the sister for screaming, while others commend her for being strong. One even calls her a "badass": high praise for courageous behavior.

Besides posting humorous remarks and suggestions for making the prank more effective, some commenters challenge Slender Man's existence. One viewer writes, "Okay, let me get this straight. Slenderman doesn't exist. People only made that up to make kids behave, because if they don't, well, they're gonna 'die.' Period." Although her tone is sardonic, her focus on the nature of reality is serious. In a few lines, she summarizes the intent of cautionary legends about frightening figures, which is "to make kids behave." Adults, she notes, have "made that up," so the death threat to children must be "made up" as well. The subtext of this comment is that adults do not always tell the truth, and kids must figure out the parameters of reality on their own. Comments like this one show how carefully adolescents consider the content of prank videos related to legends about frightening figures.

CONCLUSIONS

Although the stabbing incident in Wisconsin in 2014 was frightening and disturbing, the use of a knife by two girls to attack another and their effort to become proxies of Slender Man do not represent typical adolescents' behavior. The only part of the assault that reflects widely recognized young people's folklore patterns is two "best friends" retaliating against a third. Although we can see that some weapons have become part of games, as in the video *My Sister Has a Taser!!* (Kitty_Gaming_Wannabes 2016), weapons do not usually appear during play, and pranks tend to cause no harm other than a momentary fright. Sibling pranks, an understudied area of children's folklore, tend to express competition with siblings in a friendly, nonviolent way.

Application of Goffman's frame analysis to YouTube videos of Slender Man pranks played by siblings helps us understand the interconnection of such pranks with other forms of self-presentation, both in "real life" and on the Internet. The largest surrounding frame is competition with siblings, which includes varied interactions. Within that frame, YouTube offers rich potentiality for siblings' assertion of power. Ilinx play, which disturbs the players' equilibrium, makes this assertion of power possible. Pranks, which startle, shock, and briefly frighten victims, epitomize ilinx play, which gives adolescents exciting opportunities to disconcert their brothers and sisters. It is important to note that both prank videos and comments on the videos constitute a form of performance that entertains viewers and encourages posting of similar material.

When adolescents make videos of Slender Man pranks on their brothers and sisters and post these videos on YouTube, they explore subtle gradations between truth and untruth, reality and fantasy, safety and danger, and success and failure. Although they care about all of these polarities, they seem most concerned about separating reality from fantasy and truth from untruth. Accusations of "FAAAKE!" express insistence on clarity and transparency. Video presenters may respond to commenter's complaints, discussing appropriate forms of presentation.

Since Slender Man is a threatening character who represents possible abduction of children, he stimulates lively dialogue online. Is he really dangerous? Can adults be trusted to protect children from him? And if he actually victimizes children, will the children survive? All of these questions arise in comments, demonstrating the complexity of young people's concerns and interactions.

Another important issue is the prank's degree of success or failure. Each prank involves a delicate balance between respect and victimization; pranks that are deemed successful usually cause momentary disorientation and fright without completely terrifying the victim. Commenters on sibling prank videos tend to object if the victim gets too scared or if he or she does not seem scared at all. Failures of this kind tend to evoke scornful suggestions for improvement. It is noteworthy, however, that "failed" prank videos may get attention and applause. Sometimes pranks that go wrong are even more entertaining than the ones that succeed.

As these prank videos and comments show, journalists, parents, and teachers need not worry too much about explaining Slender Man to young people. Kids who use YouTube are skilled at portraying Slender Man's threatening behavior and discussing its meaning in the context of their everyday lives. Those of us who want to understand children's and adolescents' perception of Slender Man just need to look past the "triviality barrier" (Sutton-Smith 1970) and examine the many videos that YouTube provides.

WORKS CITED

Beresin, Anna Richman. 2002. "Children's Expressive Culture in Light of September 11, 2001." *Anthropology & Education Quarterly* 33: 331–337. https://doi.org/10.1525/aeq .2002.33.331.

Beware the Slender Man. 2016. Dir. Irene Taylor Brodsky. HBO Documentary Film.

Bowman, Marion. 1987. "Contemporary Legend and Practical Joke." In *Perspectives on Contemporary Legend*, ed. Gillian Bennett, Paul Smith, and J. D. A. Widdowson, 2:171–175. Sheffield, UK: Sheffield Academic Press.

Bronner, Simon J. 2011. "Framing Violence and Play in American Culture." *Journal of Ritsumeikan Social Sciences and Humanities* 3:145–160.

Caillois, Roger. 1961. *Man, Play and Games.* Glencoe, IL: Free Press.

Close Encounters of the Third Kind. 1977. Dir. Steven Spielberg. Columbia Pictures.

Danet, Brenda. 2001. *Cyberpl@y: Communicating Online.* New York: Berg.

Ellis, Bill. 2003. *Aliens, Ghosts and Cults: Legends We Live.* Jackson: University Press of Mississippi.

Goffman, Erving. 1986. *Frame Analysis.* Boston: Northeastern University Press.

Goodwin, Marjorie Harness. 2006. *The Hidden Life of Girls: Games of Stance, Status and Exclusion.* Hoboken, NJ: Wiley-Blackwell.

Grider, Sylvia Ann. 1973. "Dormitory Legend-Telling in Progress: Fall, 1971–Winter, 1973." *Indiana Folklore* 6 (1): 1–32.

Huizinga, Johan. 1950. *Homo Ludens: A Study of the Play Element in Culture.* Boston: Beacon.

Jones, Abigail. 2014. "The Girls Who Tried to Kill for Slender Man." *Newsweek*, August 13. http://www.newsweek.com/2014/08/22/girls-who-tried-kill-slender-man-264218.html

JOOGSQUAD_PPJT. 2014. *BEST OF SLENDERMAN!!! (Prank Compilation 2014).* YouTube, September 1. https://www.youtube.com/watch?v=GoScrW27u5o.

Jorgensen, Marilyn. 1995. "Teases and Pranks." In *Children's Folklore: A Sourcebook*, ed. Brian Sutton-Smith, Jay Mechling, Thomas W. Johnson, and Felicia R. McMahon, 213–224. New York: Garland.

Kitty_Gaming_Wannabes. 2016. *Game of Slenderman (My Sister Has a Taser!!)* YouTube, August 15. https://www.youtube.com/watch?v=NfwVtCH0wS0.

Mieder, Wolfgang. 2007. *The Pied Piper: A Handbook.* Greenwich, CT: Greenwood.

Miller, Lisa. 2015. "If These Girls Knew That Slender Man Was a Fantasy, Why Did They Want to Kill Their Friend for Him?" *New York Magazine*, August 25. http://nymag .com/daily/intelligencer/2015/08/slender-man-stabbing.html.

Miller, Montana. 2012. *Playing Dead: Mock Trauma and Folk Drama in Staged High School Drunk Driving Tragedies.* Logan: Utah State University Press. https://doi.org/10.7330 /9780874218923.

MrPilot817. 2011. *FAILED SLENDERMAN PRANK!* YouTube, May 30. https://www.youtube
.com/watch?v=0IZqtakEcqo.

Opie, Iona, and Peter Opie. 1959. *The Lore and Language of Schoolchildren.* London: Oxford
University Press.

Posen, I. Sheldon. 1974. "Pranks and Practical Jokes at Children's Summer Camps." *Southern Folklore Quarterly* 38:299–309.

Sarris, Greg. 1993. *Keeping Slug Woman Alive: A Holistic Approach to American Indian Texts.* Los
Angeles: University of California Press.

Slender Man. 2016. Creepypasta Wiki. wikia.com/wiki/The_Slender_Man.

SpintwistVideos. 2012. *Scary Slenderman Prank on My Brother!* YouTube, August 26.
https://www.youtube.com/watch?v=O5Yq_4e_Tg8.

SpintwistVideos. 2013a. *Scary Slenderman Prank on My Brother 2!* YouTube, June 29.
https://www.youtube.com/watch?v=vfL_kIQsIys.

SpintwistVideos. 2013b. *Slender Man Prank! GONE WRONG!* YouTube, October 1.
https://www.youtube.com/watch?v=MgbMC3_oENM.

SpintwistVideos. 2013c. *Slender Man Prank on Halloween 2013!* YouTube, November 11.
https://www.youtube.com/watch?v=RcjfDVJSC5E.

SpintwistVideos. 2014. *Scary Slenderman Prank on My Brother 3!* YouTube, March 10.
https://www.youtube.com/watch?v=NbGIQ4hmrd8.

Sutton-Smith, Brian. 1970. "Psychology of Childlore: The Triviality Barrier." *Western Folklore* 29 (1): 1–8. https://doi.org/10.2307/1498679.

Sutton-Smith, Brian. 2001. *The Ambiguity of Play.* Cambridge, MA: Harvard University Press.

Tallman, Richard S. 1974. "A Generic Approach to the Practical Joke." *Southern Folklore
Quarterly* 38:259–274.

Tucker, Elizabeth. 2005. *Campus Legends.* Westport, CT: Greenwood.

Tucker, Elizabeth. 2007–2008. "Levitation Revisited." *Children's Folklore Review* 30:47–60.

Tucker, Elizabeth. 2008. *Children's Folklore: A Handbook.* Greenwich, CT: Greenwood.

Tucker, Elizabeth. 2011. "'LMAO, That Wasn't Even Scary': Legend-Related Performances
on YouTube." *Contemporary Legend* 3 (1): 44–57.

Tucker, Elizabeth. 2014. "The Endangered Child: Choking and Fainting Games in the
Online Underground of YouTube." *Children's Folklore Review* 36:19–34.

Wallace, Kelly. 2014. "Slenderman Stabbing Case: When Can Kids Understand Reality vs.
Fantasy?" *CNN.* June 5. https://www.cnn.com/2014/06/03/living/slenderman
-stabbing-questions.../index.html.

Warner, Marina. 2007. *Monsters of Our Own Making: The Peculiar Pleasures of Fear.* Lexington:
University Press of Kentucky.

Widdowson, John. 1971. "The Bogeyman: Preliminary Observations on Frightening Figures." *Folklore* 82 (2): 99–115. https://doi.org/10.1080/0015587X.1971.9716716.

Woolf, Nicky. 2014. "Slender Man: The Shadowy Online Figure Blamed in Grisly Wisconsin Stabbing." *Guardian,* June 4. https://www.theguardian.com/world/2014/jun/04
/slender-man-online-character-wisconsin-stabbings.

Chapter 8

Monstrous Media and Media Monsters
From Cottingley to Waukesha

Paul Manning

THIS CHAPTER TAKES AS ITS POINT OF DEPARTURE the singular "Slender Man stabbing" incident in Waukesha, Wisconsin, an incident that defines one extreme of a continuum of "ostension," an attempt to act out or *show* the (legend) narrative in real life. I compare this case, which begins with a set of photographs of paranormal phenomena, to the equally singular case of the Cottingley "fairy photographs." I will compare these incidents to rethink ostension as a kind of *indexicality*—a sign that works by real existential contact or contiguity, as a photograph indexes its object. I will also attempt to locate discussions of the ostension of this monster within an explicit consideration of media forms for portraying the monstrous. I will treat monsters as a species of "character" defined by its portability, its ability to move across a series of linked genres or media forms. From the very outset Slender Man, as I will show, was created as a character inviting certain kinds of "transmedia storytelling," what is called in Japanese media studies, from which I draw inspiration here, the "media mix" (Nozawa 2013). The varied genres and media forms in which Slender Man appears, the "monstrous media mix," are those genres or media forms that make some appeal to realness, to indexicality. And after all, what is ostension ("pointing out, showing") but a kind of indexicality, since a pointing gesture is the prototypical indexical sign. I attempt here a sustained discussion of the relations of monsters to media forms, distinguishing between media forms that suggest an indexical contact or immediacy with the monster and those that leave the monster in a wholly unreal media space of hypermediacy. This opposition between immediacy and hypermediacy (adapted from Bolter and Grusin 2000), I will suggest, remediates the opposition

DOI: 10.7330/9781607327813.c008

between legends (understood to take place in "the real world") and folk tales (understood to take place in an unreal space of "once upon a time"). Finally, I will suggest that while photographs of monsters produce a claim to indexical immediacy, the possibility of ostension, of real contact with the media monster in our world, they also work by the "weird" indexical relation of alterity: the absolute alterity of the monstrous figure (Slender Man, fairies) set against the prosaic, banal realism of the real-world "ground" of the photographed scene (see also Manning 2017; Fisher 2017; Evans, chapter 6 in this volume). The "weird" works by producing a liminal space of destabilizing indexical contact, immediacy, between worlds of media and real life that are understood at the same time as being wholly opposed (hypermediacy). This "weird" relation between the ordinary and the wholly other is akin to Japanese subcultural fantasies of interdimensional contact between fictional characters (who live in a media world of pure fantasy called "2D") and the ordinary world of real life ("3D"): what is called fantasies of "2.5D" (Nozawa 2013).

****

The 2014 Waukesha "Slender Man stabbing" incident represents a fairly clear example of what folklorists call "ostension," that is, acting out or *showing* the legend narrative in real life. The attempted ostension of Slender Man in this incident—an attempt to really encounter the quasi-legendary monster by some form of attempted ritual sacrifice—depends on a prior act of media ostension, the creation of realistic photoshopped images of a completely invented monster on an Internet forum thread. As other chapters in this volume make clear, the Slender Man stabbing is the culmination of a series of attempts at ostension; Slender Man's reality/unreality limns the boundaries of the virtual world of the media (Internet) and quotidian reality (in real life, or IRL) and also limns the boundaries of the unreal (in this case, monsters, figures excluded from our naturalist ontology) and the real world in which the real monsters are human. The question of ostension is thus framed in part around what I will call the "weird" relation of media worlds to everyday life, and the relation of the fantastic or unreal (monsters) to the real.[1] Thus, the moral panic that results can be figured either by the media form ("monstrous media") or by the monster whose original ecological habitat—and context of first encounter—is in that media ("media monsters": creepypasta monsters like Slender Man). (What is horrifying about a monster like Sadako from *Ringu* [1998] is that she moves between both ontological dichotomies simultaneously when she literally crawls through the TV screen.) The "moral panic" that resulted from the Waukesha incident could locate the monstrous either in the media form (the monstrous media of the Internet) or the character living in the diegetic space the media form projects (the media monster, Slender Man).[2]

Almost 100 years before that incident, in 1917, two girls (Frances Griffiths was nine and Elsie Wright was sixteen) living in Cottingley, England, photographed themselves in the company of fairies who allegedly lived in their garden: similarly to the Slender Man case, here we find an attempt at photographic ostension that later produced attempts to repeat the alleged ostensive encounter with the photographed fairies in the company of visiting clairvoyant theosophists Edward L. Gardner and Geoffrey Hodson (Owen 1994; see also Smith 1991; Bown 1996).[3] As Owen summarizes:

> In the popular imagination, the name Cottingley invokes a series of famous or infamous photographs. These are photographs of supposedly real fairies that were taken in 1917 and 1920 by two young girls in the village of Cottingley, in the North of England, and which have since found their way into countless books on the paranormal and supernatural. The most famous of the photographs recently and rather typically made its appearance in the "Unexplained Mysteries of the World" picture card series promoted by a well-known British tea company, and has thereby presumably found a place in the hearts and minds (as well as the picture card albums) of the collecting youth of the nation. The Cottingley fairy photographs or, perhaps more accurately, the Cottingley fairies have attained the status of popular icons, and represent in part an ongoing cultural fascination with a proposed veiled or secret world. (48)

These photos, because of the strongly *indexical* connotations of the photograph as being ostensive evidence of the real, were famously taken as proof of the real existence of fairies by Arthur Conan Doyle, himself a spiritualist and a believer in fairies. The incident became well known because of an article written by Doyle in the *Strand* magazine in 1920 (Doyle 1920, 1922), in which the fairy photographs were reproduced. Doyle was a heretic within the spiritualist movement for subscribing to a belief in the parallel existence of fairies. (After all, his uncle Richard Doyle—along with his father—was perhaps the most famous Victorian illustrator of fairies; his 1871 illustrated gift book *In Fairyland* was a paradigmatic example of the conversion of fairies from drab beings of folklore to colorful creatures of the Victorian "fairyland" of new media forms) (Owen 1994, 50–54). At that time, for spiritualists and others in the media public, while ghosts seemed appropriate figures to pose for a photograph, fairies manifestly did not, so Conan Doyle's disclosure of these girls' attempt to photographically show fairies—real fairies in real gardens—produced a secondary furor within the occultist world, damaging Doyle's reputation before a broader public. The girls later admitted that some of the fairies were traced from images of fairies in *Princess Mary's Gift Book* of 1915, with butterfly wings added by the girls, though they maintained that one of the photographs "was real" (for an excellent summary and analysis, see Owen 1994; see also Smith 1991; Bown 1996). In both cases, then, we have an additional layer of weirdness, in which the private fantasy worlds of two girls became an object of adult public concern.

PHOTOGRAPHY, OSTENSION, AND INDEXICALITY

But for the stabbings and the blood, these cases both seem to illustrate a similar desire for ostension. In both cases, the *indexical* medium of the photograph, albeit "faked," began the chain of events of ostension. Slender Man began as a character in a photograph circulated on an Internet forum attended by "eyewitness accounts"; taken together, they were designed to produce an aura of reality. The presence of a photograph of a mysterious character allowed that character to circulate through the Internet independently from narratives, and thus to become independent of its original context, which labeled it as "unreal," and to accrete both legendary narratives and even, for some, a sense of reality. Similarly, the Cottingley photographs quickly were taken from the private play world of two girls and published in the pages of the *Strand* in 1920 as veridical proof of the existence of fairies. Thereafter, sundered from their original contexts, the photographs themselves—precisely because they were photographs, circulating apart from their original contexts—told the story of the existence of fairies, and continued to inform fantasies of ostension based on photographic proof. Photographs, which contain their own evidential claims, carrying them around wherever they go, speak for themselves, and circulate autonomously from narrative contexts, allowing characters to circulate separately from narratives and affording fantasies of ostension of the characters portrayed in the photographs.

The fact that each attempt at ostension of a monster begins with a photograph is crucial, since photographs are understood to directly index their referent, and to produce a photograph is thus to make a claim about the reality of its referent. Indexicality is a quite general semiotic property that is still strongly associated with photographic media, but as I will show, it also extends to a range of other media forms associated with a sense of authentic "contact," "realism," and "presence":

> Photography . . . combine[s] both the privileging of the visual and the
> indexical "yearning" for what the Reverend Joseph Mullins . . . described

as "stern fidelity." This stern fidelity was later theorized by C. S. Peirce in terms of a photograph's "indexicality." Peirce identified three types of signs: symbols, icons and indexes. Symbols were arbitrary and conventional—this is how we understand most linguistic signifiers since Saussure. Iconic signs are those that have a relationship of resemblance to their referents (such as painting and, some would claim, onomatopoeic sounds). Those signs are indexical which have some natural relationship of contiguity with their referent. Thus, smoke is an index of fire; and photographs, as well as almost always being iconic, are also indexical. They are iconic because they resemble whatever was originally in front of the lens and they are indexical because it is the physical act of light bounced off an object through the lens and on to the filmic emulsion which leaves the trace that becomes the image. (Pinney 1997, 20)

Peirce (1894) famously used the photograph as a singular emblem of his category of indexicality. Around the prototypical indexical media form the photograph, there has grown a kind of folk ontology of media that groups together media forms based on a shared sense of indexicality and contact. This construal of varied media forms as being similar in that they involve indexicality I will call, following Nozawa, *indexicalism* (Nozawa 2015, 386, 395n15). As I argue, the perceived indexicalism of media forms, as well as the parallel indexicalism of certain, but not all, monstrous others, is what affords—enables and constrains—the felt possibility of ostension. A shared sense of indexicalism is what links together folkloric genres and what Foster and Tolbert (2016) call "folkloresque" genres and media forms, that is, nonfolkloric genres and media forms that seek to retain the "odor" of folklore. The Cottingley fairies and the Slender Man photographs both have the "odor of legend" based on a common *indexicalism*, affording fantasies of ostension.

In both these cases, Waukesha and Cottingley, we see an entanglement of monsters and media grounded in a sense of indexicalism of a media form (the photograph).[4] The indexicalism of the photograph of the monster is what gives the monster a sense of potential reality, which in turn affords the possibility of ostension. The original act of ostension in both cases was the manipulation of the photograph to place a monstrous character within a real, everyday context. The Cottingley photographs involved a laborious process of tracing the printed images of fairies (so strongly associated with the new color printing technologies epitomized by the Victorian illustrated gift book), pinning them to flowers in the garden, and taking pictures of oneself with them, so that they would eventually be printed in the *Strand* using slightly different but equally new image-printing techniques.[5]

The original "paranormal images" of Slender Man also involved a kind of ostension, showing Slender Man as part of the "real world" involved photoshopping techniques that acted similarly to laminate the monstrous character against real, everyday backgrounds. In both cases, a media character was resituated within a real-world context. The act of ostension seeks to transcend the opposition between the media world and the real one and— what is not quite the same thing—between the fantasy world of the monster and the real one.

MONSTERS AS CHARACTERS:
OSTENSION AS CHARACTER ENCOUNTER

Both these incidents of ostension have in common that they begin with photographs of fictional characters with little or no narrative attached to them. These photographs, then, are not so much an attempt to *reenact a legendary narrative* as an attempt to *encounter a legendary character* (a monster) independently of its original narrative context, but in real life. Therefore, I believe that it is crucial to adopt a distinction often made within Japanese subcultural contexts between different kinds of characters: those (called "characters," *kyarakutaa*) that are still embedded in, subordinated to their original narrative worlds and consumed as part of them, and those (called "chara" *kyara*) that have become detached from their original narrative contexts and are "portable" to new narratives and media forms, able to be consumed independently, thus taking on a life of their own and imparting a feeling that they truly exist and actually live (Lamarre 2011, 129).

The fantasy that characters have a life beyond their originating narratives is what affords the fantasy of ostensive character encounter. I therefore seek to resituate ostension from a logic of reenactment of legendary narratives to one of "character encounter," analyzable in a manner comparable to the general semiotics of media "characters" as discussed by Nozawa (2013). Nozawa (building on a rich literature on the semiotics of characters: Steinberg 2009; Ōtsuka and Steinberg 2010; Lamarre 2011) argues that the animated "life" of Japanese media "characters" (in the second sense above of *kyara*) in the media mix as well as folkloric and folkloresque monsters must be analyzed in terms of their "portability." The life of characters, their sense of being real living beings, is maintained through processes of "decontextualization" and "recontextualization," creating a diversity of contexts of "character encounter." I take my inspiration from Nozawa's observation that there might be a kind of similarity or symmetry between folkloric monsters and media characters. Folkloric monsters, like many media characters, initially inhabit narratives and are consumed as part of those narratives ("narrative consumption") (Ōtsuka and Steinberg 2010). Like media characters, they can also be extracted from narratives and consumed separately for their own sake ("character consumption"). As a result of this autonomy and portability from their original narratives, they can also be resituated within new media genres and narrative contexts (e.g., genres of fanfic depend on this kind of character portability). Lastly, characters can be further classified, taxonomized, and analyzed into characterological components in an encyclopedic fashion ("database consumption"), which allows characters to be consumed no longer with respect to narratives, nor even as individual characters, but with respect to a whole database of characters that have similar elements (Ruh 2014).

I'll give an example of such a monstrous character's career from folkloric narrative to media mix character. Foster, drawing in part explicitly on this literature on characterization (Foster 2015, 92–95), shows how Japanese *yōkai* monsters can be consumed as part of folkloric narratives but also as part of a thriving set of media practices from the Edo period onward in which characters are extracted from narratives and given autonomous representation as characters with no narrative context (Foster 2009, 54). Different monstrous media mix contexts are associated with different forms of monstrous character consumption in the Edo period: illustrated encyclopedias by artists like Sekien lead to "encyclopedic consumption"; collectible monster cards in games lead to "ludic consumption" (30–76). But both kinds of consumption are character consumption, as they involve the "extraction of yōkai, of weird or mysterious *characters*, from narrative or event" (54):

> By extracting yōkai from other texts and from local legends, Sekien helped disconnect them from their particular places of origin and from the narratives in which they played a part. This made them more generic and more versatile. They could become, in a sense, free agents employable in all sorts of new contexts. And in fact, during the latter part of the Edo period, yōkai haunted literature, art, and popular culture, everything from wood block prints to kabuki drama to *rakugo* storytelling. They especially thrived in the lighthearted illustrated texts know as *kibyōshi*, or "yellow covers" produced mainly between 1775 and 1806 . . . [An] important effect of *kibyōshi* is that they transformed yōkai into "characters." Removed from their connection to a particular legend or belief, they became iconic images—like advertising mascots—with a life of their own. (Foster 2015, 49–51)

Slender Man himself is interesting in this regard as an example of what Tolbert (2013, chapter 1 of this volume) calls "reverse ostension": a character assembled from stereotypical characterological elements of the monstrous (database consumption), first given life as a photographed character with very little actual narrative (character consumption), and finally accreting a series of narratives of transmedia storytelling as this photograph circulates (narrative consumption). Folkloric characters, extracted from their original narrative contexts, are portable folkloric beings that can be transported to other media forms to become "folkloresque" characters (Foster and Tolbert 2016; Manning 2016), and folkloric beings and characters engage parallel fantasies of ostension involving similar practices like cosplay. So, it seems reasonable that monsters might be treated *symmetrically* as being, in the first instance, a special subcase, or even a paradigmatic case, of media character. After all, most monsters exist only as narrative or media characters. As Nozawa (2013) points out, if anthropology (and, I add, folklore studies) "can illuminate or at least recognize special and important roles played by fairies, ghosts, gods, angels, the dead, and other fantastic and liminal actants . . . then it might as well do the same with characters."

MEDIA AND MONSTERS

Perhaps we could deepen the terrain of ostension of monsters as indexicality by starting with the fact that the term *monstrum*, as nearly everyone always points out (e.g., Henriksen 2013, 405), is in itself indexical or ostensive, by popular etymology deriving from the term *monstrare*, which means "show, point out" (as in the class of inherently indexical signs we call "*demonstratives*"). Of course the monsters in question that were *monstra*—signs, warnings, prodigies—typically really could be seen, displayed, or pointed at (Friedman 2000, 108), very unlike the distant fabulous "monstrous races" (see generally Friedman 2000; Daston and Park 1998), exotic races first collected together into an encyclopedia by Pliny (hence "Plinian races"), including cyclops, *blemmyae* (headless people with faces on their chests), *cynocephalae* (dog-headed people), and many others, which no one had ever seen firsthand. Monstra were typically singular, one-of-a-kind monstrous births (Peircean singular signs, tokens, unlike fantastic monstrous races, which were Peircean types: races). These were singular events as much as creatures, which were themselves grouped together with various omens and portents as indexical signs that pointed to God's will, warnings of future events (Park and Daston 1981; Daston and Park 1998). That kind of monster could be the object of ostension in the literal sense of being pointed at, and it in turn was interesting insofar as it pointed at something else, something really bad coming down the road. The "monstrous races" were ostensive in neither sense—you couldn't point to them, and they didn't point to anything, either: they lacked any sort of indexical significance as portents.

Medieval "monstrous races" were the kind of monster that couldn't be pointed out by ordinary people; though usually felt to be real, they were so distant from experience that they lived most of their lives as media monsters: they lived primarily in illustrated narratives and pictorially on maps of the world (*mappae mundi*), and were typically located in distant regions, somewhere in India or Africa (see the classic study by Wittkower [1942]). Such monsters were primarily creatures of media, and they were part of a class of monsters that occupied the margins of media forms. Depending on the kind of map, different margins were generated and different monsters: for medieval mappae mundi, with Jerusalem at the center, the Plinian races typically occupied the extreme east and south, most distant from the implicit indexical "You are here" of Europe; for Macrobian maps of climate, monsters were found at climatic extremes and especially in the antipodes (Friedman 2000); Portolan coastal charts, used for real sailing along real coasts, define "the real" (that which can really be encountered, be the object of ostension in the indexical sense) as the coastline, and so generated two kinds of vacuums that were filled with monsters—on the one hand, the oceans filled with decorative ships and evocative sea serpents; on the other, the equally fantastic interior of the land filled with savages, barbarians, and yes, the occasional Plinian blemmyae.

As Michael Camille shows in his classic *Image on the Edge* (Camille 1992) and other work (Camille 1998), homologous oppositions between the experienceable center and the monstrous margin inform most medieval media forms. Just as the margins of the world (which are defined relative to the kind of map) are places of the monstrous, so too the margins of the manuscript are filled with special purely ludic, completely chimerical monsters, impossible combinations of human, animal, and vegetable, image and text, that no one believed in and about which no one told stories—*babewyns*—as well as chimerical hybrids of textual characters and plants and animals that limn the boundary between central text and image and monstrous margin. Such "hybrid fantasies that adorned not only the margins of books but all manner of precious objects and buildings of the period" (Camille 1998, 44) "draw attention to themselves as artifice" (241). They exceed even the acceptable monstrousness hybridity of Plinian races and actual monstrous births. For example, alongside babewyns, textual monsters include hybrids that Camille calls "mock-writing" in which textual capitals or divisions come alive, sprouting the heads of dragons appended to leafy branches, combining image and text and forming "a spidery code that seems a sort of mock-writing, every element springs into disordered life" (Camille 1992, 50). Stylistically these monstrous ornaments of the margins of the medieval text systematically differ from "real" human, animal, and monstrous figures, in particular by their dead "button-like, unexpressive eyes" (Camille 1998, 234), underlining their status as unreal creatures that live only in media forms.

As Camille shows, monstrosity in the medieval imagination is strongly associated with material mediality, which allows the monster to appear, and monstrosity is powerfully associated with marginality across diverse media forms (text, building, mappa mundi). Different, but comparable, monsters occupy the margins of each media form: completely imaginary monsters like babewyns and gargoyles occupy the profane margins of the medieval sacred text and architecture respectively, while monstrous races occupy the margins of the mappae mundi, the maps of the Jerusalem-centered world. Some of these monsters, like babewyns and gargoyles, are pure media monsters; unlike monstrous races, which were felt to exist in the world "out there," these creatures exist only in the margins of the media they haunt and have no separate existence from their media.

PROJECTION AND OSTENSION: HYPERMEDIACY AND IMMEDIACY

As these examples suggest, the connection between media form and the form of monster is an intimate, even constitutive, one. As Henriksen (2013, 405–406) points out, this isn't exactly news: at precisely the time that ghosts and goblins were being dismissed from the real world as superstitious nonsense, new media forms such as the phantasmagoria and magic lantern were making it more and more possible to encounter these monsters in mediated form. But these media forms presumably had the pedagogical function of restricting monsters to the unreal world of the diegesis, even as they made them visible to the eye. Such monsters were admixtures of the real (they really exist as media characters) and the unreal (because they were creatures of media and not the real world). Henriksen (407) uses the nonce term *projection* to talk about those purely diegetic monsters that can be encountered only through a projective media form reserved for portraying the unreal. This particular entanglement of monster and media produces a sense of what Bolter and Grusin (2000, 34, 41–42) call "hypermediacy," where the world of the viewer and the world of the monster are strongly segregated and the monster is experienced as something that is part and parcel of the medium: "In every manifestation, hypermediacy makes us aware of the medium or media and (in sometimes subtle and sometimes obvious ways) reminds us of our desire for immediacy" (34).

Certainly, some monsters paid the price of becoming characters projected via "hypermediate" media forms, gaining visible bodies but becoming unreal at the same time. But the nineteenth century also provided an array of media forms, beginning with the photograph, that emphasized reality and authentic contact with the referent, media forms that seemed to provide indexical "ostension" rather than hypermediated "projection." Bolter and Grusin (2000) call this sensibility "immediacy" (as opposed to "hypermediacy"). As their definition makes obvious, "immediacy" is precisely what I am calling indexicalism, whose paradigmatic media form is the photograph: "a family of beliefs and practices that express themselves differently at various times among various groups . . . The common feature of all these forms is the belief in some necessary *contact point* between the medium and what it represents. For those who believe in the immediacy of photography, from Talbot to Bazin to Barthes, the contact point is the light that is reflected from the objects on to the film. This light establishes *an immediate relationship* between the photograph and the object" (30, emphasis added).

Both projection (hypermediacy) and ostension (immediacy) make possible an encounter with a kind of character (in this case Slender Man). To use the terminology of Bolter and Grusin (2000), they both remediate monsters of narratives of various kinds, but projection makes you aware of the mediation involved (hypermediacy), so the monster is produced as a spectacle, but its reality is denied (it is a chimera); ostension seeks instead to produce immediacy, to background or hide the mediation, so that the encounter has the feel of the real.

MEDIA REMEDIATE THE FOLKLORIC GENRE

New media often remediate the presuppositions of older media and genres about their monstrous objects. Just as some media project the monster, producing it but at the same time denying its reality (hypermediacy), other (indexical) media show the monster ostensively; that is, they produce it as evidence of its existence (immediacy). Taxonomies of folkloric narrative genres between folktale (fairy tale) and legend (Bascom 1984) involve precisely parallel contrasts. Legends, after all, are stories presented as being real: there is some living source alluded to and they take place in "this world," whereas folktales take place in an unreal narrative spacetime of "once upon a time" (8–11). Similarly, different monsters are often strongly or loosely associated with different genres of narrative (legends, folktales, myths) and share their attendant presuppositions of "realness": for example, in the country of Georgia it is possible to tell legendary narratives (*naambobi*) about certain kinds of goblins such as horned devils (*kaji, ch'in'ka*), but other kinds of goblins (three-headed *devi*, for example) are strongly associated with entirely fantastic "fairy tales" (*zghap'ari*) in some regions, while in others they are associated with mythic foundational narratives or appear as villain characters in fantastic medieval epic poetry (Manning 2014). These different narrative proclivities of folkloric monsters are indirectly reproduced in their popular "folkloresque" trajectories. In Georgia narratives of legendary monsters like kajis were taken as indexes of the superstitious "backwardness" of rural people from the nineteenth century onward. As a result, kajis are "abjected" from popular literature and never illustrated. Devis, as creatures of fable and fairy tale, had no such stigmatization but were respectable objects of "folkloresque" interest and illustration. As a result, when I ask Georgians to give me a description of legendary beings like the kaji or ch'ink'a, the question elicits very vague verbal descriptions; the kaji is usually presented as an aggressive horned being, similar to a goat, and the ch'ink'a is small. By contrast, the devi has very concrete images associated with it, and one can find plenty of images in an image search on Google, too, which one cannot for the other legendary beings. This probably has to do with the fact that the former two, as creatures of legend, are emblematic of superstition and backwardness, and thus there is no real interest in telling stories of such characters in print media, whereas devis, safely ensconced in the unreality of children's fairy tales, have no such negative connotations, and therefore have made the transition from folklore to folkloresque (Manning 2014).

Folkloric monsters of various kinds (including not only monsters but ghosts, fairies, and goblins), whether they are believed to exist or not, all have in common that they begin as *characters* specific to different *genres*, and each genre proposes a specific narrative model of space and time—a Bakhtinian "chronotope" (Bakhtin 1981; see also Manning 2017). Genres contain a narrated "world" of a specific kind as well as an indexical relationship between the narrated world and the one in which we live, where the narrative occurs. In a traditional folkloric taxonomy of genres (Bascom 1984), different kinds of narratives stipulate some sort of *indexical alignment* between the speech event, told in the here and now (E_S), and the narrated event (E_N). Legends, stories told as true, are narratives in which these two "worlds" coincide ($E_S = E_N$)—the world of legend is our own world.

Folktales are narratives in which there is no stipulated indexical linkage between the "Once upon a time" world (E_N) and our world (E_S), and myths are narratives in which the two worlds are the same, but all the events of myth (E_N) belong to a prior cosmological order supplanted by the one in which we live today (E_S).

Legends obviously occupy a special place within this system, for legends are the only genre in which the space and time of the haunting narrative belong to the same narrative world as the space and time of the telling. The domain of legend, then, is precisely the domain of ostension of monsters, because the indexical connection between the event of speaking and the narrated event ($E_S = E_N$) is precisely what potentiates the movement between these worlds, the traffic that we are calling "ostension." Certain genres like legends, then, afford ostension, while others do not. The same is true of media forms: some media forms have a powerful aura of indexicality about them, like photographs, and others have an equally anti-indexical quality: some media forms proffer the *immediacy* of realism, of indexical contact with the monster, affording the fantasy of ostension in the real world, and others deny it, emphasizing the *mediation*, producing the monster as an artifice of the media world, something that can be seen but never encountered in reality. As I will show, the location of the "weird" in the "weird tale" is precisely a space of contact between our banal, everyday world and a being that is entirely other (see also Evans, chapter 6 in this volume; Manning 2017): the permeability between worlds that affords a weird "ostension" is precisely afforded by genres, or media, that have the property of indexicality.

The "weird tale" designates a specific form of literary tale strongly associated with American writers like H. P. Lovecraft and Clark Ashton Smith, but *weird tale* had already come into use in the midnineteenth century as an informal term for genres of the supernatural like the ghost story, at approximately the same time that the word *weird* came to have its completely novel meaning of "strange or supernatural." While both the generic late nineteenth-century ghost story and this more self-conscious American trend in literature are often now assimilated into contemporary genre categories like "supernatural" or "fantastic," their common designation as "weird" tale deserves special attention. For one, the ghostliness of the weird is not specifically reducible to specific kinds of supernatural characters like ghosts, and unlike fantasy fiction of the later Tolkienian variety, weird fiction is defined by a space of contact between a diegetic world of prosaic realism and an otherworld or an otherworldly element (Manning 2017; Fisher 2017). The weird tale, for Lovecraft, requires a strongly realist frame setting into which there is an irruption of destabilizing otherness or alterity (see also Evans 2005, chapter 6 in this volume; Fisher 2017; Manning 2017): "Serious weird stories are . . . made realistically intense by close consistency and perfect fidelity to Nature except in the one supernatural direction which the author allows himself" (Lovecraft 1927). Similarly, an earmark of the ghost story is parallel to that of folkloric legends of ghostly hauntings in that it situates the ghost within "the prosaic detail of modernity to establish a credible context for supernatural violation . . . Everyday detail abounds in the Victorian ghost story: details of decor and dress, food and drink, furniture and transport, landscape and architecture, as well as the realities of social and sexual relationships" (Cox and Gilbert 1991, xvi–xvii; see also Fisher 2017; Manning 2017; Evans, chapter 6 of this volume).

Linda Dégh pointedly notes, "While 'lie' translates as fiction, 'truth' does not necessarily mean that people believe the legends they tell, but rather that legends are about what real people experience within their own topographically delimited territory in the real world. The real world is the referent of the legend" (Dégh 1996, 41). Such connections are equally important in weird fiction in general. Susan Stewart likens the horror story, which plays with the boundaries of reality and fiction, to the legend genre. She suggests that the world of the horror story is "neither true nor false," but the narrative itself employs "metanarrative devices [that] continually assert it to be a 'true story.'" Oral recounting of "horror" narratives includes formulae that situate the story within the real world, and these serve to "map the story onto the landscape or social relations of the reader/listener's everyday lifeworld" (Stewart 1982, 35). These serve as *quasi-indexical* metanarrative devices situating the irruption of the otherworldly within the banality of the everyday, giving the frame narrative an aura of reality. This trend is also characteristic of the faux-realist semiotics of contemporary "creepypasta," digital horror stories such as the Slender Man Mythos (Tolbert 2013, chapter 1 of this volume). Similarly, Shane McCorristine and others see in the Victorian ghost story a kind of liminal "factional" genre that is constituted as such at the undecidable boundary of fact and fiction (McCorristine 2010, 10, 16–18). On another level, fictional horror stories may make strategic "folkloresque" use of "legendary" materials, either by incorporating real-world legends into their narratives or by creating whole bodies of lore within their fictive universes that resemble real-world folklore (see Foster and Tolbert 2016).

In this chapter, then, I group together under the umbrella of *indexicalism* a whole range of genres (legends, ghost stories, weird tales, creepypasta) that are *told in the manner of a legend*, as a potentially "true" story, set in historical times and known place(s) and involving human actors as well as elements of the fantastic. Metanarrative devices from legend (appeals to an indexical chain of transmission—"I heard it from my cousin Nick, who knew the guy who saw it"), real places, times, events, and so on (see also Evans, chapter 6 of this volume) seek to produce an aura of indexicality, the "odor" of legend, and are constitutive of what I am calling *indexicalism*. In general, folkloric genres (legends), folkloresque genres (ghost stories, weird tales), and media forms (photographs) all have a shared indexicalism, as do derivative practices of ostension such as "legend tripping" and other practices that seek to bring legendary texts to life in experienceable reality. As Catherine Tosenberger notes, "It is not surprising that ostension usually occurs with legends—since the performance of ostensive acts is intended to produce real-world results, it makes sense that the narratives chosen for performance usually make some claim to real-world truth" (Tosenberger 2010, 1.7).[6]

The aesthetics of the Slender Man Mythos depends on a general aesthetics of indexicalism that is characteristic of weird fiction: the stories are generally characterized by an intense realism but for the irruption of Slender Man himself into this "real" setting (Tolbert, chapter 4 of this volume). This is aptly illustrated by Marble Hornets," a Slender Man video series that, as any legend narrative would, positions itself in a real relation to its object (see Tolbert, chapter 1 of this volume).[7] The videos are framed as real, part of an ongoing documentary series chronicling the disappearance of a college film student, with Slender Man as the primary antagonist. The backgrounds against which the drama unfolds are also real ones, and quite prosaic ones at that: everyday locales such as apartments, lonely streets, woods.[8] Similarly, what is striking about the Cottingley fairies incident is a similar juxtaposition of the otherworldly (fairies) with the utterly prosaic context of a garden in Cottingley. In both cases, metanarrative devices of indexicalism (photography) serve to produce a "weird" indexical relation of an otherworldly figure against an ordinary realistic background. The reality of the background serves, on the one hand, to give the figure an odor of legend as a creature that can be encountered in this world (immediacy), but on the other hand, it produces a laminated "weird" image that contains both worldly and otherworldly, real-life and media elements (hypermediacy), a weird juxtaposition encapsulated in the phrase most closely associated with the Cottingley incident (see Bown 1996): "There are fairies at the bottom of our garden."

THE FOLKLORESQUE TRAJECTORIES OF MEDIA
MONSTERS: GHOSTS AND FAIRIES

Folkloric monsters are creatures that inhabit genres of specific kinds: each monster has a specific chronotopic vicinity, a set of genre-internal spaces and times of its appearance. The same seems to be true of what we could call "folkloresque" monsters. Each folkloresque monster prefers media forms that have associations similar to those of the original folkloric genre, thus retaining the "odor of folklore" even as the monster is resituated within nonfolkloric channels of circulation. Just as Victorian media forms produced a whole series of new media forms that could be haunted by folkloric creatures of legend, the two primary kinds of Victorian haunters, ghosts and fairies, parted ways. Legendary ghosts became associated with a set of media genres of immediacy like the photograph, and fairies distanced themselves from their legendary backgrounds, becoming figures of hypermediacy, the unreal fantasy figures of color illustrated books and all the dazzling new media forms, from electric lighting to glass architecture, that became synonymous with the ubiquitous term *fairyland*.

This parting of the ways between two creatures of folkloric legend— the ghost and the fairy—was a long time in preparation before they came to occupy opposed niches in the new media worlds of the Victorian era (see also Manning 2005, 2016; Forsberg 2015). As Davies notes, the fairy was already a vanishing race in England, where from the eighteenth century ghosts increasingly came to usurp fairies as characters of legend narratives, because somehow ghosts seemed more "realistic" (Davies 2007, 23). In popular discourse, "belief in fairies" marks an end point on a scale of reasonableness, suggesting imminent departure from consensus reality: fairies (along with unicorns) being the accepted name for the *most unreal* of unreal things.[9] While folklorists like Bascom (1984, 8) eschew the use of "fairy tale" for folkloric genres whose "timeless and placeless" worlds and characters are excluded from the order of what exists (what folklorists call the folktale) because fairies are actually usually folkloric creatures of legend, in popular usage "fairy tale" is used more or less precisely as folklorists use "folktale," indicating how completely fairies have departed the order of the real.

Both folkloric ghosts and fairies are originally creatures of legend whose haunts are real places just down the road. But somehow in the process of becoming detached from these original folkloric narratives, these two legendary beings parted ways. Ghosts, indexical traces of living humans, become associated with genres and related media associated with indexicalism, reality, and realism, while fairies take on all the opposed properties, becoming associated with genres and media of the unreal: illustrated children's books and later children's cartoons.

The nineteenth-century movement of spiritualism produced such an influential and fascinating entanglement of the ghost and new media forms of the nineteenth century that the topic of spiritualism, ghosts, and media has become central in media studies in recent years (see the discussions in Peters 1999; Sconce 2000; Harvey 2013). As these writers show, spiritualism gathered together a range of new media forms fraught with appeals to indexicality as the metaphoric basis for their pretense of offering real contact with the departed. Spiritualist "haunted media" forms like the "full materialization" séance, the "spiritualist telegraph" séance, and spirit photograph all share an explicitly indexical, ostensive, "pointing" quality, producing tangible evidence for the existence of ghosts. As each ghostly media form receded, it would be replaced by new ones that similarly sought to produce signs of indexical contact across various channels (see Sconce 2000; Harvey 2013; Manning 2018).

Spirit photographs—double exposures on glass plates—were emblematic objects of this pervasive indexicalism. Spirit photographs at least initially offered persuasive tokens of real contact with the departed because of the parallelism of qualities between the ghost and the image— the diaphanous ghostly qualities of photographic negatives and double exposures seemed to mirror the way that ghosts were imagined (Cheroux 2005, 45)—but also because the indexicality of the photograph, first stressed by Charles Peirce, ensured that ghosts retained their most distinctive property, their legendary pretensions to being real. As Harvey (2013, 55) notes, spirit photography "literalized" the metaphoric, iconic relation between the ghost and the photographic image, since both ghosts and photographs are indexical: they point to real presences of something absent. Since then, technologically savvy hungry ghosts, typified by Japanese horror films like *Ringu*, are the rule rather than the exception, and have been known to haunt various media offering indexical telepresence and immediacy: haunted videotapes (*Ringu* [1998]) or televisions (*Poltergeist* [1982]), cameras (*Shutter* [2004, 2008]), the Internet (*Kairo* ["*Pulse*"] [2001]), even Korean web comics that typically tell scary stories about ghosts (*Killer Toon* [2013]). As John Harvey puts it: "Spirits capture technology in order for technology to capture them," that is, "spirits desire and achieve technological embodiment . . . to become Psi-cyborgs" (Harvey 2013, 63). The primary quality shared by these "haunted media" and the ghosts that haunt them is not electricity (as Sconce 2000 suggests), but indexicality, the promise of real contact and presence, crossed by a kind of qualitative alterity emphasizing absence, faint diaphanous double exposures, white noise on the television.

In contrast to this diaphanous gray ghost world of faint, but real, presence, in the Victorian period fairies became decidedly unreal fantastic characters that colonized the colorized fairyland worlds of new print technologies like illustrated children's picture books and later animated cartoons along with other creatures of fairy tale and fable, such as talking animals (Silver 1999; Bown 2001). If ghosts took on the properties of the media forms they inhabited and conferred their own ghostliness upon those media in turn, producing surprisingly durable fantasies of "haunted media" as a gray, electrical ghost world, then fairies in the nineteenth century became the prototypical inhabitants of the colorful illustrations of Victorian print media, a multimedia fantasy world of hypermediacy that, as Beverly Gordon shows, was captured under the term *fairyland*. As Gordon (2006, 40) argues, "fairyland" became a leitmotif to describe "any event, object, or space felt to be aesthetically charged, enchanted, and otherworldly. . . Fairyland was . . . sometimes understood as a beautiful, ideal place—a dreamland or wonderland that existed far away, apart from any painful realities or practicalities. It was a brightly colored, sensually rich, happy world," and its emblematic realization was in the new color illustrations of Christmas gift books like Richard Doyle's 1870 *In Fairyland*. As Gordon (2006, 2007) shows, in addition to denoting the eponymous diegetic world populated by fairies depicted in the ubiquitous fairy paintings of Doyle and others reproduced with new color print technologies (Owen 1994, 50–54), more broadly the term *fairyland* collected together a series of dazzling colorful new media forms in which the emphasis was not on the fantastic creatures the media represented but the fantastic spectacle of the medium itself. "Fairyland" described a condition of hypermediacy created by new Victorian media forms like glass architecture, color print technology, and electrical light shows, since the term drew attention to both the fantastic nature of the medium and the fantastic creatures that inhabited that medium, to both a premodern fantastic world populated by fairies and the very modern technologies of enchantment that opened doors or windows onto that world. Ghostly media emphasized immediacy and ostension that proffered faint, but real, indexical contact with the departed (ghosts); by contrast, folkloresque fairies became not creatures of immediacy (remediating the legend), but fantastic creatures of dazzling hypermediacy, creatures with no existence apart from the fantastic media world that projected them. Each kind of monster, ghost and fairy, even as it colonizes new media forms, in turns lends some of its monstrous qualities metaphorically to the new media form, even aligning different media forms together into categories by the kind of monster they can remediate: gray ghostly photograph or vividly colored fairylands.

In this context, the Cottingley case is interesting as an exception that proves the rule. Part of the central contradiction in the Cottingley incident is that the girls attempted to move precisely the unreal winged fairies of Victorian print culture (the girls actually traced their fairies out of such a book and then added the wings themselves) into the real world of their own garden, using photographs to make these unreal beings real. For many who might have accepted a ghost photograph, the anti-indexical connotations of the fairy combined with the indexical connotations of the photograph was simply a bridge too far.

BORDERLAND FORMS: FROM WAUKESHA TO COTTINGLEY

Both the story of Slender Man and the story of the Cottingley fairies begin with attempts to move fantastic creatures out of a domain of hypermediacy, pure media fantasy, into a domain of immediacy, to reground them in the indexical order of the photograph, and later, to reground them in reality. Since the case of the Slender Man photographs has been discussed at length in the other chapters of this volume, I will concentrate here primarily on the Cottingley case. The story of the Cottingley photographs emphasizes, as Owen notes, the public interpretations of three older influential men— Arthur Conan Doyle and a few other middle-aged theosophists—over the private narratives of the two rather shy working-class girls who made the photographs (Owen 1994, 79), who were apparently not amused by having their private childhood fairy garden invaded and publicized by these elderly theosophist birdwatchers.

Almost all the photos contain both a human figure and a fairy figure, but in the theosophical interpretations (Gardner 1982) the human figure is erased, representing at most a "medium" (inasmuch as it was felt that the *devas*—the theosophical term of art for fairies—might require the "thought forms" of the girls in order to take the somewhat conventional forms they chose, primarily adaptations of fairy illustrations). For the girls, however, the human figure had deep personal significance: "The whole point of the photograph [made famous by Conan Doyle under the title *Alice and the Fairies*] for Frances Griffiths . . . was that it is 'of me.' As far as [Griffiths] was concerned, she is as much the subject of the photograph as the fairies. There is also a sense in which Elsie Wright, as the photographer, is equally

present. It was she who organized the figures according to her vision of a
world she inhabited with the younger girl" (Owen 1994, 78).

As both Owen (1994) and Bown (1996) argue, the photographs were
produced to commemorate and give a sense of reality to a private childhood
realm and, perhaps, as a testament to an intensely private fantasy world
shared by the two girls, who by all accounts were shy outsiders, the older
girl (Elsie) still playing with dolls at age sixteen and long fascinated with
fairies, the younger girl (Frances) raised abroad and possessing a "much
derided Canadian accent." This may have explained her creation of fairy
playmates that "perhaps brought 'glamour' and 'mystery' to the austere con-
ditions Frances encountered at Cottingley, and helped replace playfellows
of the human variety" (Owen 1994, 72). "The Cottingley fairy photographs
are a fragment of 1917 childhood which Conan Doyle appropriated and
invested with new meaning, and the intentions and dreams of the girls were
subsumed in the process. Intended by Elsie Wright and Frances Griffiths
to stand as a personal record and confirmation of their relationship to the
Cottingley fairy world, the photographs were instead circulated by Conan
Doyle for public consumption to support his own dearly held beliefs about
spiritualism" (79).

The Cottingley fairy photographs themselves are a "weird" hybrid: produced as private testaments to a singular childhood relationship of "shared
fantasy," they became public photographic evidence of a hidden kingdom
of nature. As media objects, too, they are hybrids—fairy photographs
whose images of fairies were literally drawn by one of the girls after fairy
illustrations from a book in which one of Conan Doyle's own fictional stories appeared, the very kind of fairy illustrations that Conan Doyle's father
and uncle had both made professionally. For their producers, the fairy
photographs owe little or nothing to the naturalizing specular discourse
of immediacy and indexicalism of the spirit photograph; rather, they com-
prise the aesthetics of hypermediacy of the fairy picture, which they incorporate physically, blending it with the aesthetics of the personal portrait,
revealing not a hidden side of nature (fairies) but a hidden side of the girls
themselves, not "the 'real' Elsie—the adult, working and shopping Elsie"
but "the 'phantasmic' Elsie—the child-Elsie who saw fairies" (Bown 1996,
68). As Bown powerfully glosses Elsie's own account of the photographs:
"Elsie's description 'pictures of figments of our imagination' should therefore be taken as an accurate and revealing description of the photographs.
When they took the pictures, Frances and Elsie looked at themselves and
each other, and recorded what they saw: girls-who-see-fairies, caught in the
act, one might say, of imagining themselves in relation to the distinctions

between adulthood and childhood, illusion and reality, and of playing with these distinctions as if, well, they were purely imaginary" (79).

In the wake of Doyle's (1920, 1922) publication of these photographs, the girls, fully three years after the original pictures were taken, were forced to endure what must have seemed like an equally long time of torment when they spent a number of days with a theosophist named Hodson on a fairy bird-watching expedition in the garden where they saw the fairies (Gardner 1982). (All further attempts to produce fairy photos, of course, failed, a circumstance that Doyle and the theosophists blamed on the girls' loss of mediumship as a result of the advent of sexuality!) By all accounts, the incident of clairvoyant bird-watching, which occurred over a period of days, was a torment for the girls, but the clairvoyant, Hodson, produced interminable fairy-watching notes of the fairies that he or the girls saw, such as the following:

> *Fairies* (Tuesday, August 16th, 10 p.m., in the field by the light of a small photographic lamp). Elsie sees a circle of fairies tripping around, hands joined facing outwards. A figure appears at the centre of the ring; at the same time the fairies face inwards. (Gardner 1982, 39) . . .

> (In the Glen, 18th, 2 p.m.) . . . *Golden Fairy*. One specially beautiful one has a body clothed in iridescent shimmering golden light. She has tall wings, each of which is almost divided into upper and lower portions. The lower portion, which is smaller than the upper, appears to be elongated to a point like the wings of certain butterflies. She, too, is moving her arms and fluttering her wings. I can only describe her as a golden wonder. (41)

In these attempts at clairvoyant ostension, the naturalized fairies of theosophy (devas) were well on their way to becoming little more than disenchanted psychic insects (Silver 1999, 190), the subject of "occult naturalist" forms of clairvoyant ostension, fairy bird-watching. For the girls, however, the fairies in the photographs seem rather to be an attempt at reenchantment, bringing the aesthetic enchantment of the fairy painting to life, to *their lives*, in photographs that were as much pictures of fantasy selves as fantastic others. Unlike spirit photography, where the producers and interpreters were largely agreed on the interpretative apparatus, the Cottingley photographs were truly "borderland forms"; although they were interpreted within the same epistemic and ontological framework as spirit photographs by Doyle and others, they were produced by the girls in a framework that owes more to the fantastic aesthetic premises of the fairy painting. Indeed, they were precisely assembled from fragments of fairy paintings that were resituated from the hypermediacy of the fairyland of the Christmas gift book (to be specific, *The Princess Mary's Gift Book* of 1915) into the immediacy of the garden at the back of their house in Cottingley.

INTERDIMENSIONAL TRAVEL: ONTOLOGY OF THE WEIRD AND THE 2.5D

Slender Man is precisely the kind of entity whose very aesthetics works via the sort of ostension we see in the weird narrative: Slender Man is always found in "real" places, as Tolbert points out in chapter 4 of this volume, and there is an intense realism but for the "irruption" of Slender Man into this real setting. Creepypasta monsters like Slender Man, then, echo the general aesthetic tendencies of the American weird tale (see also Evans, chapter 6 of this volume), producing "a 'liminal' space of contact between a diegetic world of prosaic realism and an other world or an otherworldly element" (Fisher 2017; Manning 2017, 83). Slender Man and creepypasta in general not only remediate the legend and the weird tale, they are modeled on the specific aesthetics of the weird as a space of interdimensional, indexical contact. The aesthetics of the weird tale, you might say, is basically all about ostension. And yet the fabrication of such images speaks instead to a hypermediacy that playfully absorbs this indexicality while at the same time exhibiting a kind of yearning for transdimensional travel into the fantastic.

The weird is a space of ostension but also a liminal space that depends for its effects on the monster being somehow wholly other to the world in which it is encountered. The monster is *from another world* but is encountered *in this world*. The original Slender Man photographs and the Cottingley photographs have in common that they proffer a weird image of interdimensional contact, where the real world contains both prosaic real human figures and something wholly other. The case of the Cottingley fairies more strikingly underlines this latent theme of interdimensional travel, for here the fairy photographs seem to reground fairies in reality, something that, unlike ghosts, are indigenous to the world of hypermediacy, attempting to make a purely fictional media character come to life in this world, moving from the two-dimensional illustrated page of the gift book to the three-dimensional world of the here and now alongside three-dimensional humans.

By underlining this language of interdimensionality, I seek to draw out striking parallels here with the folk semiotics that inform Japanese media cultures having to do with the ostension of (purely fantastic) manga/anime characters into this world. In indigenous *Otaku* and *Fujoshi* fan culture idiom, the domain of ostension is the domain of "2.5D" interdimensional transfer (Nozawa 2013), essentially ostensive practices by which manga/ anime characters are brought across dimensions from the 2D world of the media forms in which they are first encountered into the 3D world in which the fans live: dressing up as Slender Man as discussed by Andrew Peck in chapter 2 of this volume, for example, is comparable to cosplaying a character; pilgrimages to allegedly or fictionally haunted places are akin to anime pilgrimages to the real places against which characters are portrayed (ostensive practices of ghost hunting, pranking, hoaxing, and the like appear to be parasitic on the quasi-legendary status of Slender Man, which distinguishes such ostensive practices from those of other fan communities). Thus, ostension can be understood as a form that parallels fantasies of 2.5D "interdimensional travel," containing the same ambiguities of real/ unreal that Kitta stresses in chapter 3 of this volume. According to Nozawa (2013), "While the two realms, 2D and 3D, are kept separate, people fantasize what I will call cross dimensional travel, where a double desire is expressed: keeping the boundary intact while at the same time 'traveling' to the other dimension. This ambiguous moment is often playfully encapsulated by the expression 2.5 *jigen,* or '2.5D': not completely virtual 2D but not entirely actual 3D, either."

Slender Man and the Cottingley fairies, then, have in common that they are characters in Nozawa's sense and, like Nozawa's characters, they are first and foremost creatures indigenous to their specific media forms. Whether they can travel to other 2D media of the media mix or engage in 2.5D interdimensional travel out of the 2D media mix into 3D reality depends on character "portability," the cross-contextual stability of the character that allows it to "live," to remain recognizable across media contexts while still being plastic enough to inhabit new contexts of character encounter (whether new media forms or embodied forms): "Media mix must presuppose or must create a situation where characters can move beyond one media format and beyond one narrative context. Animated characters do not simply 'move' on a screen; they must be able to move out of the frame, and enter into other media forms and other narrative contexts. So movement-in-society is what is at stake . . . Characters' life is maintained through processes of 'decontextualization' and 'recontextualization,' . . . which create a diversity of contexts of character-encounter" (Nozawa 2013).

By attending to the varied practices of ostension through which Slender Man "lives," I have attempted to read this monster as a "media monster," a kind of "character" shaped and adapted to the varied contexts of the media forms he can inhabit.

ACKNOWLEDGMENTS

Much of what I say here is directly or indirectly indebted to conversations with Jeff Tolbert, who helped a linguistic anthropologist and remedial folklorist to understand the dimensions of folkloristic discourse in general and Slender Man in particular. I'd like to also thank my fellow monsterologists, folklorists and anthropologists Anne Meneley, Shunsuke Nozawa, Michael Dylan Foster, Robert Brightman, Yasmine Musharbash, Charles Stewart, Ron James, Ilana Gershon, Teri Silvio, and Debra Occhi.

NOTES

1. See also Evans's chapter 6 of this volume; Manning 2017. My use of the term *weird* here is primarily in Lovecraft's (1927) sense, but by appropriating it as a key term I am also influenced by Foster (2009), who uses it in preference to loaded terms like *uncanny* whose connotations take analysis directly—and unhelpfully—back to Freud.

2. My use of terms like *monstrous media* and *media monster* is inspired by Figal (2010) and Foster (2009, 160–203).

3. For the fairy photographs, see https://en.wikipedia.org/wiki/Cottingley_Fairies.

4. I'll include fairies as monsters since we are saying these are things that aren't real in the usual sense.

5. You see from this list of media (photographs, printed images, traced copies of printed images that are then photographed and then printed) that I can't quite bring myself to talk about the monster without talking about the media that allow it to exist in the first place as a character that can be encountered first in a medium's diegetic space and then can also transcend that space using other media.

6. Importantly, Tosenberger (2010) goes on to demonstrate that in the TV series *Supernatural*, ostension is not limited to the legend genre (1.7).

7. *Marble Hornets*, YouTube video series (DeLage, Wagner, and Sutton 2009).

8. I thank Jeff Tolbert (personal communication) for all these observations.

9. I think this would correspond to the intuitions of most readers, but if not, I offer this citation from the website of the philosopher Stephen Law, who uses "belief in fairies" as marking an end point of a scale of reasonableness: (http://stephenlaw.blogspot.ca/2007/11/sleight-of-hand-with-faith.html).

WORKS CITED

Bakhtin, Mikheil. 1981. "Forms of Time and of the Chronotope in the Novel." In *The Dialogic Imagination*, ed. Michael Holquist, trans. Caryl Emerson and Michael Holquist, 84–258. Austin: University of Texas Press.

Bascom, William. 1984. "The Forms of Folklore: Prose Narratives." In *Sacred Narrative: Readings in the Theory of Myth*, ed. Alan Dundes, 5–29. Berkeley: University of California Press.

Bolter, Jay David, and Richard A. Grusin. 2000. *Remediation: Understanding New Media*. Cambridge, MA: MIT Press.

Bown, Nicola. 1996. "'There Are Fairies at the Bottom of Our Garden': Fairies, Fantasy and Photography." *Textual Practice* 10 (1): 57–82. https://doi.org/10.1080/0950236 9608582239.

Bown, Nicola. 2001. *Fairies in Nineteenth-Century Art and Literature.* Cambridge: Cambridge University Press.

Camille, Michael. 1992. *Image on the Edge: The Margins of Medieval Art.* London: Reaktion.

Camille, Michael. 1998. *Mirror in Parchment: The Luttrell Psalter and the Making of Medieval England.* Chicago: University of Chicago Press.

Cheroux, Clement. 2005. "Ghost Dialectics: Spirit Photography in Entertainment and Belief." In *The Perfect Medium: Photography and the Occult*, ed. Clement Cheroux, Andreas Fischer, Pierre Apraxine, Denis Canguilhem, and Sophie Schmit, 44–71. New Haven: Yale University Press.

Cox, Michael, and R. A. Gilbert. 1991. "Introduction." In *Victorian Ghost Stories*, ed. Michael Cox and R. A. Gilbert, ix–xx. Oxford: Oxford University Press.

Daston, Lorraine, and Katherine Park. 1998. *Wonders and the Order of Nature, 1150–1750.* New York: Zone Books.

Davies, Owen. 2007. *The Haunted.* New York: Palgrave Macmillan. https://doi.org/10.1057 /9780230273948.

Dégh, Linda. 1996. "What Is a Belief Legend?" *Folklore* 107 (1–2): 33–46. https://doi.org /10.1080/0015587X.1996.9715912.

DeLage, Joseph, Troy Wagner, and Tim Sutton. 2009. *Marble Hornets.* YouTube video series. https://www.youtube.com/user/MarbleHornets?feature=watch.

Doyle, Arthur Conan. 1920. "Fairies Photographed. An Epoch-Making Event." *Strand*, December.

Doyle, Arthur Conan. 1922. *The Coming of the Fairies.* London: Hodder & Stoughton.

Doyle, Richard. 1870. *In Fairy Land: A Series of Pictures from the Elf-World.* London: Longmans.

Evans, Timothy. 2005. "A Last Defense against the Dark: Folklore, Horror, and the Uses of Tradition in the Works of H. P. Lovecraft." *Journal of Folklore Research* 42 (1): 99–135. https://doi.org/10.2979/JFR.2005.42.1.99.

Figal, Gerald. 2010. "Monstrous Media and Delusional Consumption in Kon Satoshi's *Paranoia Agent.*" *Mechademia* 5:139–155.

Fisher, Mark. 2017. *The Weird and the Eerie.* London: Repeater Books.

Forsberg, Laura. 2015. "Nature's Invisibilia: The Victorian Microscope and the Miniature Fairy." *Victorian Studies* 57 (4): 638–666. https://doi.org/10.2979/victorianstudies .57.4.03.

Foster, Michael Dylan. 2009. *Pandemonium and Parade: Japanese Monsters and the Culture of Yōkai.* Berkeley: University of California Press. https://doi.org/10.1525/califor nia/9780520253612.001.0001.

Foster, Michael Dylan. 2015. *The Book of Yokai: Mysterious Creatures of Japanese Folklore.* Berkeley: University of California Press.

Foster, Michael Dylan, and Jeffrey A. Tolbert. 2016. *The Folkloresque: Reframing Folklore in a Popular Culture World.* Logan: Utah State University Press. https://doi.org/10 .7330/9781607324188.

Friedman, John. (Original work published 1981) 2000. *The Monstrous Races in Medieval Art and Thought.* Syracuse: Syracuse University Press.

Gardner, Edward L. 1982. *Fairies: The Cottingley Photographs.* London: Theosophical Publishing House.

Gordon, Beverly. 2006. *The Saturated World: Aesthetic Meaning, Intimate Objects, Women's Lives, 1890–1940.* Knoxville: University of Tennessee Press.

Gordon, Beverly. 2007. "Crazy Quilts as an Expression of 'Fairyland.'" *CQ Magonline* 6 (3). Accessed October 28, 2016. http://cqmagonline.com/vol06iss03/articles /701/index.shtml.

Harvey, John. 2013. "The Ghost in the Machine: Spirit and Technology." In *The Ashgate Research Companion to Paranormal Cultures*, ed. Olu Jenzen and Sally R. Munt, 51–63. Burlington, VT: Ashgate.

Henriksen, Line. 2013. "A Short Bestiary of Creatures from the Web." In *The Ashgate Research Companion to Paranormal Cultures*, ed. Olu Jenzen and Sally R. Munt, 405–416. Burlington, VT: Ashgate.

Kairo ("Pulse"). 2001. Dir. Kiyoshi Kurosawa. Japan: Toho.

Killer Toon (Deo Web-tun: Yeo-go-sal-in). 2013. Dir. Kim Yong-Gyun. South Korea: CJ Entertainment.

Lamarre, Thomas. 2011. "Speciesism, Part III: Neoteny and the Politics of Life." *Mechademia* 6 (1): 110–136. https://doi.org/10.1353/mec.2011.0005.

Lovecraft, H. P. 1927. "Supernatural Horror in Literature." *Recluse* 1:23–59. https://ebooks.adelaide.edu.au/l/lovecraft/hp/supernatural/chapter10.html.

Manning, Paul. 2005. "Jewish Ghosts, Knackers, Tommyknockers, and Other Sprites of Capitalism in the Cornish Mines." *Cornish Studies* 13 (1): 216–255. https://doi.org/10.1386/corn.13.1.216_1.

Manning, Paul. 2014. "When Goblins Come to Town: The Ethnography of Urban Hauntings in Georgia." In *Monster Anthropology in Australasia and Beyond*, ed. Yasmine Musharbash and Geir Presterudstuen, 161–177. New York: Palgrave Macmillan. https://doi.org/10.1057/9781137448651_10.

Manning, Paul. 2016. "Pixie's Progress: How the Pixies Became Part of the 19th Century Fairy Mythology." In *The Folkloresque: Reframing Folklore in Popular Culture*, ed. Michael Dylan Foster and Jeffrey Tolbert, 81–103. Logan: Utah State University Press. https://doi.org/10.7330/9781607324188.c003.

Manning, Paul. 2017. "No Ruins. No Ghosts." *Preternature* 6 (1): 63–92. https://doi.org/10.5325/preternature.6.1.0063.

Manning, Paul. 2018. "Spiritualist Signal and Theosophical Noise." *Journal of Linguistic Anthropology* 28 (1): 67–92.

McCorristine, Shane. 2010. *Spectres of the Self.* Cambridge: Cambridge University Press.

Nozawa, Shunsuke. 2013. "Characterization." *Semiotic Review*, no. 3. https://www.semioticreview.com/ojs/index.php/sr/article/view/16.

Nozawa, Shunsuke. 2015. "Phatic Traces: Sociality in Contemporary Japan." *Anthropological Quarterly* 88 (2): 373–400. https://doi.org/10.1353/anq.2015.0014.

Ōtsuka, Eiji, and Steinberg, M. 2010. "World and Variation: The Reproduction and Consumption of Narrative." *Mechademia* 5 (1): 99–116.

Owen, Alex. 1994. "'Borderland Forms': Arthur Conan Doyle, Albion's Daughters, and the Politics of the Cottingley Fairies." *History Workshop Journal* 38 (1): 48–85. https://doi.org/10.1093/hwj/38.1.48.

Park, K., and L. J. Daston. 1981. "Unnatural Conceptions: The Study of Monsters in Sixteenth- and Seventeenth-Century France and England." *Past & Present* 92 (1): 20–54. https://doi.org/10.1093/past/92.1.20.

Peirce, Charles S. 1894. "What Is a Sign?" https://www.iupui.edu/%7Epeirce/web/ep/ep2/ep2book/ch02/ep2ch2.htm.

Peters, John D. 1999. *Speaking into the Air: A History of the Idea of Communication.* Chicago: University of Chicago Press. https://doi.org/10.7208/chicago/9780226922638.001.0001.

Pinney, Christopher. 1997. *Camera Indica: The Social Life of Indian Photographs.* Chicago: University of Chicago Press.

Poltergeist. 1982. Dir. Tobe Hooper. America: MGM/UA Entertainment.

Ringu. 1998. Dir. Hideo Nakata. Japan: Toho.

Ruh, Brian. 2014. "Conceptualizing Anime and the Database Fantasyscape." *Mechademia* 9 (1): 164–175. https://doi.org/10.1353/mec.2014.0012.

Sconce, Jeffrey. 2000. *Haunted Media: Electronic Presence from Telegraphy to Television*. Durham: Duke University Press.

Shutter. 2004. Dir. Banjong Pisanthanakun and Parkpoom Wongpoom. Thailand: GMM Grammy.

Shutter. 2008. Dir. Masayuki Ochiai. America: 20th Century Fox.

Silver, Carole. 1999. *Strange and Secret Peoples: Fairies and Victorian Consciousness*. Oxford: Oxford University Press.

Smith, Paul. 1991. "The Cottingley Fairies: The End of a Legend." In *The Good People: New Fairylore Essays*, ed. Peter Narvaez, 371–405. Lexington: University of Kentucky Press.

Steinberg, Marc. 2009. "Anytime, Anywhere: Tetsuwan Atomu Stickers and the Emergence of Character Merchandizing." *Theory, Culture & Society* 26 (2–3): 113–138. https://doi.org/10.1177/0263276409103114.

Stewart, Susan. 1982. "The Epistemology of the Horror Story." *Journal of American Folklore* 95 (375): 33–50. https://doi.org/10.2307/540021.

Tolbert, Jeffrey A. 2013. "'The Sort of Story That Has You Covering Your Mirrors': The Case of Slender Man." *Semiotic Review*, no. 2: Monsters. https://semioticreview.com/ojs/index.php/sr/article/download/19/19.

Tosenberger, Catherine. 2010. "'Kinda Like the Folklore of Its Day': 'Supernatural,' Fairy Tales, and Ostension." *Transformative Works and Cultures* 4. https://doi.org/10.3983/twc.2010.0174.

Wittkower, Rudolf. 1942. "Marvels of the East: A Study in the History of Monsters." *Journal of the Warburg and Courtauld Institutes* 5:159–197. https://doi.org/10.2307/750452.

Notes on the Authors

TREVOR J. BLANK is associate professor of communication at the State University of New York at Potsdam. He is the author or editor of eight books, including *Folklore and the Internet* (2009), *Folk Culture in the Digital Age* (2012), and *The Last Laugh: Folk Humor, Celebrity Culture, and Mass-Mediated Disasters in the Digital Age* (2013). His research interests span digital culture, mass media, humor, public health, and the intersections of folk belief and contemporary legends.

TIMOTHY H. EVANS, associate professor of folk studies in the Department of Folk Studies and Anthropology at Western Kentucky University, has a Ph.D. in folklore and American studies from Indiana University. He has worked in both public folklore and academia and has published in a number of areas, including public and applied folklore, the culture of the American West, folk art and architecture, folklore and literature, and fantasy and science fiction. He has published articles on H. P. Lovecraft, William Morris, Philip K. Dick, Neil Gaiman, and others.

ANDREA KITTA is an associate professor at East Carolina University. She is the author of *Vaccinations and Public Concern in History: Legend, Rumor, and Risk Perception*, which won the Brian McConnell Book Award in 2012. She received the Bertie E. Fearing Award for Excellence in Teaching (2010–2011) and has been nominated for numerous teaching awards. Dr. Kitta is currently finishing her next book, *The Kiss of Death: Contamination, Contagion, and Folklore*, to be published by Utah State University Press. Her interests include medical folklore and the folklore of health systems, disability studies, belief, the supernatural, pandemics, stigmatized illnesses, and contemporary legends.

MIKEL J. KOVEN is senior lecturer in film studies at the University of Worcester. He is the author of *La Dolce Morte: Vernacular Cinema and the Italian Giallo Film* (2006), *Film, Folklore and Urban Legends* (2008), and *Blaxploitation Films* (2010). His essays covering the relationship film has with folklore and folklore with film have appeared in a number of academic journals and in a variety of edited books. He does not believe in Slender Man.

PAUL MANNING, professor of anthropology at Trent University, specializes in linguistic and cultural anthropology. He has conducted historical and ethnographic research in Wales and Georgia and has published, along with numerous articles, three recent books dealing in whole or in part with Georgia: *Strangers in a Strange Land* (2012), *Semiotics of Drink and Drinking* (2012), and *Love Stories* (2015).

LYNNE S. MCNEILL is an assistant professor in the Folklore Program at Utah State University. Her research interests include legend, belief, fandom, and digital folklore. She is the cofounder of the Digital Folklore Project and the author of *Folklore Rules* (2013).

ANDREW PECK is an assistant professor in the Department of Media, Journalism, and Film at Miami University. He earned his Ph.D. in communication arts from the University of Wisconsin–Madison, where he also served on the editorial staff of *Western Folklore*. His research focuses on how digital media offer new possibilities for the practice of everyday communication and frequently deals with topics such as humor, play, Internet memes, vernacular authority, and contemporary legends. His work has appeared in the *International Journal of Communication* and in the *Journal of American Folklore*.

JEFFREY A. TOLBERT is assistant professor of American studies at Penn State Harrisburg. He holds a Ph.D. in folklore from Indiana University. His research focuses on two disparate but increasingly interconnected areas: vernacular belief and popular culture. With Michael Dylan Foster he is co-editor of *The Folkloresque: Reframing Folklore in a Popular Culture World* (2016).

ELIZABETH TUCKER, Distinguished Service Professor of English at Binghamton University, specializes in children's and adolescents' folklore, folklore of the supernatural, and legends. Her books include *Campus Legends: A Handbook* (2005), *Haunted Halls: Ghostlore of American College Campuses* (2007), *Children's Folklore: A Handbook* (2008), *Haunted Southern Tier* (2011), and *New York State Folklife Reader: Diverse Voices*, coedited with Ellen McHale (2013). She has edited *Children's Folklore Review* and served as president of the International Society for Contemporary Legend Research and the Children's Folklore Section of the American Folklore Society; she is also a Fellow of the American Folklore Society.

Index